TRANSFORM
TO
PERFORM

– A Study of Total Performance Management

TRANSFORM TO PERFORM

– A Study of Total Performance Management

Dr. V.R. Katkhede
M.A. (Sociology), Ph.D. (HR)
Corporate Advisory/HR,
Uttam Galva Steels Ltd., Mumbai.

First Edition : 2011

Himalaya Publishing House

• MUMBAI • NEW DELHI • NAGPUR • BENGALURU • HYDERABAD • CHENNAI • PUNE • LUCKNOW
• AHMEDABAD • ERNAKULAM • BHUBANESWAR • INDORE • KOLKATA

First Edition : 2011

Published by : Mrs. Meena Pandey for **Himalaya Publishing House Pvt. Ltd.,**
"Ramdoot", Dr. Bhalerao Marg, Girgaon, **Mumbai - 400 004.**
Phone: .022-2386 01 70/2386 38 63, Fax: 022-2387 71 78
Email: himpub@vsnl.com Website: www.himpub.com

Branch Offices

New Delhi : "Pooja Apartments", 4-B, Murari Lal Street, Ansari Road, Darya Ganj, New Delhi - 110 002. Phone: 011-23270392/23278631, Fax: 011-23256286

Nagpur : Kundanlal Chandak Industrial Estate, Ghat Road, Nagpur - 440 018. Phone: 0712-2738731/3296733, Telefax: 0712-2721215

Bengaluru : No. 16/1 (Old 12/1), 1st Floor, Next to Hotel Highlands, Madhava Nagar, Race Course Road, Bengaluru - 560 001. Phone: 080-22281541/22385461, Telefax: 080-22286611

Hyderabad : No. 3-4-184, Lingampally, Besides Raghavendra Swamy Matham, Kachiguda, Hyderabad - 500 027. Phone: 040-27560041/27550139, Mobile: 09848130433

Chennai : No. 85/50, Bazullah Road, T. Nagar, Chennai - 600 017. Phone: 044-28344020/32463737/42124860

Pune : First Floor, "Laksha" Apartment, No. 527, Mehunpura, Shaniwarpeth (Near Prabhat Theatre), Pune - 411 030. Phone: 020-24496323/24496333

Lucknow : Jai Baba Bhavan, Church Road, Near Manas Complex and Dr. Awasthi Clinic, Aliganj, Lucknow - 226 024. Phone: 0522-2339329, Mobile:- 09305302158/09415349385/09389593752

Ahmedabad : 114, "SHAIL", 1st Floor, Opp. Madhu Sudan House, C.G.Road, Navrang Pura, Ahmedabad - 380 009. Phone: 079-26560126, Mobile: 09327324149/09314679413

Ernakulam : 39/104 A, Lakshmi Apartment, Karikkamuri Cross Rd., Ernakulam, Cochin – 622011, Kerala. Phone: 0484-2378012/2378016, Mobile: 09344199799

Bhubaneswar : 5 Station Square, Bhubaneswar (Orissa) - 751 001. Mobile: 09861046007, E-mail: orissa@himpub.com

Indore : Kesardeep Avenue Extension, 73, Narayan Bagh, Flat No. 302, IIIrd Floor, Near Humpty Dumpty School, Narayan Bagh, Indore- 452 007(M.P.), Mobile: 09301386468

Kolkata : 108/4, Beliaghata Main Road, Near ID Hospital, Opp. SBI Bank, Kolkata - 700 010, Mobile: 09910440956

DTP by : HPH Editorial Office, Bhandup (Asmita Pankar)

Printed by : Shri Krishna offset Press Delhi-93

PREFACE

Think about your company. Perhaps, your CEO may be talking about employees being most important variable for business success. If so, does he have a vision, mission and objectives of success? How it connects to business results? How to systematically grow over time? Who is accountable to deliver the results? If he does not have the vision clear, certainly he cannot transform your company to perform. For such people, this book will certainly help chalk out roadmap to understand, implement and achieve desired performance. This book, in addition to general organizational issues, focuses on human resources and other effective systems for achieving organizational performance and proves measuring and managing human behaviour and its performance is possible. Employees will be satisfied only when they see that their work makes a meaningful contribution to the business and to them. And that requires a system that measures, develops, manages and celebrates employee's contribution. With no objectives of performance management and measurement, employees will be evaluated by their diligence, loyalty, not by results. But if you truly care about people, your people then measure, manage and celebrate their results. We often hear that insanity is continuing to do the same thing and expecting different results. This fails to move our theme transform to perform.

Over the last several decades, employee management, development, services have emerged as the primarily determinants of business success. Today's economy is increasingly driven by knowledge, information and services. Learning that works. The management, therefore, must venture beyond traditional norms of performance. Learning and leveraging of human resources and knowledge resources require much more.

Transform to perform is all about understanding what is Total Operating Performance (TOP). What does it mean to be performance and non-performance? Performance Managed companies are the companies really more successful than their Non-performance Managed counterparts? And if it is so, why and what are the characteristic required to manage performance-oriented companies. The whole book narrates various characteristic of performance managed company.

My main objective in writing *"Transform to Perform"* is to examine the role of performance management, measurement and development, and to provide guidance on how to manage Total Operating Performance at work.

Performance Measurement is the first step that leads to control and eventually to improvement. If you can't measure something, you can't understand it. If you can't understand it, you can't control it. If you can't control it, you can't improve it (H. James Harrington). Measurement provides us clear, visible targets throughout the organization. It also gives us team-based environment, a rallying point for galvanizing group efforts.

This book lays the foundation, providing historical perspectives on performance of human resources. Secondly, it focuses on human side of enterprise and how employee's skills, knowledge, attitudes and capabilities can be channelized to achieve desired performance. It also takes a look at performance management, measurement and development, as an integrated process for performance mapping. It guides on how plant, corporate and employees performance can be improved with proper action plan. And lastly, it presents supplementary reading to know about high-performing organizations attributes, so that readers/organization leaders can understand down-to-earth requirements of high-performing organization. It is hoped, this book may prove a pioneering book in a field that needs pioneers who have the discipline and 'can happen attitude' to make their organization high-performing entity. I hope this book will be directly helpful to those who are perusing management education, who are managing men and organization including academic institutions and other type of organizations.

This book is intended for organizational leaders, senior executives, researchers, academicians and students of management studies, who are interested in making change happen in self and their respective organizations to produce results.

– Dr. V.R. Katkhede

ACKNOWLEDGEMENT

This book is the product of thirty-two years of study of various organisations, I worked. My special tribute to all these organisations. Their forceful responses to emerging new ideas for performance improvements, motivated me to collect, compile and implement improvement interventions at work. I bow down in the gratitude before late Dr. R. J. Rathi, Chairman and Managing Director, Sudarshan Chemicals Industries Ltd., Pune, who thoroughly shouldered on me the responsibility of Zero Defects implementation in all its three manufacturing facilities. This transaction to transformation process educated me deeply why and what of performance management. This teaching has set up working model of best performed organisation. This book *Transform To Perform* is the same model I am presenting to readers. This book is not only the product of theoretical reading and compilation, but also a research work experienced while serving different organisations, under the leadership of different CMDs, MDs with their different personality traits and styles. Their active, reactive, positive and sometimes proactive styles of 'people management' taught me how to balance people management issues in a systemic way. Transform to Perform is again the outcome of such leader's culture, styles and commitment for organisational improvement. These management leaders with whom I worked and on whose shoulders I stood upon have shaped so much of my philosophy, thinking and strategies and skills, I acknowledged them in gratitude and I salute them once again.

A book like this would not have been possible without the interest, support and cooperation of key senior executives in each of the companies I worked. Although it is impossible to recognise every contributor individually, I greatly indebted to the individuals in the companies who provided access, answered my endless queries and offered issues I addressed here. Thanks to each and every one of you.

I also gladly acknowledge the very special contribution of Miss Shraddha Yewale, my Personal Assistant, who not only helped to type, but most important, maintained calm in the midst of my often frenetic, out of control activity. She all the time remained cheerful and supporting in her secretarial and typing assistance. This book could not have been completed without her unswerving faithfulness.

However, no list of acknowledgement would be complete without recognising the indulgence and moral support provided by my wife Mrs. Kamal, who continuously helped me a lot during the lengthy preparation of this book.

And finally, thank you to a whole host of behind – the – scenes colleagues who supported me a lot. These people never accepted that something was impossible. Their support, encouragement and assistance have made this undertaking much easier.

– Dr. V. R. Katkhede

BRIEF CONTENTS

1. In Search of Confirmation 1 – 7
2. Introduction 8 – 14
3. Human Side of an Enterprise 15 – 30
4. Performance Management 31 – 44
5. Basics of Business Objectives – I 45 – 84
6. Performance Measurement 85 – 107
7. Performance Development 108 – 137
8. Workplace Performance Improvements 138 – 181
9. Reward Management and Performance 182 – 185
10. Supplementary Readings 186 – 273

DETAILED CONTENTS

1. **IN SEARCH OF CONFIRMATION** 1 – 7

2. **INTRODUCTION** 8 – 14

2.1 Human Resources at Work
2.2 Break the Past for Better
2.3 Present Business Crises – Danger and Opportunity
2.4 Facing Business Crises and Competition
2.5 Facing the Environment (Internal)
2.6 Establishing Performance Management

3. **HUMAN SIDE OF AN ENTERPRISE** 15 – 30

3.1 The New People Economy
3.2 The New People Organisation
3.3. The New People Management
3.4 Change Management and New People Management (NPM)
3.5 Organisational Structure
3.6 Organisational Leadership – CEO Profile
3.7 Organisational Culture
3.8 Company Philosophy
3.9 Statement of Corporate Objectives
3.10 Purpose of Company's Corporate Vision
3.11 A Mission
3.12 HR Training Commitment
3.13 Company's Strategic Intent

4. **PERFORMANCE MANAGEMENT** 31 – 44

4.1 Managment People to Perform
4.2 Performance Management – A Continuous Process
4.3 Performance Management – An Integrated Process
4.4 Total Performance Process

4.5 Investigating Full Process
4.6 Corporate Performance
4.7 The New Management Paradigm
4.8 Performance Management at Work
4.9 Performance Agreement
4.10 Summing Up on Performance Management

5. BASICS OF BUSINESS OBJECTIVES – I **45–84**
5.1 Setting Foundation
5.2 Creating Business Objectives Awareness
5.3 Defining Business Processes
5.4 Process Mapping and Analysis
5.5 Strategy Planning for Total Performance Plan
5.6 Key Critical Performance Factors
5.7 Exploring Business Objectives
5.8 Business Objectives – Scope for Action
5.9 Performance Scope at Plant Level
5.10 Performance Scope at Departmental Level
5.11 Performance Objectives – Models
5.12 Objective Planning in Action – Total Operating Performance

6. PERFORMANCE MEASUREMENT **85 – 107**
6.1 Performance Standards
6.2 Setting – Smart Goals
6.3 Performance – Goal Setting Exercise
6.4 Price System in Performance Measurement
6.5 Goal Setting Methodology

7. PERFORMANCE DEVELOPMENT **108 – 137**
7.1 Performance Development
7.2 HR and OD
7.3 Performance Appraisal
7.4 Potential Appraisal
7.5 Assessment Centre
7.6 The Critical Mass Techniques

7.7 The Workout

7.8 MBWA

7.9 Employee Counselling

7.10 Employee Mentoring

8. WORKPLACE PERFORMANCE IMPROVEMENTS 138 – 181

8.1 Introduction

8.2 Quality Circle – Management by Participation

8.3 Kaizen – A Continuous Improvement

8.4 Innovation and Innovativeness

8.5 Employee Coaching

8.6 Team-work

8.7 Personal Assessment, Positive Thinking and Positive Attitude

9. REWARD MANAGEMENT AND PERFORMANCE 182 – 185

10. SUPPLEMENTARY READINGS 186 – 273

10.1 Changing Workplace Basics

10.2 A Quality Management

10.3 Skills and Their Primary Attributes

10.4 Emotional Intelligence

10.5 Learning Organisation

10.6 Work Excellence and World-class Companies

10.7 Training and Development of People

Chapter 1

IN SEARCH OF CONFIRMATION

Can you imagine playing in cricket where no one knows the score? Your team is scoring, the other side is also hitting and the spectators are also cheering. But how long will you maintain real interest in the game? A score makes the action interesting by defining what it means to win and whether the team has a chance to won. It tells players how the team is doing and how their individual efforts contribute to its success – in short what they need to do to win.

The situation is not so different for the players in the game of industry. Employees are intelligent individuals who are motivated by work that keeps them informed about how their efforts affect the outcome, and given them power and responsibility to reach their goals. The factory game today is fast changing. Modern manufacturing strategies can be adopted successfully in a conventional organisation too. They require a partnership among employees, managers, skilled and technical staff in which the parties are responsible to each other for the outcome: performance, and to produce the desired performance, all partners must be informal while working together.

Never start instantly with the idea of changing organisational culture. Always start with the issues the organisation faces. Only when those business issues are clear, and then only ask yourself whether the given culture aids or hinders resolving the issues. Always think of culture as your source of strength. It is residue of your past successes, core principles of contributing to society, the practices of manufacturing high quality products, services, your business practice, activities, created beliefs, values and business methods that all are known collectively as organisational culture..

The question reflects what are the underlying cultural traits about what makes a high performance organisation works. The assumptions are: A set of technical and social systems, procedures, practices, policies, values which can be defined as main barriers or barometer of a successful performance. The answer to the question may be good or bad management systems. Weed out bad systems and replace it with good management systems to transform to perform your organisation. See the following two contrasting organisations to make you sure where you stand before transformation.

	Performance managed organisation	*Weak performance managed organisation*
1	They have clear agreement on the strategic intend of business.	They focus on financial measures to the exclusion of most other types of performance.
2	They have good cooperation and teamwork among management and staff.	Their focus is at short-term performance.
3	They linked unit, department and individual performance to strategic company measures.	They guard and held of performance data without much use.
4	They shared information within the organisation openly and candidly.	Their review meetings are often tactical in nature. Performance discussions tend to use focus on a single symptom.
5	They follow effective communication at each level of organisation.	Communication is restricted to few levels in the organisation.
6	Their employees are willing to take risks as they are involved and empower in their tasks management.	Understanding of strategy is inconsistent across the organisation.
7	They linked individual performance to overall company performance.	Performance measures across the organisation tend not to be linked or integrated.
8	They have high level of self-monitoring and discipline of performance at each level.	Many initiative are begun, few seems to be effectively completed.
9	They are culturally different because having strategy better communicated, they follow one language and thus language provides clear, visible targets throughout the organisation.	Bureaucratic decision processes push decisions up the organisation. Performance management and reward systems send messages to employees concerning what is important.

From the above traits of performance managed organisation one must learn following lessons;

- ❖ Need for consistent and committed leadership.
- ❖ Top-down mechanistic structures do not drive deep change.
- ❖ Arrogance never wins.
- ❖ Bottom-up organic change is powerful for cultural change, but limited, without top management and infrastructure support.
- ❖ There are natural ups and downs in the process of transformation.
- ❖ Stick with change and progress can be made.

CEO – as a change manager must have positive mind-set, while executing change in the organisation.

(a) **Leader must lead** – It starts at the top. Leader must change themselves to become transformational leader. Long-term change depends on continuity of leadership.

(b) **Change requires a reason and vision** – People need to know the reason. People need a future vision. You can't copy any organisational systems but to evolve your own.

(c) **People must be taught and supported** – People will resist change because they are human. For people learning by doing is more powerful than learning by listening. To cope with certainty of change people need support, involvement and empowerment.

(d) **Change needs a plan and a process** – Attitude and behavioural change must be supported by structural change. Metrics do not produce change but can be key enablers. Break-up change journey into small steps.

This way we are all potential change agents as we discipline our skills, systems, knowledge. We sharpen our perception about what is possible? and we develop respect for tools, techniques and relationships that surround us. Only facts, fear and force do not work. The three real keys to transformation are three Rs.

- **Relate** – Form a new emotional relationship with a person or community that inspires or sustain hope.
- **Repeat** – The new relationship helps you learn practice and master the new habits and skills that you need.
- **Reframe** – The new relationship that helps you learn new ways of thinking about your situation and your worklife.

You and your organisation are service provider to society at large. Great service providers do not always have state-of-the-art technology, rather they have state-of-the-art social or people skills, systems and network.

Transform to perform strategy demands Mental Revolution on the part of manager, managed, customers and stakholders. Individual and collective change starts and ends with the mental map people in organisation carry in their heads. Likewise Mental Revolution is also required on the part of organisational head – CMD, CEO, MD to examine his organisation value systems existing today and then try to transform the same in the value system of best managed companies. Value management, pre-measurement, management and development are the critical areas where you must examine your organisation before implementing transforms to perform strategies.

Value Systems of Organisation

In the world of Liberalisation, Privatisation and Globalisation companies are searching for new ways to instill a sense of commitment in their employees. For many this means new workforce values focused on increased ownership and opportunities for professional and personal growth. Many organisations are learning that they need to encourage greater employee participation in order to gain higher commitment, productivity and innovation. In short, Total Operational Performance (TOP), the key to success is determined not by accident of possession, but by the capacity to generate new knowledge, attitude, skills and the ability of the organisation to apply that knowledge, skills and attitude skilfully in the production and service processes. I do agree wholesale change of culture is nearly impossible for an established organisation. Start with understanding your strengths, developing positive future vision. The journey to evolving your culture to the desired future state is long and you want to learn as you go, continually planning, doing, checking and acting. Start with an analysis of your own culture's strengths and weaknesses and build on your strengths.

It is possible to get significant wins without the CEO being involved in the transformation process. But it is impossible to transform an entire organisation without absolute commitment, dedication and leadership from the top. It takes energy, a sense of purpose, forging a vision and the charisma to sell the vision everyday.

Conformance to requirements for transform to perform strategy must be fulfilled by organisational leaders in confirmation with his partners in business.

Organisational values, behaviours are well demonstrated in its day-to-day operational systems. following operational "7 S's systems" depict the systematic contrast in two organisation. Learning of this contrast makes you aware of your today's organisations image. Decide your SWOT accordingly and try to transform to perform better and better.

7 S's in Organisational Context

On surface one organisation may appear to be like all others in the same line of business. Worklife within one may seem similar to life in another, but it will be different in practice. Each organisation is unique. This uniqueness emanates from its culture, which grows and changes during the life of organisation. The structure and style of the organisation influences the managerial style and staff behaviour at work.

McKensey's 7 S's is for evaluating efficiency and effectiveness of operating performance of the organisation. Nothing shall be effective, if people in organisation are not effective. People produce everything else at their personal, interpersonal, managerial and organisational levels. Hence, any change and improvement must begin with 'self'; with his commitment, whether he is a CEO, manager, staff or worker. It is, therefore, necessary to rediscover the status of 7 S's in the organisation. 7 S's examine how organisational reality differs from organisational records.

Organisation - A	Organisation - B
(1) Style	
Participative style of leadership creates more leaders on shop floor, creates innovation, initiative and commitment. Manager must weigh benefits of participatory style against the predictability of high control. To talk participation but practice control only creates cynicism.	The predominant managerial style is laissez faire, which in practice, means that training and development activities are allocated ad hoc, as unfocused responses to individual needs. The organisation may be in communication business, yet relies on internal grapevine to keep the staff informed.
(2) Skills	
Skills such as delegations, communication, negotiation, self-management which are fundamental to high performance. Company competencies in technology, human resources, organisational developments, and best-in-class are also a part of skills developed by the company.	The strategy proposes applications that will require skills not currently available. The computer staff's skills are out of date. Acquiring them and updating the staff would require intensive investment in training.
(3) Shared Vision	
How we are going to get the work done? Defined relationships of people, performance agreements, rewards and clarity of vision liberate employees to do what they must do to get the job done and the manager are considered to be source of help.	The organisational stated policy is to promote and reward individuals on the basis of achievement. The reality that those who drink after work with CEO is the ones to get plum job. The organisation says that it puts customer first, but it is not unusual for staff to be called off the customer care training centre by their managers to attend to more urgent matters. In this situation either the organisation has no mission, intent or there is no deep understanding and commitment to the mission at all levels.
(4) Structure	
Communication of information, organisation chart, management levels, MIS, organisation reporting, feedback system, performance review, performance development, roles and goals KRA's, recognitions all are structured, documented and transparent to all in the organisation. To implement strategies there is a need to re-orient and tone up organisational structure. Reviews and redesign on the structure is necessary to translate the plan into clear-cut responsibilities for different positions to ensure organisational objectives.	Having no alignment between structures, staffing and shared value, the organisation poorly serves and reinforces the strategic path of performance. Centralisation absolves to take timely decision by manager and managed. Having unstructured working there breeds low trust resulting in closed communications, little problem-solving and poor cooperation and teamwork.

(5) Systems	
The design and implementation of good management systems start with customer and end with suppliers. It stresses that everyone must take responsibility for the adoption and documentation of management systems with the aim to provide operators of the process with consistency and satisfaction in terms of methods that ensure specified performance requirements.	The systems are old fashioned and laborious. They are self-perpetuated, have in-built opportunities for errors and require duplicate records to be maintained. They do not provide the information needed for managerial decision-making, so necessitate the creation of supplementary system.
(6) Staffing	
Manpower planning, allocation of job roles, manpower audit, skill upgradation, absolence, career management is well defined and standardised.	The leader in the organisation do not subscribe to its goals. They are time servers and resist change. They effectively lay dead hands on the aspirations of more committed staff.
(7) Strategy	
Read map for company performance and its perspectives, future plans, modification, expansion, acquisition, diversification, policy on marketing, product developments are made well known to all. Strategy professed mission, with available resources and with market conditions. Moreover, strategy monitors and changes to reflects shift in the wind, including the status of the competition. Operational environment outside/inside is monitored periodically to make sure strategy is in alignment with the realities outside and inside.	The published strategy consists of generalised statement of intent. No resource implications or contingency plans have been considered and there are no indications of who is going to do what by when. Having no well-defined road map to follow nor strategy is well developed, the organisation fails to meet the needs and realities or both – organisation and individuals therein.
Thus, any organisation who are transforming their management thinking similar to the above one has to embrace the principles of fairness and kindness, making better use of people for increased efficiency, and personal and organisational performance.	Thus, any organisation with these values similar to the above one is not likely to encourage individual employees of their skills. One could not expect the employees to be motivated to learn or take the risks needed. The culture will not welcome questioning or challenge to its existing systems or modes of behaviour. Many organisations transmit this sort of message without intending so. The desire for change may exist but making it happen in real is another matter. Unless deliberate action is taken, while organisation is learning how to learn, it may block, de-motivate or lose many good potential learners. Obviously, if we want to move ahead in a major way we need to shift the present situation in a totally new ways like organisation – 'A'.

For an organisation to be truly performance-oriented, each part of it must work properly like 'A' type of organisation. Each part, each activity, each person in the organisation affects and is in turn affected by others. Errors have a way of multiplying and failure to meet the requirements in one part or area creates problems elsewhere, leading yet more errors, yet more problems and so on. The benefits of getting it right first time everywhere (like "A" type organisation) are enormous.

Chapter 2

INTRODUCTION

Structure:

2.1 Human Resources at Work

2.2 Break the Past for Better

2.3 Present Business Crises – Danger and Opportunity

2.4 Facing Business Crises and Competition

2.5 Facing the Environment (Internal)

2.6 Establishing Performance Management

2.1 HUMAN RESOURCES AT WORK

According to natural law and principle, one must prepare his land, put in the seed, cultivate, weed and water it if one expects to reap a harvest. There is no instant success formula where you can just move and fetch money for produce. So, is the law with management paradigm.

You can buy man's time, muscular motion, his knowledge, skills and behavioural pattern, you can buy his physical efforts for certain time per day. But you cannot buy his enthusiasm, initiatives, dedication and devotion of heart, soul and mind. For this you have to learn and understand him, creating favourable conditions to make him work. There is no quick fix formula to motivate him at work.

Under scientific management, Human Resource Management practices are "pay him well" and ask him to produce. Keep him under tight supervision to get maximum from him without paying due attention to his welfare. Under Human Relations Management. "Treat him well" understand him and his needs as those affects on his work contribution and therefore he must be taken care at work. Under Human Resource Management paradigm "Use him well" he is knowledgeable person with right skill, attitude and aptitude. Create a culture that helps tap his talent and release his creative energy. Human Resource Management recognizes that human resources want to make meaningful contribution to the organisation. They want their talents to be identified, analysed, developed and recognised in the Organisation. The organisational goal is then to identify and develop their capacities, abilities and capabilities to accomplish the objectives of the organisation. It should try to create an environment in which people can contribute their full range of talents to the achievement of the organisational goals. Thus, HRM today works with the 'whole person'.

Using the paradigm of HRM, we must manage people by set of principles as the natural law of farm and harvest. It is well recognized that people are the highest value because people are the programmer. They produce everything at their personal, inter-personal, managerial and organisational levels. Obviously, the management leaders must have to change/reexamine their present management paradigm and this change, reexamination and renewal process must begin from the top CEO with strong commitment to bring thebest out of people involving and utilizing them in every process of organisation.

You cannot change the fruit unless you change the roots is universally true and largely tested fact.

2.2 BREAK THE PAST FOR BETTER

Management paradigm shifts means adapting distinctively new ways of thinking, redoing about old organisational issues. It is a road map for explaining and understanding certain aspect of reality. While a person may make small or big improvement by developing new skills, quantum leap in performance and revolutionary advances in technology requires new map, new paradigm, and new ways of thinking about seeing the world around.

Throughout history, leaders like Columbus (discovered America); Copernicus (discovered Earth moves round the Sun): Mahatma Gandhi (discovered Non-violence movement to win freedom from Britishers): and Bal Gangadhar Tilak (declared freedom is my birth right and I will get it), thus, they discovered the new leadership trends to unite people together. These leaders have used various models, road maps and modalities to manage people. They changed the old thinking of the world. Likewise in the business world carrot-and-stick approach, where rewards and punishment are used to generate productivity, changed to more sophisticated human relations and human resources models based on influence strategies and involvement techniques. Thus, leaders can transform their organisation and their people by communicating organisation's vision, mission, clarifying purposes, making behaviour congruent with belief and aligning procedures with principles, roles and goals. People may then achieve a heightened sense of personal contribution through their commitment to the organisation's mission.

Organisational growth is thus characterised as step-by-step developmental process where leaders train people the new management principles. They are liberated from old habits and increasingly motivated and directed from within. And when people in organisation respond to this change, they find new ways to make their systems, styles increasingly congruent with organisation's values, roles and goals. To implement any change in the organisation transactional leadership roles are important.

Transactional leadership role is basically focuses on the "top" leadership and cause realities of organisation to confirm to new values and ideas. They separate causes, symptoms and work at prevention in proactive and catalytic manner. They focus more on mission and strategies making full use of human resources to lead the organisation in a new direction. While transformational leadership role focuses on an efficient interaction with changing realities, it focuses on "bottom line" and is event-centred. It supports structure and systems that reinforce the bottom line, maximising efficiency. It relies on human relations to lubricate human interactions. The goal of both the leadership is to transform people and organisation to change them in mind heart and enlarge vision, insight and understanding. It clarifies purpose, principle and makes behaviour congruent with beliefs or values and brings about change that is permanent, self-perpetuating and momentum building.

2.3 PRESENT BUSINESS CRISES – DANGER AND OPPORTUNITY

Today business environment is dynamic, turbulent and unstable. It presents opportunities for organic, flexible, adaptive and innovative companies. It is perilous for rigid, mechanistic ones. Tom Peter describes, "Today's business environment is thriving of chaos and further ...Violent and accelerating change now common and will become the grist of the opportunistic winners and the losers will view such confusion on a problem to be dealt with skill ful competitors will ride the whirlwind of chaos, turbulence and change. The same tempest will sweep the losers away."

2.4 FACING BUSINESS CRISES AND COMPETITION

Thunder clouds do not fear lighting, hurricane do not fear wind. To prosper in a turbulent chaotic marketplace, become storm. An agile, flexible organisation is like this – a whirling but purposeful thunderstorm only an organisation with discipline and commitment can feign disorders. Such discipline and commitment do not come from rule and laws. They must come from adherence to immovable principles by all organisational members. And thunder heads contain the potential energy to release the organisation from whirlwind for positive gains. They persevere despite thousands of diversions. Organisation must always pay attention to the competitive environment. Sun Tzu observes environment this way "And therefore I say, know the enemy; know yourself; your victory; will never be endangered. Know the ground; know the weather; your victory will then be total." If ignorant both of your enemy and yourself, you are certain in every battle to be in peril.

Facing the Competition: Organisation, people and systems win market share, popularity. They use social and technical skills. Simultaneously to this, competing organisations assess their surroundings with each other. They act according to their perceptions and get feedback from their action. For this:

- Organisation uses their senses to assess the environment with each other.
- Act on their perceptions.
- Receive and analyse feedback from their actions.
- Culture, customs, attitudes and values affect an organisation decision process.
- The control system is an organisation's brain and nervous system.
- Each organisation has a physical capability and a competitive organisation is a living entity. It has a brain, nervous system and body. The ground it stands on its competitive environment, opposing organisations stand to the same field. Each uses its strengths and advantages of the ground to win its goals. Thus, the winning organisations do not do different things but they do the things (strategies) differently.

2.5 FACING THE ENVIRONMENT (INTERNAL)

If industries are to survive and grow in competitive environment, industries must learn to change and grow. They must learn to develop and use their own thought, power to work, communicate and trust the workplace. The changes in management beliefs, practices and systems will certainly help to remove the fear that management can't be trusted and make the employee feel more secure. However, in order to participate the employees will need to feel more confident in their own ability to contribution. They need to be willing to accept more responsibility and not just want to react to orders. In pursuing open, continuous two-way communication they must be willing to speak-up and express their concern confidently and clearly to the top management. They must be willing to participate in the corrective action process and deal with the facts without emotions. They instead of looking for reasons why the change won't work, they must be willing to listen and change. Changing people's attitude will be greatly facilitated by training and development of human resources.

Total performance management refers to both a philosophy and a system for simultaneously addressing quality, productivity, profitability and innovation. A good sign that an organisation is managing for total performance uses three types of measures on a broad basis for implementation:

Quality	=	quality and timeliness
Quantity	=	yield and accuracy
Profitability	=	cost and value addition

If these measures are managed in an integrative way on every major/minor work activities, there will be an objective basis for constant improvement. Creating such systems responsive to both management and employee will help to establish total performance management.

Any management has three primary business objectives:

- ❖ To enhance customer satisfaction – Internal and external,
- ❖ To strengthen organisations competitive position,
- ❖ To improve earning.

These objectives should guide the overall organisational performance, development strategies and these strategies are built upon the feedback received from following performance track systems.

- ❖ Current performance of product, people, processes.
- ❖ Trend analysis of product, people, processes.
- ❖ Problem identification of product, people, processes
- ❖ Management action, priorities for product, people, processes
- ❖ People issues relating to employee relations, rewards and development
- ❖ Needs/issues requiring review of by Senior management: strategy structure, style, systems, skills, staffing and shared values; organisation and people's character, climate, culture and commitment.

Unless an organisation is working towards total performance in all operations any effort to raise the level of quality will be seriously handicapped.

2.6 ESTABLISHING PERFORMANCE MANAGEMENT

The purpose of human resources strategy is to improve performance of corporate competencies by creating and managing a system for improving top-down performance people in the organisation – leaders, key positions, executives and operating staff play critical roles. Consider these roles as good seeds. And good seeds need good soil – the larger and responsible organisational context within which these critical roles reside. The soil is often called as high performing organisation. The objective of performance management is to show road map to get there. Therefore, corporate leaders must push the right leavers of organisational performance called: goal setting, feedback, appraisal or measurement is a cycle that begins with goal setting and ends with compensation.

The cornerstones for performance are:

- A context that shapes expression of all works, its vitality, creativity and quality.
- Empowering people with the information, resources and support they need to fully express their capabilities and competencies.
- Intense and pervasive communication about direction, cooperation, problems and results.
- Constant discovery and elimination of barriers to people performance.

Processes for Performance Improvement

- Quality Management – Establish accuracy and timeliness measures for key performance indicators.
- Do pareto and trend analysis to evaluate performance in each area of observation.
- Set realistic business performance goals.
- Productivity Management – (a) Average value forecasting methods.
  (b) Do capacity planning
  (c) Develop contingency plan to handle backlogs.
- Management Reporting – (a) Identify key information about what you do – volume, productivity, accuracy, timeliness, backlogs.
- Track performance of key indicators against established goals.
- Identify positive or negative variance from forecasted and goals achieved.
- Design clear, concise reporting formats.
- Communicate results to all management levels.

Thus, shared vision becomes the constitution of the organisation which helps create synergistic empowerment to unleash and combine the energy, talent, competencies and capabilities of all involved. It is the sum total of the work activities which increase productivity, quality and work improvement as per planned results.

Chapter 3

HUMAN SIDE OF AN ENTERPRISE

Structure:

3.1 The New People Economy
3.2 The New People Organisation
3.3 The New People Management
3.4 Change Management and New People Management (NPM)
3.5 Organisational Structure
3.6 Organisational Leadership – CEO Profile
3.7 Organisational Culture
3.8 Company Philosophy
3.9 Statement of Corporate Objectives
3.10 Purpose of Company's Corporate Vision
3.11 A Mission
3.12 HR Training Commitment
3.13 Company's Strategic Intent

New Economy, Organisation and People in LPG era

Historical change represents not a straight-line extension of individual society but a radical shift of direction. It adds up to nothing less than a complete transformation at least as revolutionary in our days as.. old industrial civilisation. Every civilisation has its own ideology – a kit of powerful culture assumptions that structures its view of reality and justifies its operations, "Pay me well", "Treat me well" and "Use me well". The principle of Human Resource Management has its standing of that time ideology, assumptions and thus, they justified their management of people.

In the LPG era it is now apparent bringing revolutionary and self-reinforcing changes at all levels of business at once. The consequence is not merely the distinction of the old industrial value but the creation of foundation for the new. Must we remain for ever trapped between absolute vision and values? We shall have to invent, discover scores of innovative strategies for magnifying people to perform. The new global economy is dominant by the great transformational organisations. Emerging business organisations bring with it not merely changes in how people be managed but also bring changes in their mind-set, attitudes and skills. Every new civilisation plucks idea from the past and reconfigures them in ways that help it understand in relationship to the world.

For companies to be innovative and efficient it is necessary to adopt a new and different approach to assuming work and people. The hard aspects of organizing people must be combined with the soft aspects of values, visioning, new way of thinking, doing and new means of influencing behaviour at work. Attracting, managing and nurturing knowledgeable worker is the single most critical issue that we will have grapple with in the new people-management. Doing this, calls for a slew of proactive measures on three fronts. First, companies have to have an organisational ambiance where talent can bloom, secondly, they have to put in place systems that help unleash their potential and thirdly, they have to build in a reward-and-recognition mechanism that provides value for people.

If organisations are to thrive in new economy with new people-management, they must focus on the challenges posed by the changing business environment. The principles underlying the new form of organisations are to some extent known to us. We have most of the tools, techniques as well as structure, style, systems of the implementing process. What is required is to apply these to produce results for themselves. And while doing so deepens our own understanding of new economy, new organisation and new people that will require in implementing total performance management.

3.1 THE NEW PEOPLE ECONOMY

In new economy major changes in business are making far reaching effects in business world. These changes are making knowledge vital. So, people are crucial to every work operation. In the past it was the strategist within the organisation typically, the owners to set the corporate objectives while the processes were meant to contribute to in itself. None of the process owners approached the company's goals directly. The combined effect however was meant to add up rewards that end.

Today's CEO are aiming each of their processes at customer satisfaction be customer-internal or external. From taking product order to dispatching product it is people lie at the heart of core functions of the organisation. Thus, all corporate strengths are dependent on people. Companies that compete on the strength on its products have no choice but to use people as source spring for winning concepts. Product improvements can be generated by people. Inter-dependent systems that convert articulated and implicit customer satisfaction/expectation into specific features. Development of successful product depends crucially on using knowledge as a core competence of the corporations. Companies manufacturing will be more effective than rival, not because its people are using the technology more cleverly. Technology is mechanising, many of the monotonous job, allowing employees to improve this productivity manifold. Marketing people through their service component generating customer value and introducing new and exciting forums of customer interacting. People are becoming the principal instrument to delight the customers.

Organisational restructuring or business process reengineering will not succeed unless the right people with appropriate set of skills are in place to manage the new process. CEO ensures that their people minds are reengineered too by proper training and development. It is company's people who will make or break the application of any new management tools. The objective of course, is to ensure that the resources of each individual are applied directly to the task they have to perform. CEO is practising new organisational forms dismantling vertically functional departments and replacing them with horizontal cross-functional and process centred teams.

The objective is to assign ownership of each process to a group of people, making them responsible for its success or failure to ensure that it meets targets. As a result, the onus of performance is no longer on rigid systems but on the resourcefulness, initiative and responsibility of the process-owners. Today's professional is much more demanding as they possess the capabilities to determine their performance. Recognising these successful techniques are focusing directly on people instead of technologies or processes, operating on the principles that devising for getting the best out of people will automatically maximise corporate performance. So, companies are developing their people in teams on the shop floor, offices using them to solve problems innovatively and meet stretch targets.

3.2 THE NEW PEOPLE ORGANISATION

The organisation is build on an effective business philosophy, vision and mission not merely or organisational systems. It believes that it is only human resources take the organisation at desired competence. It encourages people to learn to produce the results – the desired competence. It encourages people to learn to produce the results they desire and nature's creative and innovative patterns of collective sharing and learning. It develops fresh organisational realities, capabilities all the time to remain best-in-class race. It is essential because only it can survive tomorrow's knowledge-based economy to manage today's and tomorrow's intense global competition, then only it can cope up with tomorrow's rapid fire technological and social changes, only it can handle tomorrow's demanding and fragmented markets. Such organisations only can build a people-based work system in a company. And it can be created by keeping the company in a state of constant change, cultivating diversities in the functioning of an organisation and create mechanism to unlearn old and absolete knowledge and build setting where people collectively learn, involve and take decisions, Using people's knowledge as competencies and skills as a competitive advantage for survival. It is, therefore, constantly tries to attain total quality in every sphere of work actively at workplace. It builds evolutionary bond with customer and vendors best suited to cope with global change and thus create energised workforce that evolve with the company. This ever-learning, ever-evolving, ever-innovative, ever competitive organisation of tomorrow will wrest advantages by marrying the development of every single employee to organisational performance by creating and implementing the new people-management.

3.3 THE NEW PEOPLE – MANAGEMENT

This new approach to managing human resources is undergoing a revolutionary change and it is acknowledged of the fact that it is people and not money, machines, methods and material that must run organisation. Global competitiveness can be achieved not through the best technologies and state-of-the-art plants but by effectively your employees, to perform at global standards. A new approach to managing people becomes absolutely critical one. As a result, the human resources function has acquired a new and crucial responsibility ensuring that corporate and individual objectives are melded into one and individual rewards are available only if corporate goals/objectives are met.

In any business strategy, people are more crucial than plans. Effective implementation is possible only with motivated implementation. Michel Treacy and Wiresema, management gurus rightly revealed that winning corporate, dominate the market by offering one of the three competitive benefits to their customers; best product, best price and best service created by people. Creating new people-management means recruiting people with appropriate knowledge, skills, creating a corporate culture for individual excellence and providing training and developing for their assigned roles by appraising and rewarding them for meeting corporate goals. For this NPM sets its agenda ensuring that the mind-sets of people irrespective to change by facilitating change management intervention like organisational renewal or management engineering. Total quality management intervention like organisational renewal or management engineering and get manage cultural transition; may it be merger, alliance or acquisition. This is managed by following processes and practices with proper evaluations and measurements and performance standards. Without managing people effectively no organisational transformation can take place.

3.4 CHANGE MANAGEMENT AND NEW PEOPLE MANAGEMENT (NPM)

Every form of organisational transformation needs the whole-hearted support of people at all levels. This can only be actuated by linking the top management vision for change to the bottom line employees who will be its instruments and or change agent and it is the function of the new people-management to establish a powerful coalition within the company by communicating that vision. As said by management guru Udai Pareek "There must be grater involvement and participation of people in decision-making, decentralisation and delegation of power that is the only solution and it must be done pragmatically, not philosophically". Top management relies on champions for new projects, products and processes. Human Resource Management will play a vital role in providing them say M. Athrey. He is right in the sense that, after all, the people management must not only give power to your people, it is a must and in the ultimate analysis also give power to your profits.

3.5 ORGANISATIONAL STRUCTURE

Organisational structure can help or impede performance. Organic systems are for flexible and responsive than mechanistic ones. Quality of individual employee is a factor in organisational performance. Mechanistic organisation relies on rules and procedures and there is a rule to cover everything. While an organic system is adaptive. Participants apply judgement and initiative to their work. Judgement means reaching a decision without a rule. Initiative means using judgement to respond to a new situation. The person responsible for the job should decide how to do it. Upper management staff not interferes much in their processes of decisions. Sometime subordinates want to take responsibility but the organisational structure won't let them. Hence, the CEO must think these major lessons on organisational structure:

- The management system must be organic to survive in turbulent and chaotic environment, mechanistic system can handicaps their own members.
- Large companies often need to deploy independent small business unit. Success depends on successful use of both large and small forces.
- Make the organisation as flat as possible.
- Defer decisions to the lowest possible level. Do not hamstring line managers and employees with committees. Owners and CEOs must avoid micro-managing line operations. They need to define goals, but delegate responsibility for achieving them to the front-line. Organisation survival in a dynamic competitive environment requires change. The organisation must recognise when change is necessary. Using proper techniques helps to overcome resistance to change. No matter how good the management system or its success records, it must be adopted to changing conditions.

3.6 ORGANISATIONAL LEADERSHIP – CEO PROFILE

Zhuge Liang, a Chinese author wrote that "Generals do not say they are thirsty before the soldiers have drawn from the well, generals do not say they are hungry before the soldiers food is cooked; generals do not say they are cold before the soldiers are kindled; generals do not say they are not before the soldiers canopies are drawn. Generals do not use fans in summer; do not wear leather in winter; do not use umbrellas in the rain. They do as everyone does".

Leader's behaviours must convey desirable attitudes and values to their followers. Leader's actions must accord with their statements. The leader must import confidence to his followers. To do this the leader must have genuine self-confidence, pretensions are not enough. "When troops are strong and officers weak the army is insubordinate, when the officers are valiant and the troops ineffective the army is in distress." – Sun Tru the art of war. "Independence is my birth right and will get it." – Bal Gangadhar Tilak, Indian freedom fighter – For any programe to succeed, leader must show commitment and support supplying resource and recognising successful results.

A business leader's goal is to win success for employee, clients, customers, stakeholders. For this he uses appropriate physical, organisational and management tools to do this. The tools can be physical, mental, organisational and managerial. A professional is a product of extensive training and lifelong experience. Continuous improvement applies to people as well as organisations. Quality, productivity, competitiveness and performance begin in the leader's mind. The intellect of the leader is the keystone of performance. Excellence depends on the leader's attitude, values, beliefs and conduct. This must be the right conduct of the leader and accordingly he adopts to the situation, choose the right organisational or managerial tool for the situation. Accept change and new ideas are always critical for individual employee and organisational success. Keep open mind and avoid preconceptions, prejudices and procrastination. Murphy's law has rightly described the character of uncertain leadership "The fewer the people who care whether it goes wrong or right the greater the certainty it will go wrong. The less authority vested in those closest to the problem, the more the problem lingers and spreads." Hence, grooming of the leadership should be a constant preoccupation of the organisation. Because he shapes the company's output, he encourages new ideas, stimulate right things, thrive on tough competition, think of involvement programes and empower others to make decisions. He thinks of a dynamic, caring human system, think of improving initiative and innovation. Thus, he shapes organisational character, culture and climate. He creates the vision and creates more leaders in the organisation. It is the leader who motivates his people for better and continuous performance. Teams provide the best means of distributing authority and accountability; thus they facilitate leadership that operates at bottom-up as top-down.

3.7 ORGANISATIONAL CULTURE

An economic organisation is not a purely economic creation; it is simultaneously a social creation. Like any other social system, a work organisation involves a subtle form of coordination between individuals. Each person and each group within an organisation is indeed like an organ in the body. If the coordination mechanisms between the eyes and the hands are disrupted then work by both the eyes and the hands will fail to improve their joint productivity. Industry does not need managers and employees to toil more assiduously. Instead the mechanism of coordination between them must be more attuned to subtlety of relations that are essential to their joint productivity.

Organisation succeeds largely because its culture offers employee a stable social setting in which they get bearing and draws support to cope with and build the other social relations in their lives. Tradition, climate and values that set a pattern of activities. Opinions, actions instill their pattern in their employees by their examples and pass it down to succeeding generation employees with this base of values, managers begin to look carefully at their approaches to managing people. The unmistakable sense of intimacy, trust and reliance are the unique ways of working together and are the cornerstone of the culture, both in and out of the business setting. Trust that exists makes implementing decisions far earlier because others tend to accept the idea that the decision probably made for the right reasons even though they may not seen it. Trust is the way of working together in a good company culture a way of communicating to people that they matter as people, not as parts of the organisation. The company culture makes people happy and their work enjoyable if it operates on positive values. Company culture is a total of the inherited ideas, beliefs, values and knowledge which constitute the standard, the shared bases of social action. These sets of share values affect organisational behaviour at work. Organisational culture thus plays a critical role in productivity, quality, competitiveness and performance. It is a critical factor in success or failure. Hence, a company culture is its soul or true name. We create a better corporate culture by evoking the virtues of our employees. Organisational culture, norms and values are the best way to assure predictable behaviour. Norms and culture strongly influences organisational performance. The corporate culture must recognise the need for and then encourage continuous improvement. The emphasise must be on the developments and cultivation of a proactive customer – oriented teamwork environment. Most company find it worthwhile to examine their culture before launching any performance improvement programme then only company can demand that employees added value to the organisation and design their actions in the same direction as the organisation desired. It is therefore, obligatory on CEO behalf to ensure that the corporate vision, mission and objectives are communicated clearly to employees; equipping them with all the information they need to synchronise their reactions with the company objectives. CEO to keep evolving company system, methods, values to remould employees continuously to absorb the changes. For a company either it can be a chain that keeps employee shackled or it can be a dynamo that spurs reform and change on a continuous basis. It is up to its corporate culture to determine which a company shall be?

3.8 COMPANY PHILOSOPHY

Development of a consistent philosophy must begin by understanding of set values and beliefs that are internally consistent with each other as well as being externally consistent with the realities of the economic marketplace and the social environment. Therefore, a corporate philosophy must include the objectives of the organisation and the operating on the organisation by its social and economic environment. It thus specifies not only ends but also means. A complete statement of philosophy will be stated in general manner that provides each employee and managers with guidance.

An organisation is a bit like "Our personalities" just as we have belief, attitude, objectives and habits that make us unique. So, an organisation overtime develops a distinctive personality – the culture of the organisation. Some individuals exhibit stability while others seem erratic, depending on their broadly accepted beliefs. Organisation spans a similar range of corporate culture or personalities. A philosophy can help an organisation to maintain it sense of uniqueness by stating explicitly what is and is not important. It also offers efficiency in planning and coordination between people who share in this common culture. The company philosophy thus states the goals and practices that the community of employees in trying to enact. It leads overtime to the development of a host of smaller practices and modes of conduct that becomes a corporate culture. An organisation philosophy generally underlies the moral philosophy of one or a few individuals who have shaped a company through their actions. Their sense of right from wrong, articulated in a particular social and economic setting, visibly emerges over the years as a culture and a philosophy. If corporate is to provide for a consistent development of policy across the whole range of corporate activity, its statement must specify three things:

- The relationship of the firm to its social and economic environment,
- The basic objectives or ends of the firm, and
- The essential means used to achieve those ends. Any group of managers and employees who commonly understand these principles will be capable of putting into practice the kind of common sense so elusive in modern organisational life. Thus, the company philosophy gives people a sense of values to work and to live by. It suggests way to behave in responsive to its people, its customer, vendor and the community it serves. It clearly set forth the company motivating spirit for all to understand where directly or indirectly that philosophy determines how insiders-outsiders alike appraise trust and value of the company, its product, culture, climate and commitments. Company philosophy based on objectives, beliefs, values, attitude and norms make the organisation a distinctive entity and presents corporate culture and image in society.

3.9 STATEMENT OF CORPORATE OBJECTIVES

Company mission statement provides a valuable management tool to an organisation and an invaluable tool for measurement of organisational performance. Corporate objectives are the guiding principles for achieving total organisational performance. People in organisation will continue to assume that they are true and operate accordingly. The organisational success is the result of combined efforts of each individual in the organisation working towards common objectives. These objectives should be realistic, should be clearly understood by everyone in the organisation and should reflect the organisation's basic character and personality focused through company philosophy.

As a part of company corporate objectives you can in corporate objectives this way, followed by other objectives.

Corporate Objective

Our primary objective is to be premier in every facet of our business. We aspire to be recognised as premier in fulfilling our obligations to all our constituencies: customer, employees, shareholders and communities.

Further, we strive to be innovative and at the forefront of the manufacturing/service industry in its continuing evaluation. Achievement of this objective assumes attaining premier status in the manufacturing and services. While profit is our reward for serving society well, it is also a requisite for continuing to serve society at all times. Following is the summary of other objectives of the company.

(1) Management Objectives

To foster initiative and creativity and allowing the individuals, working teams, with greater freedom of action in attaining well-defined performance objectives. Management must make sure that each individual; understand the immediate objectives as well as corporate goals, policies. Employees must take interest in their work, plan it and propose new solutions to old problems and to stick their neck out when they have something to contribute for creating an environment where an employee will develop ownership with his job, for people and company is management's primary responsibility. Management by objective is always superior to management by directives.

(2) People Objectives

To help people share in company success, which they make it happen and to provide job security based on their performance. To recognise their individual and collective achievement and to ensure the personal satisfaction that comes from sense of accomplishment in their work. The company has to built around the individual the personal dignity of each and recognised his contribution personnel and personal relations will be good only if people have faith in the motives and integrity of their superiors and the company. An opportunity to share in the success of company is evidenced by fair wage/salary level, well supported by profit-sharing plan like ESOP, etc.

(3) Customer Objectives

To provide product and services of the greatest possible value to our internal as well as external customers, thereby gaining their retention, respect, satisfaction and loyalty. The management's responsibility to customer beings with product development to personal development. Product and service must be designed to provide superior performance all the time. The product must be manufactured at a reasonable cost and with superior workmanship. Prime objective of marketing department is to see that the finished product is backed by prompt and efficient service. Good communication should be maintained with the customer. Confusion and competition among sales teams must be avoided by clear assignments of sales and responsibilities.

(4) Growth Objectives

Company cannot maintain position of strength and leadership in its respective line without growth. Growth is important in order to attract and hold calibre people. Opportunities are greater and more challenging in a growing company. Continuous growth is essential for the management to achieve its growth objectives. Do not believe that large size is important for company growth-sake. Bigness of company is not the only growth of company.

(5) Profit Objectives

To create sufficient profit to finance company growth and to provide resources, the company needs to achieve its other corporate objectives. The day-to-day performance of each individual add-to or subtract from company profit. Hence, profit is the responsibility of all. Meeting this objective company designs and develops each and every product/service, so that it is considered a good value by the customers. Maintaining this spirit and competitiveness in the marketplace also requires that the company performance, its manufacturing, marketing, technical and administrative functions as economically as possible. Profit may vary from year-to-year and company plan, bank loan for short-term basis. Loans are costly and must be paid in time. Hence, management objective is to rely on reinvested profits as it is main source of capital.

(6) Field of Interest – Objectives

To enter new field only when the ideas we have together with our technical, manufacturing, marketing skills assure that we can make a needed and profitable contribution to the field. Company growth must lead to a continuing expansion of our field of interest. Diversification shall come from applying our resources, skills and competencies to fields technically related to our existing ones. To meet customer objectives, we must continually generate new ideas, innovation and success stories for delivering better kind of products and services.

(7) Citizenship Objectives

To honour company obligation to society by being an economic intellectual and social asset to nation in which we operate, all employees should strive to improve the environment in which they live. The company must strive to provide employment opportunities of widely different background and participate in social reform, programme sponsored by society. The betterment of society is not a job of to be left to a few. It is the responsibility to be shared by the company and its people. The corporate objectives of the company must be identified because any plan inconsistent with existing management principle is unlikely to succeed.

3.10 PURPOSE OF COMPANY'S CORPORATE VISION

An organisational vision offers a compelling method for forging employees into an empowered, highly motivated team. It adds purpose to employee's worklife. Vision is the hallmark of an enlightened forward looking organisation. Enlighten people in an organisation need passion that they can follow with missionary zeal. People give their lives for a flag. A vision brings out that kind of commitment. Vision to a leader, is a personal perspective on a condition that he knows to be the best to his followers. To his followers it is an articulation in words that they understand of where their leader is taking them. Vision preserves the core of the company while stimulating progress towards the future. Vision links your company's core values to a perception of how you want your future to look that is where the process should begin. Vision is a kind of tool to be redefined, reassert just what kind of company it wanted to be known. For example, Cadbury India vision states "Cadbury India will continue to maintain its leadership position in the confectionery market as well as achieving a strong national presence in food, drink sector." Mercks Ltd's vision, is "to preserve and improve human life". Thus, your vision must become the starting point, of the process that culminates in setting specific quantifiable objectives for every division, department and every employee.

It is necessary to bolt your vision to the scaffolding of mission, strategies, goals and or targets. The core function of the company vision is not to stroke your owndreams, but to ignite your people into thinking beyond your company's existing capabilities and present environment. And only a shared vision whatever is the associated risk can achieve that. After all a vision does not depict a personal paradise, it presents the 'Promised Land'. To fulfil the vision, you must have a mission.

3.11 A MISSION

It is a statement of strategic intent of what company wants to create and through which line of business. Strategic intent envisions a desired leadership position and establishes the criterion the company will use to chart its progress. The mission of an organisation explains what business the organisation is attempting to fulfil in the economy. In formulating its mission, an organisation must answer three primary questions:

(i) What function do the organisation meet when it performs its core competencies?

(ii) For whom does it perform those core competencies?

(iii) How does it use its driving force?

The driving force dictates whether the organisation will be a low cost producer or a technological leader and whether the organisation will resolve around its distribution channels or production/service or human resource upgradation. Specifically, it is the force that keeps product, market, or business development on track with the vision statement. It causes the organisation to accept or reject new product or market opportunities based on focus.

Mission has a PURPOSE and it is an articulation of the functions that a company intends to fulfil through its businesses. It nurtures VALUES – a set of cherished notions and beliefs that guide every move that a company makes. It follows – GOALS – the business targets that a company vision, mission and purpose are translated into strategy. STRATEGY – the method that a company employs to achieve the goals that its vision provides.

Please remember the vision portrays the future of the company but do not necessarily dictate how to get there.

Company's General Behaviour

All take pride in being the company's premier quality and service provider of customer satisfaction, in fact company values are the foundation for the corporate drive and behaviour. To perform up to highest measure of competence, the company and its people always;

- Take initiative and risk.
- Adopt to changing business environment.
- Make and take timely decisions.
- Work cooperatively as team.
- To be open with information, knowledge and news of forthcoming or actual problems.
- To trust and be trustworthy.
- Respect others – customers, suppliers, colleagues and subordinates.
- To judge and be judged, regard and be regarded on the basis of performance.

These are the positive work values through which company culture comes in.

Company Values: Guiding Principles

These are the corporate drive to excel.

(1) Customer Satisfaction: Internal and external are the top priority of every employee and the purpose of every one's job. Cost-effective, ongoing achievement of customer's satisfaction is the foundation of our business.

(2) Strategies, goals and objectives established to ensure consistent customer satisfaction. Corporate financial health and employee development and support are closely defined, communicated and understood.

(3) Management believes into promote and pursues excellence throughout the organisation. Excellence is expected in the quality of work done right the first time is the dominant pattern of every work activity.

(4) Initiative and ingenuity applied to the conduct of the business and the resolution of the problems are encouraged and supported throughout the company.

(5) The role and responsibilities of every employee are clearly defined. Aggressive cooperative fulfilment on behalf of our customers and in support of company's strategies and goals are valued.

(6) Reward structure recognises contribution to and achievement of results which enhance customer satisfaction, improve cost-effectiveness and strengthen profitability. The results of imbedding these values are:

- Quality service for our customers.
- A rewarding work environment for our people.
- Adequate return to our shareholders.

We want all people to be an extension of the values of the company. They must respect and practice these values.

3.12 HR TRAINING COMMITMENT

By this time CEO has gained understanding of the basic principles of effective organisational performance. But his vexing question is how to implement it? Because there may be hesitancy to change. His dilemmas are: how can culture characterised by change, flexibility and continuous improvement to implement and still maintain a sense of stability? How do we get our people the culture aligned with the strategy, so that every one in the organisation is as committed to the strategy as we have devised. How do we turn a vision, mission and values into code of conduct? How do we create culture, where managers and all treat employees as customers and use them as local experts? How do we create spirit, leadership and harmony among departments and people? How do we unleash the creativity, resourcefulness, talent, skills and energy of the people. Although we are clear that people feel hesitate to change but with change can come growth, opportunities, innovation and improvement for the organisation. You are in dilemma because you do not have full proof system for the organisation. You are in dilemma because you do not have full proof system for communication and problem-solving. The fool proof system is: commit to train your resources.

Training and education empowers employees and increase their flexibility. They instill confidence and pride. They increase the organisation's agility and competitiveness. By constantly training and developing people from shop floor to Senior managers, to upgrade the knowledge and skills pool of each one; a company will give them freedom to handle their work confidently. Training – as planned programme designed to improve performance helps bring about measurable changes in knowledge, skills, attitudes and social behaviour of employees.

Training is imperative not just for boosting operational ability but to handle difficult job tasks in assertive and confident manner. CEO will have to insist on comprehensive, systematic and continuous training linked closely to the strategy and systems between customers and organisation. Training agenda must be training and retraining which will involve unlearning old concepts and acquiring new skills – for all employees. Ultimately, the real objective of training will be to teach people how to learn: to develop their mind-set that craves for a consistent upgradation of knowledge and skills demanded by new change management.

Those who choose to implement total performance, management will have to train their workforce in the areas of innovation, quality, customer relations, inter-personal relations, communication, teamwork, leadership, right attitude, competencies, empowerment, company objectives and strategies along with their technical/operational areas. The needs of Senior managers: how to change the organisation within to keep pace with development in the external environment and for shop floor employees, upgrading their social and technical skills levels is the prime consideration. The message to CEO: nothing binds the entire workforce to the company as effective opportunities to be trained, especially on new skills beyond their daily operations. Total performance management puts following training challenges to CEO:

- Make learning one of the fundamental values of the company.
- Commit major resources and adequate time to training.
- Use training to bridge the gap with the external world.
- Use training as a development tool for individual.
- Link organisational, operational and individual needs.
- Ensure that training allows the soft skill development.
- Use training to continuously upgrade employee skills.
- Create a system to evaluate the effectiveness of training.

Thus, the need for training for the sake of the company as well as personal development is felt strongly at every level. Training is the cornerstone of intrinsic motivation, which is primary requirement for managing and maintaining performance. A worker's tool say a lot about his skills and craft people can use complex tools to achieve outstanding results. Hence, commitment to training is a must. Commitment is priceless asset, perceived equity; mutual trust and adherence to psychological contract are vital contributors to commitment. Demoralisation is survivable; loss of commitment is a death sentence. If the company is serious about training its employees show that it also cares for them. We have seen continuous training programmes with a lot of variety at many companies and they work to change employee's mindset. It is our people who make the differences and our attitude towards each other make our people different. Great service providers do not always have the state-of-the-art technology; rather they have state-of-the-art social or people's skills. To understand anything is hard. Once one understood, action is easy.

3.13 COMPANY'S STRATEGIC INTENT

It is experienced that companies that have risen to global leadership over the past two decade invariably began with ambitions that were out of all proportion to their resources and capabilities. But they create an obsession with wining at all levels of the organisation and then sustained the obsession over the years quest for global leadership. This we term as strategic intent.

Strategic intent envisions a desirable leadership position and establishes the criterion the organisation will use to chart its progress. Strategic intent is more than simply unfettered ambition. The concept encompasses an active management process that include: focusing the organisational attention on the essence of winning, motivating people by communicating value of the target; leaving room for individual and team contributions; sustaining enthusiasm by providing new operational definitions as circumstances change and using intent consistently to guide resource allocations. Strategic intent captures the essence of winning for Coca-Cola; strategic intent has been to put a coke within arm's reach of every consumer in the world. Strategic intent is stable overtime. In battles for global leadership, one of the most critical tasks is to lengthen the organisation's span. Strategic intent provides consistency to short-term action, while leaving room for re-interpretation as new opportunities emerges. Best in class companies respond quickly for gaining competitive advantages by providing quality, then driving cost down, then cultivating export markets and then undertaking new product development, leaves room for improvisation.

Achieving strategic intent requires enormous creativity with respect to means. Creativity is unbridled but not uncontrolled, because top management establishes the criterion against which employees can present the logic of their initiatives. Middle management must do more than deliver on promised financial targets, they must also deliver on the broad direction implicit in their organisations strategic intent.

Strategic intent implies a sizable stretch for an organisation. Current capabilities and resources will not suffice. This forces the organisation to be more innovative, to make the most of limited resources; strategic intent creates an extreme misfit between resources and ambitions. Top management then challenges the organisation to close the gap by systematically building new advantages. Thus, the company's strategic intent is like a marathon run in 400 metres sprint, the top management is to focus the organisations attention on the ground to be covered in the next 400 metres. In several companies management did this by presenting the organisation with a series of corporate challenges, each specifying a next race to achieve strategic intent. One year the challenge may be a quality, the next total consumer care, the next entry into new market, the next a rejuvenated product-line, the next employee development and so on.

For a challenge to be effective, individuals and teams throughout the organisation must understand and see its implications for their own jobs. Companies that set corporate challenges to create new competitive advantages quickly discover engaging the entire organisation requires top management to:

- Create a sense of urgency – by amplifying weak signals in the environment that point out the need to improve instead of allowing inaction to precipitate a real crisis.
- Develop a competitors focus at every level through widespread use of competitive intelligence, every employee should be able to benchmark his or her efforts against best in class competitors so that the challenges become personal.
- Provide employee with the skills they need to work effectively, training in quality, behaviour, attitude, problem-solving, value engineering, team-building, employee need to work effectively. Give the organisation time to digest one challenge before launching another.
- Establish clear milestone and review mechanism to track progress: In such cases, the challenges will take root only if senior management and low level employee feel a reciprocal responsibility for competitiveness. Reciprocal responsibility means shared gain and shared pain. To achieve strategic intent, the company should not be competitive imitation but competitive innovation. The art of containing risk within manageable proportions.

The approaches to competitive innovation are:

- ❖ Building layers of advantages.
- ❖ Searching for loose bricks.
- ❖ Changing the terms of engagement, and
- ❖ Competing through collaboration.

Such organisational transformation can start only with CEO. Before Senior managers can realign behaviour and beliefs throughout the organisation, he needs to change his own priorities and ways of thinking. This means creating an organisation with which members can identify, in which they share a pride, and to which they are willing to commit. In short, Senior management must convert the contractual employees of an organisation into committed member of a purposeful organisation. By making tangible commitments to the defined objectives, Senior management substantiates such belief: provide people deep in the organisation with the motivation that comes from making perceptive progress. It is then obvious that if employees are put out extraordinary efforts to realise company targets; they must be able to identify with them. It is fine to stress what to aim for, but people also need to know what the company stands for. Because employees don't just want to work for a company. They want to belong to an organisation. More than just providing work; company can give meaning to people development. To realise the value of a committed employee, an organisation must bring its big ideas and bold initiatives down to a personal level: maintain a link between the company and each of its employees. Link does imply a mutual commitment, in which the management treats the employees not as a cost to be controlled but as an asset to be developed. And for any organisational business a sense of doing better than before becomes the clue for continuously improving organisational performance. The bull must be grabbed by its horn, so are the organisation problems by intensive identification processes. Please remember if better is possible, good is not enough. Man's great discovery is not fire, not the wheel, not the combustion engine, not atomic energy, not anything in the material world. It is in the world of ideas; man's greatest discovery is teamwork by agreement.

Chapter 4

PERFORMANCE MANAGEMENT

Structure:

4.1 Managing People to Perform

4.2 Performance Management – A Continuous Process

4.3 Performance Management – An Integrated Process

4.4 Total Performance Process

4.5 Investing Full Process

4.6 Corporate Performance

4.7 The New Management Paradigm

4.8 Performance Management at Work

4.9 Performance Agreement

4.10 Summing Up on Performance Management

TOTAL PERFORMANCE MANAGEMENT

4.1 MANAGING PEOPLE TO PERFORM

Today free market needs free men and women to discover, rediscover and invent in business future in rapidly changing business economy. The approach to managing human resources is undergoing a revolutionary change. It is the acknowledgement of the fact that it is PEOPLE – and not money, machines and material – that must run organisations. Business organisations must now ensure congruence between organisational objectives and an employee's aspiration. And therefore, proper use of human resources is a must for overall organisational performance.

Performance management is a system built on practical experience of management, managers, and employees gained while managing their company's business. It is observed that most employees will respond vitality to challenging objectives if they are involved in establishing them and if they work in organisational climate which encourages self-development, self-control, and an easy way of communication. This experience is well supported by Douglas McGregor's Theory 'Y'; which summarised as:

(1) The expenditure of physical and mental effort in work is as natural as play or rest.

(2) External control and threat of punishment are not the only means for bringing out effort towards organisational objectives. Man will exercise self-control in the service. To which he is committed. Commitment to objectives is dependent on reward associated with their achievement. The most important rewards are those that satisfy needs for self-respect and personal improvement. The average human being learns under proper conditions not only to accept but seek responsibility.

(3) The capacity to exercise a relatively high degree of imagination, ingenuity, and creativity in the solution of organisational problems is widely, not narrowly distributed in the population. Under the conditions of modern industrial life the intellectual potentialities of the average human beings are only partially utilised.

Performance management seeks to integrate the company's objectives for profit and growth with the personal goals and satisfaction of its manager, staff and employees in general. Although the system is getting constantly improved have already demonstrated its practical effectiveness. We are gaining new insight into interdependence of the business system required for good performance. Above all, now it is clear that the real key to success in business is more effective use of our human resources; the talent and drive are there, if only we release them.

What the company needs is a principle of management that will give full scope to employee's strength and responsibility and at the same time give common direction or vision and effort, establish team and harmonise the performance of the employee with common corporate goals.

Global company's challenge is: "only the fittest will survive". This has created new people economy, new people organisation and new people management. To reinvent organisations themselves in order to cope up with the post-liberalisation, privatisation and globalisation, competition; organisation leader has to transform organisational practices and processes and change mind-set of management leader and his people. It is immediate task put before him and to be competitive, it is made amply clear that one should change role boundaries for human resource management.

There must be strong conviction that every single person is capable of superlative performance. If the environment is favourable, it will enable management to harness people's talents and bring out to the organisation their fullest potentials. To stay at the top means providing the worth of all organisation again and again in newer and most challenging environment; exactly this applies at the individual level. Managing people to make them manage themselves calls for strong leadership. The purpose of a leader that of developing vision for organisation and ensuring that it is shared by everyone it affects within the organisation. Setting team goals is really a matter of convenience and pragmatism. Individual and team performance are collectively assessed as corporate performance. Getting people in harmony becomes the basic for good organisational performance. Collective performance of these groups, departments will synergise to deliver excellent corporate performance, which is usually visible to the business world. Performance is measured solely in terms of end result the organisation and individuals achieved.

4.2 PERFORMANCE MANAGEMENT – A CONTINUOUS PROCESS

Performance management is a dynamic system which seeks to integrate the company's need to clarity and achieve its profit and growth goals with the participation of managers and managed. They need to contribute themselves. It is demanding and rewarding style of managing business by involvement and ownership. It is a system, which creates a climate of opinion is recognised by providing the framework of techniques for solving them.

Looking at this, then performance management operates in a company as a continuous process of:

(1) Reviewing critically and restating the company's strategic and tactical performance plans.

(2) Clarifying each one in the company the key results and performance standards they must achieve in line with their department/units/sections and company and gaining his contribution and commitment to these.

(3) Agreeing with each one a job improvement plan which makes a measurable and realistic contribution to the department and company's plan for better performance.

Providing condition in which it is possible to achieve their key results and improvement plan notify.

(a) An organisational structure which gives a manager maximum freedom and flexibility in operation.

(b) Management control information at a frequency which makes for more effective self-control, better and quicker decisions.

(4) Using systematic performance review to measure and discuss progress towards result and potential review to identify mean with potential for advancement.

(5) Developing management training plans to help each manager/employee to overcome his weaknesses to build his strengths and accept a responsibility for self-development.

(6) Strengthening a manager's motivation by effective selection, salary and succession plans.

These are independent and dynamic in nature, depending on emergent need of business operation. It is therefore necessary to educate, train organisation's people on their role, responsibilities and goal realities. For this management development is valuable byproduct of running business efficiently.

4.3 PERFORMANCE MANAGEMENT – AN INTEGRATED PROCESS

An integrated management system is required that blends performance management into every aspect of the organisation. These integrated systems are called five pillars of performance management. PRODUCT is the focal point for organisational purpose and achievement. QUALITY in product is impossible without the RIGHT ORGANISATION. The right organisation is meaningless without proper CORPORATE LEADERSHIP. Strong bottom-up COMMITMENT is the support pillar for all the rest PROFIT AND PERFORMANCE. Each pillar depends upon the other four and if one is weak all are. Indeed, the key question is whether the organisational performance serves or squashes the human spirit. Therefore, how you choose to organize for performance can either make you perform or break your performance. These five pillars on performance are again built on the foundation of your organisational STRATEGY, STRUCTURE, STYLE, SKILL, SYSTEMS, STAFFING AND SHARED VALUES. Well supported on the plinth of organisation CHARACTER, CLIMATE, CULTURE AND COMMITMENT. If all are positive to build positive organisational image, people will be recognised you as Best-in-class corporate performance managed organisation.

All the above systems of management are inter-linked and integrated to produce performance, generally classified as:

(1) Human Process – Values, attitude, behaviour, norms, interaction and culture.

(2) Structure – Organisation layers-fat/flat management systems, policies, procedures, practices, information system, flexibility.

(3) Knowledge – Technical, administrative, human processes, skills and competencies.

(4) Non human resources equipment, plant work environment and manufacturing technology, capital, etc.

(5) Strategic Position – Business plans, marketing and customer relationship and service, human resources, environmental changes, etc.

Integration and re-examination of these systems and subsystems makes total

4.4 TOTAL PERFORMANCE PROCESS

A fundamental need of management who wants to improve their organisation's performance is to know how they operate their processes. Processes are series of steps designed to accomplish a goal – whether it is individual, departmental or organisational.

They are linear in that they have starting and finishing points. They have width based on the number of departments, individuals involved and have depth determined by the level of details at which the process is documented. In addition, processes have customers, beneficiaries and are driven by business, management and customers requirements. Processes can be measured, by a set of assumptions – business plan. Thus, processes are the infrastructure of a company and are the primary pipeline through which corporate work flows. So, when embarking one must develop both its process awareness and its process competence.

Process awareness includes:

- Identifying the number of existing processes within an organisation and their inter-dependence.
- The performance level of each process.
- The required resources to support each process.
- A vision of how they should operate.
- An executive team requires relay on insight, vision, a methodology and people skills in process activities.

Most organisations have a vision, a mission, an operating set of norms, values and a strategic plan. These four elements set the direction of the organisation and within their four, alignments is critical. The strategy needs the road map to the company/division and reflects the mission of the organisation. In addition the values set the tone for how the organisation operates and guides, how the strategy is implemented. All these elements come together in the annual budget or business plan and allow the organisation to fulfil its strategy and vision and it does reflect the desired values. If you don't know these processes where you are going, it does not matter how you get there.

The direction of the organisation must be clear before you begin to rethink and redesigned your performance processes must have requirements defined. Those are:

- ❖ Organisation development goals or objectives.
- ❖ Human resource issues.
- ❖ Customer satisfaction, relations and service.
- ❖ Goal or target setting.
- ❖ Technology needs.
- ❖ And operating costs.

And conformance to these requirements produces results – business performance, more effective information, more appropriate organisational behaviour, and increased efficiency, improved quality of product and service and more effective resources allocation. Further investigation in performance process elements shall sharpen your understanding on performance management.

4.5 INVESTING THE FULL PROCESS

The subelements of investigating performance process are:

- ❖ Input detail – what do you need to start?
- ❖ Cycle time – how long form start to finish time?
- ❖ Efforts – how many hours of people's time?
- ❖ Resources requirement – what materials or other cost-related items are to be consumed?
- ❖ Value added – what does this step contribute and to which output?

And, Performance Indicators are:

- ❖ Quality – what is done to ensure work is defect free?
- ❖ Feedback – how do you know if you have been successful?
- ❖ Competence – what skills are required and do they exist at the required level?
- ❖ Values – the corporate values exist in the process and what values are present within the process.
- ❖ Authority and autonomy levels – where and what are they?
- ❖ Behavioural requirement – what does the process require people to do?

This thorough investigation of any process gives you entire picture of process. The deeper you investigate a process mapping, the more you will find that the work successfully completed.

A great deal of information through investigation helps to set performance targets of the process. The key issue in setting goals or targets is to balance them in future. However, performance requirements should include all critical categories: Cost, time, quality, behaviour, attitude; information system; productivity/efficiency, price, etc. These are particular categories of performance management. It is at this point in the performance of particular project that a quantum leap takes place from process review to process interpenetration and action plan. And accordingly you workout performance process strategic plan based on the following information;

Process maps, existing performance data, management requirements, business requirements, process requirements, customers requirements, measurement criteria, performance targets, improvement scenario, improvement strategy, operating assumptions, problem areas identified, an array of tools and methods, accountability and authority to act, experience with the process.

The major benefit here is that there is a great deal of confidence in the decision taken forward if they are pretested by this method.

4.6 CORPORATE PERFORMANCE

Getting people to perform in harmony becomes the basis for the good organisational performance. The uniformity of perception and common understanding of a need is the very basis of collective drive in reaching a common goal. If this foundation is strong then the organisation will have the in-built resilience to absorb shocks from variable like technological change, national or global economical changes, government regulation and market condition and so on. The managers who strive for positive performance must determine and define the sequence, extent and timing of individual tasks so that people perform in step with one another. Thus, individual performance will merge into dynamic flow of collective performance. The collective performance will synergise to deliver excellent corporate performance. Therefore, any productivity, quality or performance improvement programme to be truly effective must develop and maintain the interest, awareness and participation of all members of the organisation. People caring CEO ask people to do their job themselves, delegate responsibility and ownership of the job, people takes pride in performing their jobs and produced excellent performance. Thus, the synergy of individual and organisation brings maturity in organisational success. This aspect of performance is called intrinsic.

Intrinsic performance aspects: Belonging to the real nature coming from within, inherent which do effect, positive or negative performance. Positive, proactive and learning CEO's are generally people-oriented and their people are performance-oriented. They are strongly supported by company's structure, style, skills and culture. Another aspect of performance is extrinsic aspect. These are dependent on external circumstance coming from outside items and process itself. If the organisation is flexible it will adapt change process for accommodating organisational renewal, management engineering or business process rengineering plans will yield gain from change management. Hence, this distinction in intrinsic and extrinsic will be important in measuring and assessing performance.

4.7 NEW MANAGEMENT PARADIGM

Change management may demand many organisational improvement programmes right from knowing the present position and the intended destination to determine the needed direction. Shift in paradigm cause many management policies, procedures, practices and systems correction. The past is prologue. It is only future that should really matter. And in term of performance, future destination is operational excellence. The present direction must be continuously changed and or improved. Effective performance improvement programmes require that all personnel within an organisation understand their purpose and develop interest in making these programmes work. They must eventually assume a participative position. The emphasis must therefore, be on the development and cultivation of practices of customer-oriented service and teamwork environment. Organisation will need to recognise and eventually adopt a newer management paradigm, which is founded on effective, collaborative efforts by all members of the organisation. Management in the traditional sense of the team is a member of this team with well-defined responsibilities. However, the previous, definition of planning, directing, organising and controlling as management activities is redefined and redirected to the newer, more positive role imperative as shown below:

Traditional Management	Planning	Directing	Controlling	Organizing
New Management Functions.	Creating a vision, Featuring, Setting goals and overall objectives.	Aiming, Focusing, Promoting actions, Encouraging, Persuading.	Checking results, Identifying improvements.	Removing barriers and road blocks, Facilitating, Allocation of resources.

To reach desired operational results, the management eventually need to adopt this management paradigm. The corporate culture needs to attune itself to accepting accurate inputs, analysing the information and developing and implementing any need for improvement. The management will have to carry out survey of improvement base issues and actions to achieve desired performance management.

Improvement Base Issues

(1) Developing a means of defining customer internal as well as external expectations and translating these into realistic goals and objectives.

(2) Using, developing and empowering employees, treating these resources as human capital.

(3) Planning and carrying out effective project and process management.

(4) Using appropriate, quantitative measurement techniques for status reporting and analysis of both positive and negative trends.

(5) Developing an effective root cause analysis system to identify the real causes for organisational problems for improvements.

(6) Using positive fault correction, practical, corrective, adaptive and preventive actions.

To educate our managers more on these issues, I think, we must go through 'ACHIEVE' model, developed by Hersey and Goldsmith and used by Blanchard Training and Development Institute.

4.8 PERFORMANCE MANAGEMENT AT WORK

Using human resources as competitive weapon in the management of organisational performance is certainly a new dimension in the management of organisational behaviour. But how can organisations use human resources as strategic weapon? This can't be done in isolation and need very close coordination between planning and the other performance factors. Companies can gain a competitive advantage through their human resources by making sure that employees have the appropriate skills and are suitably motivated. Managing people to perform can make a very significant difference. If we approach them in different manner. That performance is not merely a function of attributes individual possesses, but also depends on the organisation and environment. Individual can be highly motivated and have all the skills to do the job but will not be effective unless their work fits in the need of their organisational environment. Hersey and Goldsmith stated that while analysing human resource problem, two primary goals should be kept in mind: to determine key factors that can influence employee performance and to present these factors in a way that can be used and remembered by managers. These key factors are: motivation, ability, and understanding: organisational support, environment fit, feedback: and validity. These factors he has presented to ACHIEVE model. While using this model he says, the manager evaluates how each factor will affect the present potential performance of employee for a given task. Then the manager should take the steps that 'Fit' the unique causes of the performance problem. The seven factors to ACHIEVE model along with typical problem-solving alternative are broadly narrated.

A – Ability; C – Clarity; H – Help; I – Incentive; E – Evaluation; V – Validity; E – Environment.

A – Ability: (Knowledge and Skills) – This refers to employees knowledge and skills – the ability to complete the specific task successfully. Key component of ability include task – relevant education; task – relevant experience; task – relevant aptitude (potential or traits that enhance the successful completion of the task). In analysing follower/employee performance, the manager should ask, does an employee have the knowledge and skills to complete this task successfully? If he has ability problem, solutions may include specific training, coaching, and assignment of specific duties or responsibilities. These alternatives should be considered.

C – Clarity: (Understanding and Role Perception) – Clarity refers to an understanding and acceptance of what to do, when to do it and how to do it. To have understanding an employee needs to be clear on the major goals and objectives, how these goals and objectives – top priority and low priority goals. Should be accomplished and the priority of goals and objectives, if employee has a problem in clarity or understanding, there may be problem in the performance-planning phase. The manager should assure that all objectives are formally recorded. An employee should be encouraged to ask question for further clarification.

H – Help: (Organisational Support) – This refers to the organisational support, an employee needs for effective task completion. These support factors include adequate budget, equipment, facilities and skills that are suitable for task completion, necessary support from other departments, product/service availability and quality and adequate supply of proper manpower. If there is a lack of support, manager should clearly identify where the problem exists. If the problem is of fund, equipment, etc., the manager should see whether the necessary resources can be acquired. If not manager can revise objectives to avoid holding employees responsible for circumstance beyond their control.

I – Incentive: (Motivation and Willingness) – This refers to employees task relevant incentive – the motivation to complete the specific task – under analysis in a successful manner. In evaluating the incentive it is important to remember the most people are not equally motivated to complete the task. Employees tend to be more motivated towards the successful completion of task that will bring them either intrinsic or extrinsic rewards. If the employees have an incentive problem, they should clearly make to understand that performance of the task is related to pay, promotion, recognition and job security. Rewards can be tangible or intangible, feedback on performance, such as recognition or a pat people on the back, can be an important part of the overall incentive system.

E – Evaluation: (Coaching and Performance Feedback) – Evaluation refers to informal day-to-day performance feedback as well as formal periodic reviews. An effective feedback process let employees know how well they are doing the job on the regular basis. It is unrealistic to expect the employees to improve performance if they are unaware that performance problem exist. People should know how they are being evaluated on regular basis before their formal periodic evaluation occurs. If there is an evaluation problem, it may be caused by the lack of day-to-day feedback on both effective and ineffective performance. Recognition for a job well done can be a vital part of the ongoing evaluation process. It can increase motivation and cost the organisation very little.

V – Validity: (Valid and Fair Personnel Policies) – Validity refers to the appropriateness and legality of human resources decisions made by managers. Managers need to make sure that decisions about people are appropriate in light of laws, court decisions and company policies. If there is validity problem, the manager should know that the trend of the law in management is clear: Personnel decisions need to be documented and justified on the basis of performance-oriented criteria. Managers uncertain about validity issues should discuss them with the personnel department.

E – Environment: (Environmental Fit) – The term refers to the external factors that can influence performance even if the individual has all ability, clarity, help and incentive needed to do the job. Key element of the environmental factors includes competition, changing market conditions, government regulations, suppliers and so on. If there is an environmental problem beyond their control, employees should not be rewarded or reprimanded for performance. In short, employees should be expected to perform at a level consistent with the limitations of their environment edge. Thus, focusing firmly on, resources with mutual trust and reliance could provide a significant opportunity to secure a sustained edge over competitor's performance, what is required is broad strategy, integrated plan of action and psychological contact with employees to accomplish organisational goals in the given framework. Once people go through these issues, make their implicit expectation explicit, their sharing expectations regarding roles and goals in such open atmosphere emotionally charged them to perform well. They develop a kind of psychological contract with the organisation and willingly entered into performance agreement.

4.9 PERFORMANCE AGREEMENT

Performance results can be evaluated by measurement, observation and discernment. Specify how you will evaluate performance, how progress is reported, what shall be the reward. People will be much together on themselves than outside evaluator or manager. When trust is high, discontentment is replaced by so-called objective measurement.

Based on these principle performance agreement terms are included here:

(1) Specify desired performance parameters and results. Let them supervise methods and means of their work.

(2) Go heavy on guidelines, light on procedures, so that as circumstances change, employee have the flexibility to function, exercising their own initiative.

(3) Mention all available resources within the organisation as well as outside it for supporting their tasks fulfilment.

(4) Involve people in setting their goals, standards or objectives of acceptable and exceptional performance.

(5) Maintain trust and use discernment, more that quantitative measurement to assess performance.

(6) Reach an understanding of what positive and negative consequences might follow achieving or failing to achieve desired performance.

(7) Make sure the performance agreement is reinforced by organisational structure, style and systems to stand the test of time.

Managing performance by agreement is one of the core requirements of performance management.

Performance management is all about getting thing done as desired. Once this psychological contract is established employees then supervise their work themselves and managers then are the sources of help and guidance. Having participated in the formation of the agreement feel good about giving accountability and responsibility to them and they do whatever is necessary to perform as desired within the guidelines. Since they evaluate themselves, they have clear, up-front understanding of what results are expected and what criterion are used to assess their performance. People know in their heart much more than measurement system can reveal about their performance.

4.10 SUMMING UP ON PERFORMANCE MANAGEMENT

"A good coach knows how to step on someone's toes without messing up their shoeshine." Team based organisations work teams establish performance expectations, coach along the way towards reaching those objectives, provide feedback and take corrective action including discipline. And coaching is not something the CEO can order, the middle executive to do for bottom. Business that grows by involvement, development and improvement do not die. Performance management is thus based on the proposition that positively induced improvements in target/goal achievement can only arise from positively induced changes in behaviour.

Man is a problem-solving skill and knowledge using social animal. Once he has satisfied his need, two main kinds of experience are significant to him; one of his deepest needs is to apply his skills and knowledge, whatever they be to the challenging tasks to feel the exhilaration of the well solved problem. The other need is to find meaningful and warm relations with people to love and be loved to experiences, to respect and be respected, to work in common tasks. If this approach to managing men were to be adopted it would really provide as a valuable, more systematic and objective base for increasing performance.

The two fold aims of performance management can be summarised as:

- To improve the performance of existing manager in line with company objectives.
- To identify and then train, retain those with potential to meet the future needs of the business.

The performance management is not just a set of procedures and formats. Peter Drucker has rightly said that "what the business enterprises needs in a principle of management that will give full scope to individual strength and responsibility at the same time give common direction of vision and effort, establish teamwork and harmonise the goals of the individual with the common will. The only principle that can do this is management by objectives and self control". Performance management thus beneficial to both: individual and organisation.

Performance management extends following benefits to individual

(1) Knowledge as to what his superior expects to be accomplished, which assure that he directs his efforts toward what is most important.

(2) An understanding on the part of each subordinate as to where he stands with his superior in terms of relative progress.

(3) A better basis of performance evaluation then is possible through evaluation based on personality traits (ability, initiative, integrity, judgement, health, appearance and moral).

(4) Ultimate is higher individual performance and moral building.

Performance management also extends some benefits to organisation

(1) A reserviour of performance and personnel information as a periodic basis for updating employee career life.

(2) The determination of personnel development needs with organisation.

(3) A sound basis for promotion and compensation practices.

(4) A managerial method whereby the superior and subordinate in an organisation identify major areas in which employee will work, set standards for performance and measure results against these standards.

(5) An effective alternate to the largely inadequate traditional approach to measuring results in a method that establishes definite results which the individual is to achieve in a given timeframe.

(6) An unbiased method necessary to implement and maintain a performance standard aimed at improving overall performance and morale. Top management spends necessary time to define objectives and yardsticks by which performance will be measured. In turn these overall objectives must find their ways to the heads of the subordinates and finally to the individuals. This way the objectives of sub-units and individuals are integrated with the overall performance objectives of the organisation.

(7) The CEO and his management staff set objectives of the company, the individual manager formulates their own (department) objectives. When the objectives of the CEO are disseminated to the organisation and interact with the individual objectives, a reaction takes place that causes the individual to modify his goals to fit the organisations or organisation to adopt some of the individual's goals. This is the key aspect of the performance management process.

(8) Organisation budget cycle starts from the sales projections in total and the demand spread overtime; a product budget indicating the timing and quality of product, and indicate material, labour and overhead expenses is tentatively developed. Finally, budget for such discretionary areas as administration expenses, R&D and capital additions are prepared. The chain of participation makes everyone aware of his responsibilities and results. Since it is collectively approved budget revisions and trade offs is permitted if necessary. So, the performance objectives setting process is the result of compromise.

(9) Objectives developed by individuals contribute meaningfully to the objectives of the unit and to the total organisation.

(10) As far as possible objectives are challenging, specific and measurable.

(11) Reviewed periodically, the periodical counselling as to the progress is made, help change the morale, motivation of individual as it warrants.

(12) Evaluations are based on the ability to meet or exceed the previously mutually established, measurable objectives. Evaluation distinguishes between levels of individual performance.

(13) The reward structure – promotion practices, training and development, recognition, salary and benefit compensation is considered as function of explicit between delineation of performance accomplishments.

(14) The integration of objectives those which the individual sets for himself/department are tide closely to the objectives of the total organisation and in fact, contribute directly to them. This provide for more potential efficiency than under the traditional approach.

(15) Performance management improves communication – the channel of communication is automatically opened by this concept of performance management in that downward dissemination of objectives is basic and upward suggestions are encouraged. The individual feels the part of the organisation because he generates suggestions as well as contributes to their realisation.

The primary aim of performance management is to highlight their significant goals that must be accomplished if superior results are to be achieved. Setting performance objectives approach aim toward the individual and the approach describes how it is to be linked to the total organisational goals. Finally, performance management setting process helps in the elimination of overlapping responsibilities, duplication of work, misunderstanding common between workgroups within organisation, clarifies, role and responsibilities towards goal achievement thus lead to a potential increase in overall internal performance/efficiency. Performance objective setting include a commonality of purpose, an understanding to what that purpose is and an efficient use of the resources in the organisation to achieve its all-round performance.

Chapter 5

BASICS OF BUSINESS OBJECTIVES – I

Structure:

5.1 Setting Foundation

5.2 Creating Business Objectives and Awareness

5.3 Defining Business Processes

5.4 Process Mapping and Analysis

5.5 Strategy Planning for Total Performance Plan

5.6 Key Critical Performance Factors

5.7 Exploring Business Objectives

5.8 Business Objectives – Scope for Action

5.9 Performance Scope at Plant Level

5.10 Performance Scope at Departmental Level

5.11 Performance Objectives – Models

5.12 Objective Planning in Action

5.1 SETTING THE FOUNDATION

Putting business objectives in action, an organisation must have some built-in ability to make changes in response to the changing environment. Secondly, it must do so with minimal disruption of services. The ability to transform itself with little or no distress and disruption; organisation that have this transformation ability of **responsive awareness** to relate to its changing environment and **focus_flexibility** to remain focused while reconfiguring itself to meet the change required by the environment. Then only such organisations can digest and direct a new paradigm of change smoothly and firmly. The CEO of such organisation will understand that individual behaviour is shaped by the roles that people play in the organisation. He knows that effective ways to change behaviour is to put people into a new role in the organisation, which imposes new roles, responsibilities and relationships on the person. This creates a situation that forces new attitude and behaviour to emerge in the person. The inter-related factors needed to change an organisation effectively are: **coordination, commitment** and **competencies.**

Coordination of effort or teamwork is especially important if an organisation wants to benefit from the existing synergy of employee knowledge and understanding with proper coordination of effort an organisation can discover cost, quality, product development and performance development opportunities. Commitment to change is essential if management wants cooperation with an effective implementation of the changes. Finally, competencies, such as knowledge of the business as a whole, analytical skills and inter-personal skills are required if members of the organisation have to identify and solve problems as a team. If any of these elements are missing, the proposed change process will break down. It is, therefore, necessary to set foundation for future activity in two ways:

- Prepare management to accept and embrace new paradigm of change.
- Prepare organisations employees for involvement and change.

5.2 CREATING BUSINESS OBJECTIVES AND AWARENESS

The important part of every business is to know what to be done to manage change. A simple way to get started is long range planning. It is done by asking some basic question. Good places to begin with are the following objectives:

- What business am I in?
- What is my place in the industry?
- What customer am I serving?
- Where is my market?
- What is my company image to my major customers?
- What business I want to be in three to five years from now?

- ❖ What my specific goals for profit improvement?
- ❖ What improvement plan do I have to make to improve total performance of the plant?
- ❖ What is my greatest strength? Am I using it well?
- ❖ What is my greatest problem? How am I going to solve it?
- ❖ What share of market do I want? Next year, year after next?
- ❖ Are my employees/personnel policies acceptable to them?
- ❖ How can I finance growth?

These questions cover every important area of business. Generally, most companies concentrate on: Profit, Sales, Finance, Marketing, Capital addition, Production, Research, Engineering and Personnel/HRD.

The interpretation of these generalised questions/areas help us to develop business objectives in four broad types of orientations:

(A) **Commercial** – The company decides on its product policy by examination of market and from this, formulates and operates plan for profit and return on asset employed. This is sometimes, referred to as market-oriented objective.

(B) **Technological** – The company is largely engaged on either financed advanced technology or product development, usually at an agreed level of profit or return on asset employed.

(C) **Production** – The company manufactures product to customers specification, usually at low technological risk at fixed price for volume, quantities or alternatively, provides a service against a fixed price. This is sometimes, referred to as service-oriented objective.

(D) **Human resources** – The company decides its core competency in product or quality on the basis of knowledge and skills pool of its employees and accordingly plan product and manufacturing, technology transfer or acquisition and develop manpower planning and development of workforce. This is called employee-oriented objectives.

Business Objectives are Generally Classified as:

- ❖ Sr. Objectives – for top of the organisation (core group).
- ❖ Line objectives – deriving directly from senior executives (SBU / UNIT / DEPT.)
- ❖ Supportive objectives – deriving laterally from the line objectives or other supportive objectives (service-oriented functionaries).

Degrees of generality as associated with these objectives are:

(a) **General objectives** – where the objective is of necessity, vague and difficult to specify.

(b) **Specific objectives** – where the results are identified can be defined precisely or related to standards.

(c) **Quantitative objectives** – where the results are specified in numbers.

5.3 DEFINING BUSINESS PROCESSES

Any process is a set of interrelated activities, each having inputs and outputs. Inputs can be material, equipment, information and other tangible objects when converted by services of activities into output that is provided to a product/service recipient – the customer, internal or external. It can be individual, departmental, a group or processing equipment and machinery. Every process has some characteristics.

(1) **Clearly defined ownership** – department, manager, group of workers who are responsible for yield, cost, quality, work schedule and performance.

(2) **Boundaries** – these are the beginning and end of a process, operational jurisdiction.

(3) **Capacity** – it is output rate of the process.

(4) **Documentation** – a detailed record of workflow of process and its performance. I provides references through which process can be measured (chart, drawings, personnel, record, etc.).

(5) **Control points** – this regulates the quality of work or provides feedback on process results.

(6) **Effectiveness** – is assessed by measurement. It must reflect customer requirement and its conformance, non-conformance in process is termed as ineffectiveness of the process (customer complaints, poor product quality, lack of interest).

(7) **Efficiency** – it is a measure of the output against the benchmark set to achieve the output. Inefficiency symptoms are non-value-added activities (suppliers problems, excessive cost on non-value-added activities).

(8) **Adaptability** – this is the ability of the process to adjust to change (technical, personnel and other departments and profiles).

(9) **Measurement** – these are the standards against what is measured. It is a process of identifying variation in results (SPC, SQC, PARETO are some of the statistical techniques).

(10) **Corrective action** – positive action against variation and process effectiveness establishment, feedback and corrective actions are the heart of any process losses, its repeatability, quality and consistency.

These ten characteristics are present in all business processes – manufacturing, service and other business processes.

We have seen that every process has input – output inter-relations. This inter-linking is generally termed as product/service provider and product/service receiver. This is customer-supplier relationship. One department is customer to the other department and manager is the customer and *vice-versa*. Hence, the process owner must understand, analyse and agree to the following basics:

BASICS OF PROCESS

- Who are the process customers? (Production Dept. is customer to Engineering Dept.; Employees are customers of Personnel Dept.)
- What is the process output in terms of products/Services? (issuing annual increment is an output of personnel policy)
- How is the customer satisfaction being measured? What is the current level of customer satisfaction with the process output (are employees happy with rate of increment?)
- Do the customers have any particular concerns, such as quality of product/service? (do they expect that rate of increment to be reviewed?)
- Is there any performance data that can help in evaluating the process current performance? (whether increment policy was rigid or flexible in the past?)
- What are the perceived constraints of the process? (any grievance of employees on increment?)
- How does this process compare with similar processes in other organisational? (policy on normal increment based on result, incentive for results, etc.)

Once the basics of process are completed, the process owner (CEO as owner of organisation), should map and analyse the organisation (as a whole process.)

5.4 PROCESS MAPPING AND ANALYSIS

Process Mapping and Analysis Starts with

Development of work plan – describe the work flow – describe the process in an integrated manner – complete the process mapping – complete the process constraint analysis – complete the organisational behaviour (behaviour, attitude, culture of the organisation) – create the ideal process for better performance.

Once process mapping and analysis is completed, process owner must assess customer feedback that is customer satisfaction with product or service the organisation (as process) delivers.

For proper understanding of customer satisfaction, the process owner should answer the following questions:

- ❖ How well does the process satisfy your customer(s)?
- ❖ How do you find out whether you are meeting the needs and expectation of your customer?
- ❖ Do the measures being used to assess the opinion of your customer(s)?

Customer satisfaction, opinion, expectation are the feedback mechanism by which the quality of the process is measured and examined against the specific targets/objectives/goals. To properly identify and understand the opinion on process functioning look into these details.

- ❖ What critical characteristics of the process can be improved so that the product/service will meet or exceed the customer's needs and expectations?
- ❖ What objectives improvement plan should be established so that critical characteristics will meet customer's expectations?
- ❖ What additional information – internal or external is needed to define these targets/objectives?
- ❖ What should be measured inside or during the process implementation?
- ❖ Does the measurement being used for assessment?
- ❖ Is the process currently meeting the established targets for critical characteristics of the process?

If there is a gap between process inputs and process output, how will it be assessed (objectives agreed and objectives achieved; variance, fact-finding study is necessary for further process performance improvement).

To what degree will the change in process reduce the difference between the voice of the process (inputs) and the voice of the customer (output = customer satisfaction).

Above analysis of process will produce final activity that is working out business plan for long and short range duration.

5.5 STRATEGY PLANNING FOR TOTAL PERFORMANCE PLAN

Planning is a process, by which the management of an organisation envisions its future and develops actions needed to achieve that future goals, planning has three general levels:

(a) **Forecasting** – attempts to anticipate future trends; it may even use organisational reengineering to predict future activity.

(b) **Strategic Planning** – seeks five to ten years or more years plan with future VISION based on management's forecasts and the existing strengths of the organisation.

(c) **Operational Planning** – establishes yearly objectives, programmes and budgets and timetable.

However, the planning process helps the organisation create its future. Planning helps an organisation on: Developing organisation's vision, mission and guiding principles; help the organisation's SWOT analysis and core competencies identified and how it can be enhanced; create awareness and preparedness of CEO to analyse whether the organisation has the resources and capabilities to meet the future. If not, how these capabilities and resources are obtained?

Planning builds focus and total quality into all aspects of the organisation, which helps in organising corporate resources, setting operational objectives and planning performance. Only after a strategic plan is developed should the organisation develop its yearly operational plans, because only then will management know where to steer the organisation to achieve its **VISION.** For this, useful definition of the classification of the management functions is given by Dearden, it is as follows:

1. Class – I: Strategic Planning Consists of

- Determining company policies and objectives.
- Deciding on any changes in these policies and objectives.
- Deciding on the resources to be devoted to attaining these objectives.

2. Class – II: Management Control Consists of

- Dividing the strategic plans into logical subdivisions.
- Providing funds to carry out the subdivision of the plan.
- Assigning the responsibilities for carrying out each of the subdivisions of the plan to individuals.
- Following up to see that the assignments are satisfactorily carried out.

3. Class – III: Operational Control Consists of

- Determining the specific manpower, equipment, material and information necessary to accomplish the subdivision of the plan.
- Assigning the resources so that the plan can be carried out in the most efficient manner.
- Comparing actual results with plan and taking corrective action wherever appropriate.

Strategic planning is a vital top management function in any business and is concerned with the achievement of both general objectives defined earlier. Strategic planning is a deliberate, systematic and continuous consideration of all processes required in managing a successful business and deals with processes such as – forecasting, planning, organizing, directing, controlling, coordinating and employing the techniques used by manager to do these things.

(1) A comprehensive, continuing project designed to keep a business healthy, prosperous and growing.

(2) A process which involves consideration of every function and activity, men, market, materials, money and plant.

(3) A process which makes use of or links together techniques, used in managing separate functions of the business – work-study, budgeting, control, etc.

(4) A means of crystallising business objectives so that all managers can recognise how their individual activities will help to fulfil common goals.

There are generally **two phases of strategic planning;**

(a) There is the start-up phase which is evolved in the gathering of internal and external data, evaluation and company objectives setting, followed by detailed planning.

(b) There is the **periodic updating of the plan** which requires updating of the basic information and following through to the redefining the detailed functional operating plans.

For the benefit of strategic planning data collection is necessary to define objectives. Peter Drucker in his book ***"Practices of Management"*** has stated seven main areas requiring objectives in any company.

1. **Profitability** – physical and financial resources.
2. **Marketing position**
3. **Innovation**
4. **Productivity**
5. **Performance and development management**
6. **Worker performance**
7. **Attitude**

It is therefore, necessary to analyse internal data under these headings. For example data collection on: **Worker Performance and Attitude:**

Objective	Data involved	Format of cost data
❖ Worker performance and attitude.	❖ Productivity analysis ❖ Retraining programme ❖ Turnover analysis ❖ Record on employee relations ❖ Analysis of wage rate and employee benefit	❖ Training cost ❖ Recruitment cost ❖ Lost income expense and benefit cost

External data collection: The approach should be to confine the analysis to relevant data from creditable sources area covered under this data; financial, marketing, product design, development and production, management practices. However, in view of highly competitive nature of the business, these external data are a vital part of the strategic planning and have a vital part to play in the planning activities.

Objective	Data involved	Format of cost data
❖ Market position	❖ Geographical sales and profit analysis ❖ Product line sales and analysis ❖ Classification of customers ❖ Product support cost ❖ Review of marketing practices (pricing, support services, credit, distribution advertising) ❖ Projection of future changes, etc.	❖ Regional sales cost ❖ Field support cost ❖ Credit costs ❖ Merchandising costs

Evaluation – In evaluation, it is important to remember the questions that one is trying to answer, i.e., where do we stand, what business are we in, and what are the most urgent future tasks? This evaluation deals with production, R&D functions. But in addition, must deal also with attitude and management practices.

Function	Evaluation and comparison to be made	Required cost data
❖ Marketing	❖ Total market history and projections for product-lines and company's share of market as compared with competition. ❖ Analysis of breadth of marketing operation relative to total market	❖ Analysis of selling expenses by region, customer and product lines against industry average. ❖ Product-line, factory cost, distribution, support cost and

	❖ Analysis of marketing and selling techniques and customer distribution analysis ❖ Marginal net profits by product-line and geographical area ❖ Merchandising costs ❖ Analysis of possible technological or sociological changes on our position vs. competition ❖ Analysis of home and export sales per employee vs. competition	selling expenses by geographical and customer break-down ❖ Cost of publicity, advertising, exhibition, displaying, etc. ❖ Projected R&D costs

Management Control Activities

Falls into two areas during production phase;

(1) Determination of policies to minimise start-up costs.

(2) Activities leading to reduction of standard costs

Areas of Influencing Competitiveness and Performance are

- Market research – sales promotion
- Uses of customer's operational experiences
- Technical research and development
- Good design, planning of productive facilities
- Good employee relations
- Quantity of product and value engineering
- Cost control
- Good commercial relations with supplier and sub-contractors
- Availability of labour and staff
- Absence of unfair competition

The success of future company activities is critically dependent on a correct evaluation of the minimum cost in these areas. Overspending will lead to reduction in profitability. Under spending could lead to a dissatisfied customer and thus prejudice, future sales. The management control function is again closely concerned in this area in the determination of optimum support for present and future profitability.

BUSINESS OBJECTIVES

(1) The Organisation's Key Critical Performance Factors (KCPFs).

(2) Exploring Business Objectives (Departmental Objectives).

(3) Business Objectives: Scope for Action, Organisational Scope and Departmental Scope.

(4) Performance Objectives – Models A and B.

(5) Objective Planning in Action.

5.6 THE ORGANISATION'S KEY CRITICAL PERFORMANCE FACTORS

A total performance management system provides the essential framework and discipline for determining the critical factors affecting the success of the organisation. It does this by identifying its key critical performance factors, regarded on the important profit influencing performance, increasing participation channels through which employees at each level are continuously endeavour to balance and optimise typical areas of business. Generally, performance, profitability and growth are the main Key Results Areas of any business. Their subareas can be classified as productivity, market share, utilisation of physical and financial resources and management potential and human resources Performance. Now let us examine subkey-areas responsible for performance improvement.

1.Productivity – Under this KCPF following subareas are covered.

(a) **Employee performance** – their training, conditions of working, work involvement, climate of employee relations and plant industrial relations.

(b) **Production efficiency** – Production planning, application of industrial engineering and work study, plant maintenance, introduction of new production methods, work improvements, project implementation, and rationalisation of production facilities.

(c) **Raw material yield** – Subareas:

- Process control
- Application of value engineering
- Cost saving improvement projects
- Inventory management and control

2.Market share – Under this KCPF, following subareas are recovered.

(a) **Production Price** – Product cost, overhead cost, distribution cost, trade terms and discounts.

(b) **Customer Satisfaction** – Product quality, achievement of delivery promises, customer service and relations.

(c) **Sales Promotion** – Advertising effectiveness, merchandising, planning of sales campaigns, packing design and product presentation.

(d) **Sales Force Effectiveness** – Sales and Marketing training, sales force salary and benefits, achievement of sales targets and reward system.

(e) **Product and Market Development** – Market research, product's RandD, Rationalisation of sales outlets, product development.

3. Utilisation of Physical and Financial Resources – Subareas

(a) **Cash-flow** – Debt collection, credit control.

(b) **Plant utilisation** – Stability of production, programme standardisation of product processes, multi-shift working, use of subcontractor, sourcing out.

(c) **Level of inventories** – Raw materials, stock levels, level of WIP.

4. Management Potential and Performance – Subareas

(a) Selection and recruitment methods.

(b) Salary and wage compensation.

(c) Management by result and reward.

(d) Employee career progression and professional development.

(e) Human relations at work.

(f) Management development – Training, retraining, performance evaluation and performance development.

(g) Employee involvement and empowerment.

A thoroughly researched and comprehensive list of KCPFs provides the basis for a reliance selection of important factors, which calls for investigation and analysis and then improvement of results. By doing this exercise, the organisation will commit itself to the discipline of regularly setting, harmonising and reviewing objectives in each KRA. Therefore, the 'outcome operation' will feed directly into the performance planning process of the organisation.

A simple analysis sheet can be devised for recording present situation of these KCPFs and then action can be prioritised. The sheet consists of four points;

Points No. 1 – What we want? (The targets/objectives we should aim for)

Points No. 2 – What prevents us? (The obstacles which need to be overcome)

Points No. 3 – Why? (The reason the obstacle has not been overcome before)

Points No. 4 – What can we do? (The actions proposed)

This type of organisational problem analysis approach will help managers gain clarity of their proposed plan for performance improvement. For your better understanding, I have produced some selective business objectives for your guidance.

5.7 EXPLORING BUSINESS OBJECTIVES

After defining business processes characteristics, their mapping, analysis and strategies for planning of objectives on long-term and short-term basis, we developed phases of planning along with management functions, data collection, evaluation and management control activities considering these observations as prelude to discuss the interaction between management function with cost planning, monitoring and control. It is worthwhile to consider the approach to define main objectives of any business.

- To minimise (losses) cost and then maximise profit.
- To perpetuate the business.

Again, this depends on the business orientation (old or new) of company's operation, i.e., commercial, technological, production, human resource, R&D or customer service, etc.

Following broad base long-term objectives (specimen) are identified for measuring total performance. Later on we will discuss short-term objectives while framing company business objectives, departmental objectives and individual objective. This process of formulating overall short-term objectives shall be the base of objectives, functional objectives and supportive objectives.

(a) OBJECTIVES FOR MARKETING

- To achieve market share growth _____ % p.a. over the last year
- To achieve market share of ____ % in the various products by ____ year.
- To achieve sales through various categories of customers at the rate of Rs. ____ and ____ % of the total sale last years.
- To introduce the new products or phase-out existing products over next 2/3 years with a view to achieve projected sales turnover.
- To achieve the total sales among various users by ____ % in two/three years.
- To reduce the sundry debtors (receivable) to average period of ____ days by year 2009.
- To increase the sales through various promotion aid with a view to create awareness about product quality and availability by 2009 - 2010.

(b) OBJECTIVES FOR MANUFACTURING:

- To increase the production capacity and capacity utilisation by years 2009 - 2010.

- To upgrade existing equipment by addition of extra equipment or through modernisation of plant facilities and replacement of obsolete equipment in various department in order to increase the capacity additions by the years ________ to ________.
- To set up a project design and development team for interaction with marketing group and client to ensure development of new products as per the client specifications within the agreed timeframe by the year ____.
- The product development time for various new products would be reduced through design and implementation of the product development system by the year _____.
- To develop a system for storage and retrieval of all drawings, maps, documents for future reference through codification, retrieval procedures, etc., the system has to be developed by ____ and implemented by ____.
- To upgrade the skills of various personnel in different areas concerning the plant activities on continuous basis by ____.

(c) OBJECTIVES FOR PRODUCTIVITY IMPROVEMENT AND EFFICIENCY

- To improve the productivity level in various areas as per decided improvement areas, (i.e., yield, rejection, salvaging, etc.)
- To improve the operations in each department through reduction of average consumption per unit of final production through better utilisation of equipment, implementing operations as per a predetermined procedure, better maintenance activities or any other activity resulting in improvement in quality and reduction in cost per unit of product as per the schedule.
- To provide clarity of understanding of workplace and process by establishing time standards and process route sheets for various stages in the manufacturing process by carrying out process studies for specific industrial engineering projects for various areas as per the schedule.
- To prepare and document maintenance schedules for all the plant and equipment in various departments and areas and implement them so as to prevent stoppages or production losses, as per the schedule.

(d) OBJECTIVES FOR MATERIALS DEPARTMENT

- To bring down inventories level of various materials – raw, intermediate and finished and maintain them as per the schedule.
- To meet the requirements of various categories of materials for various departments within the specified timeframe as per the schedule.
- To rationalise/classify the existing items and materials into specific categories based on analysis such as ABC, Fast, Slow, Normal (FSN), vital, essential, desirable

(VED), as relevant to the plant by _____ time. Based on classification, the lead-time analysis would be carried out by ____ time and minimum quality levels and recorder quantities to be decided by ____ time.

- To identify the various sources of suppliers for different items and ensure availability of a minimum of three alternative suppliers for critical and vital materials by ____ time and document them in the form of a database complete with addresses, contact persons, terms and conditions to enable easy reference in future by ____ time.
- To decide on items to be made in-house, or subcontracted outside based on discussions with unit head/CEO by ____ time.
- To streamline the purchase and procurement policies and introduce Material Resource Planning (MRP) system based on integration with production planning and control team by ____ time and strives to computerise it by ____ time.
- To develop a system for evaluating or rating vendors on various aspects by ____ time and carryout the evaluation on a continuous basis.
- To ensure payment to various categories of vendors by a specified period in order to ensure availability of committed vendors for quality as well as time as per the schedule.
- To establish material inspection procedures and necessary equipments/laboratory for inspection of various categories of items by ____ time in order to ensure quality as per requirement.
- To ensure development of proper record and procedures regarding identification and disposal of non-conforming and obsolete items by ____ time.
- To develop a material accounting system by ____ time to keep track of the materials consumed in various stages and departments of the plant for various products in order to facilitate identification of costs for each product category.

(e) OBJECTIVES FOR QUALITY

- The existing activities are developed into a Quality Assurance Department by ____ time through defining the role of Quality Assurance Department and describing the various activities to be carried out and evolving an organisation with definite roles and responsibilities.
- To identify, draw and document all the technical specifications of various raw materials, semi-finished goods and broughtout items by ____ time for obtaining clarity in identifying vendors and incorporating them in the purchase order.
- To develop a Quality Management System for the unit as per ISO-9001 requirements by ____ time (give various activities required to be undertaken and the timeframe for such activities.)

- To identify the various inspection stages for process in different departments, identifying the quality checkpoints in process-stages and finished products, install audit review procedures for ensuring the conformity and adequacy of the test procedures followed and defining the inspection norms. This would be in conformity with ISO-9001 procedures, in case the plant is going ahead with such system.
- To identify, install or upgrade the existing infrastructure for quality testing, inspection and awareness in various departments as per the schedule.
- To establish a system for obtaining customer complaints feedback from users through the marketing team or directly as the case may be, for carrying out 100% complaint analysis and convey the necessary feedback to the concerned department/ external vendor. This is to be completed by ____ time complete with the detailed steps to be taken.
- To install/carryout measures for various activities/departments for reducing the quality rejections to the desired levels as decided by plant head and those given above (under manufacturing head). The measurement will be identified and framed up by ____ time.
- To upgrade the technical knowledge about use of equipment, procedures latest techniques of various personnel in the quality department in different areas as per the schedule.

(f) OBJECTIVES FOR PERSONNEL/HRD

- To set up/strengthen the personnel/HRD department along with relevant personnel for carrying out the relevant Personnel, Administration, I.R., Training and other statutory activities by ____ time. Complete with the required records to be maintained as per various agency requirements.
- To develop an organisational structure through joint discussion of departmental head, unit head by ____ time.
- To develop KRAs, job descriptions for various positions of the plant by ____ time in discussion with plant head.
- To develop personnel/HRD manuals for references to all departmental head and other employees by ____ time.
- To undertake training to all at least 100 hours per employee PA.
- To undertake periodical performance assessment at least three times in a year and device performance development plan for each employee by the start of the year, every year.
- To improve positive industrial relations on continuous basis.
- To improve absenteeism and employee turnover levels from current levels during the year ____ by charting out various steps.

- ❖ To develop detailed database of each employee in terms of all the activities related to him such as leave, performance appraisal, promotion, personnel particulars and other relevant information by ____ time.
- ❖ To identify the various activities and infrastructure required to be set up at the plant level for carrying out training activities by _____ time and setting up the necessary infrastructure as per the schedule.
- ❖ To introduce forum for expression of ideas, suggestions, sorting out common problems through formation of quality circles, focus groups, etc., at the plant level and departmental level. Formation of such groups would be initiated at plant level and implementation would commence by ____ time.

(g) OBJECTIVES FOR FINANCE AND ACCOUNTS

- ❖ To formulise accounting systems and procedures in line with the corporate policies and prepare detailed working procedures for accounting function by _____ time.
- ❖ To monitor the system of budgetary control on a monthly basis and ensure active involvement of all departments for the purpose by explaining the budgeting process and ensuring its implementation by ____ time.
- ❖ To coordinate with material department in establishing ABC classification and fixing inventory norms.
- ❖ To ensure profitability as follows:

Year	PAIBT / Investment	PAIBT / Sales

PAIBT: Profit After Interest and Before Tax (Sales – all variable expenses and fixed expenses including establishment expenditure and after interest on working capital as well as investment at the rate of 18% P.A. and depreciation as per written down values method at the rate being followed by company presently).

Investment – Investment (Net fixed assets after depreciation) includes all investments till date and proposed for respective periods.

The list of objectives given is indicative and could be expanded, modified or altered depending on the relevance of the objectives of your company.

5.8 BUSINESS OBJECTIVES – SCOPE FOR ACTIONS

Before framing an action plan, consider every business activity as a process and analyse its strengths and weaknesses, so that you are clean on mapping of what, why, where and how performance is to be focused. Considering it as critical process analysis, it involves crystallisation of various ideas into workable strategies and action plan. This enables CEO to achieve the objectives and goals lay down. This chapter is for the guidance of CEO for setting objectives and detailing action (proposed) plan. The action plan will have to be detailed out containing the following:

- Listing of all the activities required to implement the action plan in order to achieve the objectives set for various functional areas of plant/department/people.
- Arranging the activities based on their inter-relations such as those activities that could be done parallel and those that have to be done sequentially.
- Identifying the team responsible for specific activity/group of activities.
- Define timeframe for start and end of the activity.
- What would be the requirement in terms of resources such as Personnel, Plant, Equipment and Infrastructure required for various activities during the plan implementation? In other words, the following questions need to be answered by CEO/Manager in order to facilitate arriving at coherent set of objectives and formulating the action plan.

1. What should be done to achieve the objectives?

   (Explore-man, machine, method and money resources)

2. What are the pre-requisites for achieving the objectives?

   (Change in systems, structure, staff, strategy, etc.)

3. What are the assumptions being made in arriving at these objectives?

   (Infrastructure facilities, product mix, people, processes)

4. What are the changes/reviews/modifications required in the organisation?

   (Processes detailed capabilities analysis)

5. What is the nature of support/coordination required from others?

   (core group, general management, committee, plant management committee)

6. What is the step-wise milestone that should be reached to achieve the objectives?

   (Long-range and short-range objectives and priority)

7. What additional infrastructure, equipment required to achieve these objectives?
8. What are the additional skills, knowledge and manpower required to meet the above objectives?

9. What are the indicators based on which we monitor performance for each company objectives/departments and individuals?

Through these questions answering, we can integrate approach for defining scope of performance management.

5.9 PERFORMANCE SCOPE – AT PLANT LEVEL

Following techniques can be used to define scope of performance management at plant level.

(1) Critical analysis (SWOT) of the company's business objectives, problems for establishing specified goals.

(2) Critical analysis of business environment internal and external.

- **Internal** – Start portfolio position analysis on products/business/departments, i.e., which are the question mark, star, cash-cow and dog business.
- **External** – Examine market condition, competition, effect of globalisation, free economy and g overnment tax reforms and laws amendments.

(3) Identifying and analysing business key thrust areas, key strategic areas, growth plans, etc.

(4) Identifying and focusing (if need be) on new functions creation, i.e., corporate planning, management audit, customer relations, environment management, MIS, costing and budgeting, MIS, manpower development, etc.

(5) Present organisation's analysis and projected image improvement by analysing McKinsey's 7-S: structure, strategy, systems, skills, staff, style and shared values.

(6) Setting up task force and individual responsibilities to secure performance management.

(7) Drafting and or revising key result areas of department, individual managers and employee's job description for establishing performance standards.

(8) Reviewing employee performance and potential development plans for installing fair reward system.

(9) Devising and implementing manpower development plans – individual and group training and retraining.

(10) Establishing periodical performance presentation plan and employee coaching.

(11) Developing strategies for organisation and individual performance development plans, development planning, succession planning and career growth, etc.

(12) Devising performance linked reward plans. This coherent action plan will create healthy competition and cooperation in the organisation and will bring valuable benefits to the organisation.

For example:

- ❖ A realistic and economic way to develop employees.
- ❖ Commitment of the CEO to the programme.
- ❖ Willing involvement of all, as they are cleared on their role and goal responsibilities.

Likewise, at departmental/individual level performance scope can be defined. This will be better way to integrate departmental, individual and organisational goals to create balance results achievement. Following are some of the questions to be answered on performance scope by managers, employees and all concerned.

5.10 PERFORMANCE SCOPE AT DEPARTMENTAL LEVEL

1. PERFORMANCE

- ❖ Are you satisfied with the results being achieved now by your company / department/section?
- ❖ In what areas there is clear scope for improvement performance?
  - (a) Of the Business?
  - (b) Of the Managers?

2. OBJECTIVES

- ❖ Are you clear and specific on objectives for your company/department/section?
- ❖ Do they look beyond next year?
- ❖ What is the range of objectives? (For example, manager performance, employee relations, industrial relations, innovation, work improvement objectives included)
- ❖ Are they really committed to achieve them?

3. POLICIES

- ❖ Do you have policy statements in the important areas of the business, to provide guidance on recurring questions?
- ❖ Are minor decisions frequently referred upwards for policy clearance?

4. MANAGER RESULTS

Is each manager really clear about:

- ❖ The key results he must achieve?
- ❖ The performance standards and criteria by which he will be judged?
- ❖ The control information he received in order to monitor progress?

- The limit of his authority?

  (a) If you have job descriptions already, can you be sure that they are used as a management tool?

- Were they imposed/failed/forgotten or did managers make genuine contribution to their job description?

  (b) Does each manager have an agreed plan with standards and time schedules, to improve his performance?

  (c) Are jobs big and demanding enough to provide growth opportunities for men?

5. ORGANISATION

Is there a sound division of work to be done?

For example:

- Scope of decentralisation
- Scope of delegation
- Confusion between staff/line
- Missing functions
- How many managerial levels are there from CEO/MD to first line supervisor?
- Are there too many?
- Are there many small jobs and not enough stretching and responsible jobs?
- Is the organisation working in good spirit?

For example:

(a) Sense of collaboration

(b) Flexibility on work to rules

(c) Power politics

(d) Preoccupation with status

6. CONTROL

- Do managers have control information on all the key results they must achieve?

  (a) Is it simple

  (b) Is it relevant

  (c) Is it timely

  (d) Is it acceptable

  (e) Is it a good basis for self-control

- Do managers delegate sufficiently so that they have time to concentrate on the things only they can do well?

7. COMMUNICATION

- Do managers listen as much as they talk?
- Is there a flow of information down the line so that a sense of common purpose and understanding is built-up?

8. SPIRIT OF THE BUSINESS

- Say what you feel personally about:

  (a) Are standards and controls used mainly as tools of self-help or as threats from above?

  (b) Do you feel free to approach your boss with ideas and suggestions for change?

  (c) Does your boss consult you on problems not strictly within your responsibility?

  (d) Do you have enough information – written and oral to know how you are getting on and how the business is shaping overall?

  (e) Are mistakes generally treated as 'crimes' or opportunities to learn?

  (f) Do you feel that you are over-managed?

  (g) Does your boss help, train and guide you on the job or do you just pick it up?

  (h) To what extent do you feel you are working on your own? Or cooperating with others as a team-member?

9. MANAGEMENT DEVELOPMENT

REVIEW

- Do you have a regular manager performance and potential review scheme? If not, how do you judge and record your manager's/employee's performance and potential?
- Does your scheme focus on the results a manager achieves or on the kind of man he is or what he does?
- What practical use do you make of reviews?

For example:

- When did you last identify and given accelerated promotion to an outstanding man?
- When did you last remove a man who could or would not meet minimum job standards?

TRAINING

(1) Do you prepare a training plan for your managers? Who creates it?

- ❖ Executive management
- ❖ Staff management
- ❖ Both

(2) Do you run internal management training courses?

- ❖ How do you identify the need for this?
- ❖ How do you evaluate the benefits of the course?

(3) Think of the last training course or seminar you attended personally

- ❖ Was it useful?
- ❖ Did you make any action proposals on your return?
- ❖ How you made direct use of what you learnt?

SUCCESSION

- ❖ Do you have a company succession plan?
- ❖ Do top managers take time to discuss promising young men and problems?
- ❖ Is it difficult to fill key management posts when they become vacant?
- ❖ Are you hoarding talent which could in the interests of man and company be used better elsewhere?

REWARDS

(1) Does your salary system:

- ❖ Attract and hold the right quality and number of managers?
- ❖ Reward managers in relation to the results they achieve and their potential?

10. A PERSONAL PROJECT

(1) Do the following project and discuss the outcome with your boss:

- ❖ Define your departmental objectives.
- ❖ You are responsible for a company, a department, a function or a section?

Write out:

(2) What is the essential contribution your department is making to the company's success?

(3) What are your departmental objectives for the next year?

(a) What are the major problems, difficulties, constraints, you expect to meet in achieving them?

(b) What are the opportunities, solution, improvements, you would make, given a free hand?

Objective	Problems	Opportunities to improve

11. DEFINE YOUR OWN JOB

- Think now about your job as an individual manager?
- Look at your KRAs expected
- Now define your own job in terms of these KRAs
- When you have done this, go back to check that you have made full use of the 'suggestions for improvement' column.

(a) ORGANISATIONAL STRUCTURE

- Analyse your departmental structure
- What problems often arise?
- What improvements can you identify?

(b) CONTROL DATA

- Analyse all the management control information you received from all sources and
- Ask yourself

(a) Do the controls focus on vital results?

(b) Are they simple and relevant?

(c) Do they stimulate action?

(d) Do they encourage self-direction?

(e) Do they tell you all you need to know?

(f) Are some superfluous?

(g) What improvements can you identify?

This scope analysis may not be comprehensive and there may be other actions and areas, which will stimulate interest in designing performance improvement plan. This planned action plan is indicative and organisation can enlarge, modify it suiting to its need. This may be used as guide book for preparing and implementing your plan.

(Source – taken from: Management by Objectives – by Job W. Humble, McGraw-Hill Publication).

We have seen that without organisation's KCPFs, we can't measure desired performance. Organisational KCPFs help us explore business objectives as well as scope for defining relevant objectives for the company, its departments and individuals and accordingly performance projects are implemented for respective levels.

This implementation of objectives again force us to review present and changing trends in industries utilising human resource effectively implementing intervention of organisational development programmes to arrive at total performance systems. It is, therefore, advisable to discuss and review our present status before putting objectives in action.

Following chapter clears your dilemma on these issues and makes you aware on how effective objectives (short-term) are being set.

5.11 PERFORMANCE OBJECTIVES – MODELS

Performance management starts with company culture, corporate values, mission and corporate goals. Corporate culture and values are the most powerful tool that a company has at its disposal for motivating, retaining, developing and getting the best out of its people. Only with clearly defined corporate business objectives, CEO is able to ensure a fit with people who share the same values, morals, priorities and attitudes. When employees internalise the company culture, values they always work in company's interest irrespective of their job requirements. In this mutually beneficial relationship between the company and each of its people the expectations from each side will be clear. The company will demand that employees add value to the company and align their actions in the same direction as the organisation is. CEO must ensure that the corporate vision, mission, values and business objectives are communicated clearly to all employees, equipping them with all the information they need to synchronise their actions with the company's objectives. The central objective of any company is to maximise the long-term return on resources, which it employs. Performance management; by setting collective business objectives in a dynamic system seeks to integrate the company's need to clarify and achieve its profit and growth with the employee's needs to contribute and develop himself.

It is a demanding and rewarding style of managing a business and it has following best practices to internalise.

- ❖ Create a self-appraisal system to be followed by supervisory and team appraisals
- ❖ Establish a clear link between rewards and productivity performance increase to increase motivational levels
- ❖ Make employees fully aware about the parameters used to evaluate their results
- ❖ Set and review specific objectives for each of the department, individual periodically.
- ❖ Ensure that the performance management principles and the working of the systems are transparent.

Starting from the macro-level business objectives and then breaking them into departmental functional and finally individual objectives, the company can set performance targets. The aggregate of the objective achievement under each performance standard is presented in a periodical performance review. Thus, helps to achieve monitoring of performance, enabling individuals to set and meet developmental parameters for company and individuals during the course of the performance targeted period. The models of setting business objectives are described here as A and B.

PERFORMANCE MANAGEMENT MODEL – A

SETTING PERFORMANCE OBJECTIVES

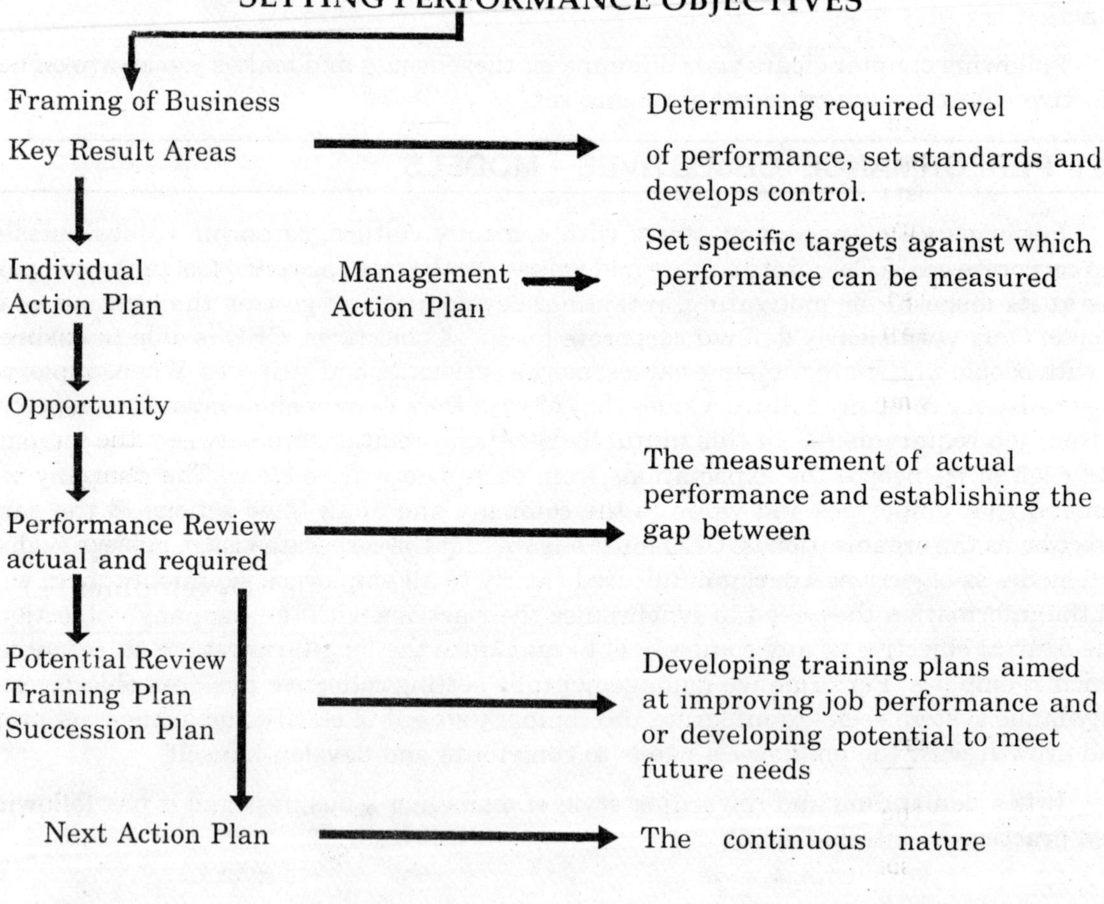

PERFORMANCE MANAGEMENT MODEL – B

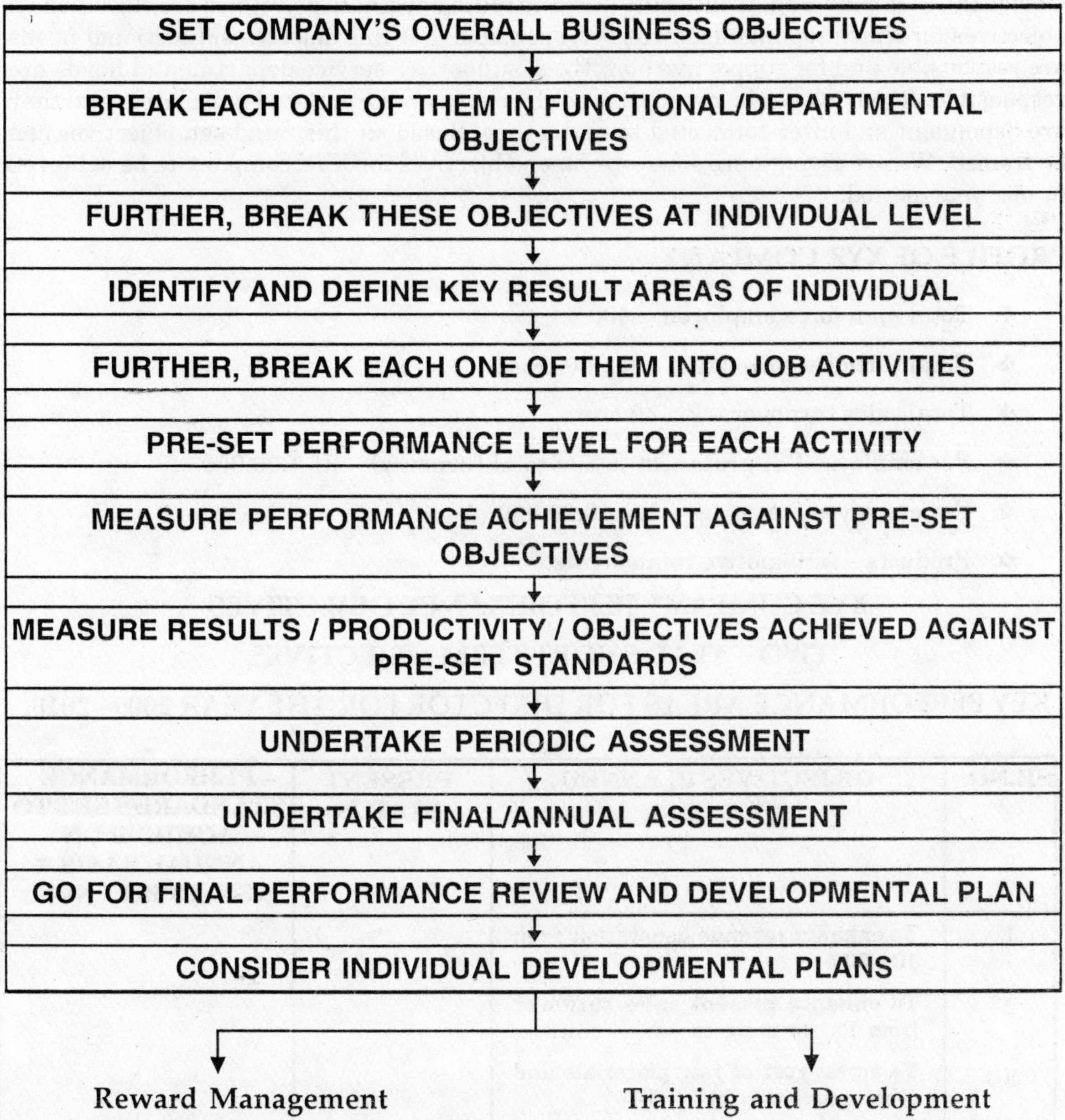

5.12 OBJECTIVES PLANNING IN ACTION

A company organises its resources and operates it to create growth and capitalise on growth opportunities offered by external market. Establishing core competencies in product leadership, customer service, R & D, technological innovations, human resources policies, etc., requires strategic planning, strategic intent to achieve challenging business objectives, it also requires clear road map for directing and implementing strategies and intent. Obviously, then planning, monitoring and controlling business objectives are classified on objectives for which top management is responsible. For line objectives, functional heads are responsible and for supportive objectives, supportive service departmental heads are responsible. It may please be noted that no objectives are formulated in isolation and they are dependent and inter-connected to each other. Based on this mind-set, objectives can be framed. We are giving here some specimen objectives for XYZ company to be achieved in one year period.

PROFILE OF XYZ COMPANY

- Total man force employed – 400
- Total turnover (after tax) – Rs. 50 crore
- Total sales turnover – Rs. 40 crore
- Per employee P.A gross cost (8% of total turnover) – Rs.1,00,000
- Per employee P.A. sales – Rs. 10,00,000
- Products – Automotive components.

XYZ COMPANY PERFORMANCE OBJECTIVES

TWO – YEAR SHORT-TERM OBJECTIVES

KEY PERFORMANCE AREAS FOR DIRECTOR FOR THE YEAR 2009 - 2010.

SR.NO.	OBJECTIVES PLANNED	PRESENT STATUS	PERFORMANCE STANDARDS SET TO ACHIEVE ON ANNUAL BASIS % AGE (IN RS. / NOS.)
1	To enhance revenue generation from 10 - 20%		
2	To enhance present sales turnover from Rs. 40 crore to ——— crore		
3	To arrest cost of raw materials and other purchases by ———		
4	To generate internal revenue by elimination of wastages, rejections, rework and other cost of doing wrong things		
5	To save on energy bills		
6	To arrest gross employee per month cost by down-sizing, right-sizing and or smart-sizing		

7	To undertake at least three/four products development		
8	To undertake work improvement projects by all departments		
9	To bring customer service improvement (internal and external)		
10	To implement ISO-9001 (2000) and ISO-14001		
11	To implement Quality Management Principles and Plans (TQM)		
12	Training/Retraining to all employees		
13	To establish new management functions such as management audit, budgeting, SBU, MIS, MCS, PPC, etc.		
14	To undertake employee satisfaction survey		
15	To undertake employee potential appraisal		
16	To implement objectives performance review plan presentation		
17	To revise human resources and employee relations policies		
18	To check and reduce employee turnover		
19	To enhance per head employee productivity by ———		
20	To undertake one-to-one coaching for employees future career advancement		
21	To undertake HR audit to gauge present and future manpower forecasting and cost.		

CASE STUDY

TOTAL OPERATING PERFORMANCE

TOP is a shared understanding about

- ❖ What is to be achieved?
- ❖ How it is to be achieved?

It is an approach to managing people that increases *the probability of achieving success.*

For achieving operating performance, *FOUR KEY COMPONENTS* are needed:

(i) **Planning and Contracting** – Against agreed objectives.

(ii) **Managing and Coaching** – For Performance Improvement.

(iii) **Feed Back** – How we are working against targeted objectives.

(iv) **Reward and Recognition** – Increments, Promotions and Development.

- ❖ The management which strives for positive performance must determine and define *the sequence, extent and timing of individual tasks* so that people perform in steps with one another.
- ❖ The individual performance will merge into dynamic flow of collective performance called *CORPORATE PERFORMANCE.*
- ❖ Collective performance synergises to deliver excellent corporate performance, which is usually, the only kind of *performance visible to the world.*
- ❖ This corporate performance approach emphasises that everyone's performance affects total performance.
- ❖ Therefore, any productivity, quality, work improvement programmes, to be truly effective, must develop and maintain the interest, awareness and participation of all members of the organisation.
- ❖ This can be done by developing a system of defining organisation's expectations and translating these into realistic goals or objectives.
- ❖ Total Operating Performance (TOP) is a performance measuring tool used for gauging corporate as well as individual performance.

To bring effective change in performance building, clarity on the following business objectives is important.

- Present state of business – Analysis of data
- Business benefits to seek – Improvement in quality of product and **Services – Internal and External**.
- Vision and strategy for performance – Road map for achieving success.

Once an agreement on above is reached, TOP implementation is undertaken this way:

- An analysis of – what has gone well last year and should be kept alive in future.
- An analysis of – what has gone bad and should be scrapped/improved.
- An analysis of – what new systems can add value to operational performance.

Based on above analysis of business operations, BUSINESS OBJECTIVE CYCLE is kept moving by **planning objective achievement action plan** this way.

(A) Key Critical Performance Factors (KCPFs) – At *Corporate* level on Key Performance Indicators (KPIs).

(B) Key Performance Areas (KPAs) – At *Manufacturing* unit level.

(C) Key Result Areas (KRAs) – At *Dept. / HOD* level.

(D) Target Setting – At *Individual* level and down the line.

Business objectives on TOP are specific work activities or projects the COMPANY, MANUFACTURING UNIT, DEPARTMENT/HOD AND INDIVIDUALS are required to achieve in a TIME-BOUND PERIOD. Objectives are the statements of intent or actions, hence are written down and made known to all.

Business objectives are devised with the support of following ***GUIDING PRINCIPLES:***

(1) To help reinforce understanding of our business and need for all-round effort with team spirit.

(2) To focus efforts, skills and competencies (contributions) where they are most needed (improving product quality, market share, cost reduction, etc.)

(3) To help build skill base of people and to empower them to improve their performance in response to changing business circumstances.

(4) To help, build and sustain an open, honest debate about continuing performance improvement at levels.

In brief, ***TOP is not new or another task but a 365 days process based on two-way communication between MANAGEMENT, MANAGER AND JOB HOLDER.***

TOP is distinctly implemented through such *ACTION PLAN*.

- Handing over objective document to Manufacturing Unit/HOD/Individual.
- Undertake periodical review to assess where we are.
- Final Performance Evaluation – Yearly.
- Planning for Reward and Recognition – Individual development.

Business objectives are generally spelt out in these areas and then translated into KPIs, KPAs, KRAs and Targets /Objectives.

- Additional revenue generation.
- Enhancing market share.
- Improving customer satisfaction.
- Improving product and productivity.
- Improving quality of products.
- Budgetary control.
- MIS.
- Cost reduction and work improvement.
- HR development – training.
- Mentoring and coaching.
- Performance development.
- Preventive and productive maintenance.
- Energy conservation and audit.
- Inventory Control – finished products, WIP, Materials and Stores.
- Plant Discipline – Safety, House keeping, Inter-personal relations.
- Quality Assurance.

TOP ASSESSMENT METHODOLOGY

Setting Performance Standards Its Measurement

Identifying deviation Corrective Action Plan.

Performance Standards – KPIs, KPAs, KRAs and Objectives are targets laid down by management are called Performance Standards.

Standards provide a clear definition and expectation for company, department and its people.

- Through standards, people know how they will be judged, hence, its supervision is less arbitrary and subjective.

- Setting standards consists of three parts.

Purpose – Why standards need to be developed? *To determine the need for standard.*

Example: To reduce total operational cost by 5%.

Expectation: What is expected from people?

Example: To implement cost reduction project throughout the year. Additional revenue generation by 5% over last year's sales revenue.

Measurement: Setting standards involves the need to make the products/service measurable against standards. *If you can't measure, you can't improve.*

Example: To implement minimum four cost reduction projects by each department.

Such standards are then translated into KPAs, KRAs and Targets on micro-level.

Performance standards are quantitative and qualitative. Some give tangible results, which can be measured – cost of non-conformance: Rejection – 3%. Some are intangible – Those are qualitative and can't be measured in quantity, volumes, numbers, etc.

Intangible is a kind of social and mental activity. Impossible to give quantity. For example, Positive Attitude, Behaviour and Mind-set, etc.

How do we measure cooperation, integrity, loyalty or positive attitude? We can measure its results, which are either positive or negative and are visible. *We only can assess it qualitatively.*

Performance Measurement – ***What was expected*** as per standards and ***what actually happened?*** The deviation is measured by way of quantity, quality, time, volume and percentage. Administering measurements guide us to take corrective action against deviation/gap removal.

DAVIATIONS

Why deviations occur?

(1) When standards and measurements are not reasonable – **SMART** (**S**pecific, **M**easurable, **A**ttainable, **R**elevant, **T**rack-able).

(2) When employee could not do the job, due to lack of skill and knowledge.

(3) When inter-department nature of product, processes are there. The preceding tasks sometime contribute to problems.

(4) Deviation from standards may occur due to service provider's fault. It may be employee's negligence, personal problem, management action, decision, etc.

(5) Deviation occurs when you adopt bureaucratic approach to service. "You will have to see the manager's attitude – our inflexible attitude".

CORRECTIVE ACTION

- Review Objectives.
- Review of process parameters.
- Review of people's skills and competencies.
- Review of people coaching and development.

BUSINESS – OBJECTIVES AND KEY TASKS

Unless the company sets demanding and exciting objectives, it runs a heavy risk of losing business vitality.

- Objectives are something to strive for more than present, to move forward.
- Objectives are aims that excite the imagination and give people something they want to work for. Something challenging to do, something they can be proud of when they achieve it.
- When there is a framework of a clearly expressed set of business objectives for future, it is much easier for people down the line to make faster and better quality decision for their own.
- Objectives are essential for company to take better advantage of the opportunities, which lie in future and forestall the threats, which it contains.
- To conclude, objectives provide an integrative and unifying power to people. *Instead of random functional and departmental objectives,* a total company view is worked out which determines where resources can best be concentrated for maximum growth, profitability.
- Without this kind of discipline, resources are left to themselves; seem to drift into those areas which have low profit opportunity for the company. Company business objectives are linked with individual's effective contribution.

(1) How company's objectives relate to individual work?

(2) How does company help him to understand where he fits in?

(3) What is expected of him?

(4) How can be judge whether he is doing a good job?

The company does this, by means of drawing results by way of defining:

HIS KEY TASKS – Essential for the achievement of the company's objectives.

THE STANDARDS – By which individual performance, key tasks may be realistically judged.

Key tasks are generally related to MEN, MACHINE, METHOD, MONEY, SYSTEM and POLICIES. Individual is employing for effective operations. The manager's basic needs to perform well are:

- ❖ Agree with the results he has to ACHIEVE.
- ❖ Give him an opportunity to PERFORM.
- ❖ Let him know how he is GETTING ON.
- ❖ Give him GUIDANCE AND TRAINING.
- ❖ REWARD him on his contribution.

Once needs are clear to the company, clarity on individual ROLE AND GOAL purpose is clear and thereafter company sets out individual's ACCOUNTABILITY and RESPONSIBILITY in context of his ROLE AND GOAL.

This is done by ANALYSIS of:

- ❖ His Key Result Areas of the job – (KRAs)
- ❖ The level of performance desired (Measurements)
- ❖ The controls that monitor – (Standards)
- ❖ His job improvement plan – (Training/Coaching)

After this analysis of individual role, it is followed by *REVIEW* using jobholders KRAs, accountability and responsibility well supported by CONTROLLED INFORMATION.

- ❖ A review of objectives achieved against the agreed objectives.
- ❖ An analysis of VARIANCES/GAPS.
- ❖ Action required for effect IMPROVEMENT.
- ❖ The REVISION of objectives, if necessary.
- ❖ SETTING new objectives, wherever necessary.

KEY PERFORMANCE INDICATORS (KPIs)

The framing of business objectives is clearly not enough to ensure its implementation. They are needed to translate the objectives through its KPIs into core processes. What the organisation must accomplish to achieve the objectives by examination and categorisation of the impacts. This should lead to a balance set of deliverables for the organisation in terms of financial and non-financial performance, customer/market satisfaction, people/ internal organisation satisfaction and environment/social satisfaction.

KPIs or critical success factors may be in some cases statements of hopes. But they provide directions the success criteria. In KPIs/CSFs determination, the organisation should follow the rule that each KPI is necessary and together they are sufficient for the mission to be achieved. KPIs provide what of the organisation, but they must be supported by measurable Key Result Areas (KRAs) that are tightly and in arguably linked. These will help to translate the directions of setting targets and in turn simplify managements thinking. The KPIs will be used to monitor progress and as evidence of success for the organisation in every direction, internally and externally.

Any organisation implementing TOP uses three types of *MEASURES*.

- **Quality** – Quality of product/service and timeliness measures for Key Performance Indicators.
- **Quantity** – Yield and accuracy of processes.
- **Profitability** – Cost control and value addition.

Creating such integrated system for company, manufacturing units, departments and individuals will help establish TOP.

Within this approach, the corporate management frames these primary business objectives:

- To enhance customer satisfaction – Internal and External.
- To strengthen organisation's competitive position.
- To improve earning.
- To commit continuous work improvements.
- To upgrade HR skills and competencies.

To achieve above corporate business objectives, CEO has to concentrate on:

- Generation of additional profits to the company.
- New product development.
- Customer satisfaction and services.
- People development.
- Plant performance.
- Quality of product and services.

These objectives are then translated at micro-level as:

- Key Performance Areas (KPAs)
- Key Result Areas (KRAs)
- Individual Targets (Performance)
- Broad Performance
- Targets/Goals

Thus, when performance is standardised and measured, it improves; when performance is measured and compared, it improves further; when it is measured, compared and suitably recognised, it improves even more drastically.

KEY PERFORMANCE INDICATORS (KPIs)

AS HEAD OF THE ORGANISATION, PRIMARILY RESPONSIBLE FOR ENTIRE GAMUT OF ***BUSINESS OPERATIONS***.

(1) **PROFIT** – To plan and achieve adequate profit to finance the company's growth and provide resources to meet targeted corporate performance.

(2) **NEW PRODUCT** – Decide new product development and existing product improvement in consideration of a good value to company customer – domestic and overseas.

(3) **CUSTOMER** – Provide products/services of greatest possible value to customers thereby gaining and holding their respect and loyalty. Enter in OEM market aggressively with requisite manufacturing and marketing skills and add value to the company's revenue.

(4) **PEOPLE** – Implement and administer organisational development interventions by upgrading HR knowledge, skills and establish core competencies in product, process and people.

(5) **PERFORMANCE** – Organise, inspire, deploy, enable, measure value adding operating performance standards. Manage with Key Performance Areas (KPAs), Key Result Areas (KRAs) and Target Setting – Total Performance Management.

— Define, Implement strategic cost reduction, ___ improvement projects in all operational areas to generate additional internal revenue.

— Implement strategic cost planning, policy decisions and resource allocation with Management Control System (MCS and MIS) and Review Systems.

(6) **QUALITY** – Institutionalise the processes of innovations excellence by adopting Quality Management System right from bottom line performers.

KEY PERFORMANCE AREAS (KPAs)

AS A PROFIT CENTRE HEAD, PRIMARILY RESPONSIBLE FOR ENTIRE GAMUT OF ***WORKS OPERATION***.

(1) Generate profit to finance the company's growth.

(2) Plan and achieve targeted production and productivity of the manufacturing facilities within the given norms.

(3) Effective utilisation of resources – man, material, money and technology.

(4) Effective implementation of budgetary norms, cost control measures to achieve optimisation in the areas of product quality, people and plant performance.

(5) Implement HRD interventions by undertaking work improvement projects, 5-S, quality circles to facilitate over all organisational development.

(6) Implement, monitor and measure key tasks /results of HODs for better performance and ultimately achieve total operating performance.

(7) Implement ISO-9001, 14001, quality systems and other innovative interventions to create core competencies in process management.

(8) Administer periodical plant and people performance targets through regular meetings and presentation.

(9) Maintain internal MIS and customer care correspondence with all our domestic and foreign buyers.

(10) Coordinate with Marketing for smooth dispatches to the satisfaction of the customers.

(11) Oversee the financial and accounting aspects of manufacturing facilities.

KEY RESULT AREAS (KRAs)

Once objectives are framed, they need to move from being words into operating reality. They must generate into work assignment. And work is always specific, measurable with deadline and with specific accountability and responsibility.

Delegation of objectives and work associated with its achievement demands involvement of HOD and his team-members who are known to be able to do the job. KRAs of individual HOD are the supportive foundation for achieving objectives.

- KRAs are the on-going results or output a jobholder is expected to achieve.
- Taken together KRAs present key outputs of a job in the areas of **MEN, MATERIALS, METHODS, MACHINE** (Technologies) **AND MONEY**.
- KRAs are accountability statements for which individual are responsible.
- KRAs referred to **WHAT HAS TO BE ACHIEVED WITHIN WHAT TIME.**
- KRAs have two elements:
  (1) ***Standards***/Goals/Targets describing the output of product/service.
  (2) ***Measurement*** which indicate how KRAs can be evaluated – Quantitatively and Qualitatively.
- KRAs/Measures/Standards and priority may change year-on-year to represent new performance benchmarks, necessitated due to changing business requirements or when jobholder's job is changed.

GENERAL KRAs FOR ALL HODs (A)

(1) To improve quality of product and services.

(2) To identify non-confirming areas in the department and reduce operating cost related to the department.

(3) To undertake work improvement projects to add value in departmental activities.

(4) To improve better utilisation of human resources, machines, and equipment through planned preventive maintenance measures.

(5) To reduce cost by undertaking cost reduction projects on employee cost, spares and other store items, raw materials, telephone, tours and travels, furniture and fixtures, product selling cost, etc.

(6) To study work activities and other processes in the department by establishing time and motion study, work measurements and other efficiency improvement techniques.

(7) To prepare and document Standard Operating Procedures (SOPs) relating to all work activities in the department.

(8) To undertake role and goal exercise by developing KRAs for executives and job descriptions for all departmental employees.

(9) To train, retrain all departmental employees by scheduling training calendar on: On-the-job, classroom, internal and external training programmes.

(10) To implement ISO-9001, ISO-14000 standards in the department and monitor it continuously.

(11) To educate, implement and monitor 5-S activities, quality circles, work improvement projects in the department and upgrade employee knowledge and skills to implement TQM in future.

(12) To maintain discipline and develop positive employee inter-relations and inter-departmental relations.

GENERAL KRAs FOR ALL HODs (B)

(1) To prepare and document Standard Operating Practices (SOPs) relating to all work activities in the department.

(2) To improve quality of product and services.

(3) To identify non-confirming areas in the department and reduce operating cost related to the department.

(4) To undertake work improvement projects to add value in departmental activities

(5) To improve better utilisation of human resources, machines and equipment through planned preventive maintenance measures.

(6) To reduce cost by undertaking cost reduction projects on employee cost, spares and other store items, raw materials, telephone, tours and travels, furniture and fixtures, product selling cost, etc.

(7) To study work activities and other processes in the department by establishing time and motion study, work measurements and other efficiency improvement techniques.

(8) To undertake role and goal exercise by developing KRAs for executives and job descriptions for all departmental employees.

(9) To train, retrain all departmental employees by scheduling training calendar on: On-the-job, classroom, internal and external training programmes.

(10) To implement ISO-9001, ISO-14000 standards in the department and monitor it continuously.

(11) To educate, implement and monitor 5-S activities, quality circles, work improvement projects in the department and upgrade employee knowledge and skills to implement TQM in future.

(12) To maintain discipline and develop positive employee inter-relations and inter-departmental relations.

(13) Identify and implement innovation in processes to meeting quality of product/service.

(14) Specific KRAs for the department.

Chapter 6

PERFORMANCE MEASUREMENT

Structure:

6.1 Performance Standards

6.2 Setting – Smart Goals

6.3 Performance – Goal Setting Exercise

6.4 Price System in Performance Measurement

6.5 Goal Setting Methodology

Effective assessments are clearly an indispensable component in achieving and maintaining organisational success. Therefore, any complete strategic plan must specify goals, strategic objectives, action and the final performance by which management and stockholders will gauge success. Top management performance can usually be measured by sales volume, market share, cash-flow, profit, RoI, etc. Operating management, however, is often disconnected from the strategic plan. As a result business processes and activities under the control of operations are not affected in the ways that will make the company more profitable or give it more market share. This misalignment of performance measurement between strategy and process performance in operations is often poorly understood. It certainly does not receive the priority it should from the top management. The critical success factors (CSF), management defines at the strategic level must be transformed to the operations level in the form of key performance indicators (KPIs) and key result areas (KRAs) and clearly linked to business performance. Successfully linking the real drivers of overall business performance at the operational level is a prerequisite of effective performance measurement.

The primary purpose of measurement is to assess performance levels and to analyse what is happening and where. The most beneficial aspect of performance management, however, is pinpointing problem areas and focusing attention on actions that will have the best impact on overall business performance.

Without good performance measurement, it is easy for companies to fall into a very common trap – employee keep busy with all kinds of activities but achieve few of the desired results. Effective performance measurement is the compass that guides management towards meaningful results at the process level results that tie directly with the companies goals.

Why Measure Performance?

The basic purpose of any measurement system is to provide feedback, relating to your goals, that increase your chances of achieving these goals efficiently and effectively, measurement gains true value when used as the basis for timely decisions. Secondly, the purpose of measuring is not to know how your business is performing but to enable it to perform better. The ultimate aim of implementing a performance measurement is to improve the performance of the company. If you can get your performance measurement right, the data you generate will tell you where you are? How you are doing?

A good performance measurement system will help you achieve success in five ways:

- Establish your current position,
- Communicate direction,
- Stimulate action in the most important areas for your business,
- Facilitate learning,
- Influence behaviour.

What are the Benefits of Performance Measurement?

It enables managers to define and track performance on metrics for every strategic objective set by the company/department. By noting performance that falls short of targets. For example, "Our goal was to reduce order processing errors by 10%, but we reduce them by 5%. Manager can address the causes of the shortfall and work to continually improve performance."

Performance measurement shows how performance in different part of the company affects performance in other parts. For example, "The company may discover that having the logistics staff achieve the objective" accelerate order delivery by 10% helps the customer satisfaction by 15%.

By seeing such or similar relationships, companies can make more informed decisions. For example, they can increase budget, add new hires or introduce a more efficient process to improve performance instead of guessing which factors need to be addressed.

Types of Measurement

Generally there are three to four bases of measurement, called

- Result base measurement (RBM)
- Activity base measurement (ABM)
- Customer base measurement (CBM)
- Skill/competencies base measurement (S/CBM)

1. Result Base Measurement (RBM):

It is a way of looking at and teaching others to create measures for really hard to measure of today's work. Customer doesn't want to hear how hard you have worked or what techniques you have tried, they want result.

2. Activity Base Measurement (ABM):

Asks "What would you see the employee doing? Or how is time-being spent? Or what do we have to do to get to our goal?" In such cases the emphasis is on activity/behaviour/ actions which are means not ends. As a result, by measuring activity, they generate more activity, because what gets measured gets done. Management by objectives has the potential to define results, but most often uses deadlines to measure completed tasks. And in many cases the timeliness of the task completion is much less important than the quality of results.

3. The Customer Base Measurement (CBM):

The customer based focus part of approach help give drives corporate success and customer satisfaction. Result flow from customer needs and values is always in the eyes of the customer. In addition, by asking what results an employee has to produce to support corporate goals, the employee's goals will be linked to organisation's direction. Instead of measuring activities, if this activity was done really well, what result would be produce which adds value, for customer and so instead of measuring "training programmes" ask if the training was done well, what result would we produce? The answer "competent employee" becomes the starting point for measurement, instead of "training programme". Therefore, instead of using MBO (Management By Objectives) which asks "what the task done by the deadline? Result base measurement defies the results and allows any combination of quality, quantity, cost or timeliness measures to apply. It is rare that customer only cares about deadline to the exclusion of quality or cost.

4. Competency Base Measurement (CBM):

Defines what skills, knowledge, experience an individual needs in order to produce results. But having skill and using it successfully are two different things. For example, a car mechanic with a certificate of training completion on the wall is not the same as a required car. What results must employee produce, which will add value for customer, or help the company achieve goals? And then "How would we know that this result was done well. Instead of using competencies, result base measurement asks". If the employee uses skills/knowledge well, what will be produced for the customer? And so instead of measuring "product knowledge" a sales clerk might be evaluated on recommendations for products meeting "customer needs" or "sales".

The Need for Performance Measurement

Organisational control is the process whereby an organisation ensures that it is pursuing strategies and actions which will enable it to achieve its goals.

Performance measurement being the central control of evaluation, solve the problems of such hard tasks through these processes:

Alignment: Goals in alignment with corporate direction and customer needs because the results are derived from these starting point.

- **Speed:** Defining good measures that used to take months can now be done in hours.
- **Creativity:** Defining results and allowing employees to seek the best way to get their rewards finding new, more efficient path to the goal. Measuring activity rewards confirm to a set procedure.
- **Cost tracking:** Tracking behaviour or competencies is very expensive. Tracking results is usually cheaper and less time-consuming, allowing more time to produce instead of measuring.
- **Activity focus:** If your employee are lost in the activity and don't know why they are doing, what they are doing, performance measurement answers the "why" question and helps them focus on producing values.

Choice of performance measures which are appropriate to a particular company. This selection ought to be made in the light of the companies strategic intensions in which it operates and the kind of business that it is dealing with whether the company is in the manufacturing or the service sector, in choosing an appropriate range of performance measures it will be necessary however to balance them, to make sure that one dimension or set of dimensions of performance is not stressed to the detriment of others. The mix chosen will in almost every instance be different. To say, while most companies will tend to organise their accounting systems using common accounting principles, they will differ widely in the choice, or potential choice of performance indicators.

The ultimate aim of implementing a performance measurement is to improve the performance of the company. Measure – managed companies perform better in three important aspects.

- They are perceived as being industrial leader.
- They are perceived as providing financial return.
- They are perceived as being adept at managing change.

A good measurement system thus will help achieve success in five ways.

- Establish your current position.
- Communicate direction.
- Stimulate action in the most important areas of business.
- Facilitate learning.
- Influence behaviour.

In short, implementing a performance measurement system can have far-reaching effects on the organisation. It can be used for;

- Deciding what the key drivers of performance.
- Refocusing and stimulating activity on these key business drivers.
- Drawing attention to goals and targets.
- Creating a culture of achievement.
- Noticing in advance any trend affecting in business so that changes can be made in good time.

Before implementing the system, it is clearly very important to agree to design a good set of measures and gain commitment to them. The measure influence behaviour and activity. So, your level of success will largely depend on how well you have set-up your system.

Kalpan and Norton is their book on Balanced Score Card identified four perspective, each card representing an important face of the company. These are:

- ❖ Financial
- ❖ External customer
- ❖ Internal process
- ❖ Innovation and learning

These four perspectives represent a balance view of any company and that by creating measures under each of these headings no important area would be missed.

1. Financial Measures

Financial measures alone are insufficient to manage business. Focus purely on financial aspect is not enough. Firstly, the focus often result people taking the earliest options to improve performance, reducing costs rather than encouraging growth. This may be beneficial in the short-term but in the longer-term, cuts in investment, research and development, will harm business. Secondly, financial measures are result measures, that is, they provide a measure of how well all the other activities have been done. They do not tell you to improve performance.

2. Customers

Customers are the life blood of the business; their orders and payment are the reason for the business to exist. That is why you need the customer perspective.

3. Internal Process

Internal process to satisfy customer and make a financial return the business must be efficient and effective at what it does. Hence, the perceptive internal process. The objective here is not to be good at everything but to be brilliant at producing the products or services which match the exact needs of your customers.

You keep up with the ever increasing demands of customers and the ever improving performance of your competitors. You need to innovative and learn.

4. Innovative and Learn

This fourth perspective is all about developing the capabilities and process you need for the future. This perceptive often contains most of the measure for people development. These four perpectives have to design to balance the financial and non-financial, the internal and the external current performance with the future. Look at the business strategy and extra palate from this what key factors are to ensure you achieve strategic intents or aims and then analyse the business needs to ensure you are really focusing to measure on the most important factors for business success. If you are sure that your strategy reflects your strategic intents of success and business needs then it is as well, go back to consider the needs of various interested parties in your business customers; employees, shareholders, owners, regulators, the local community and suppliers. Once this exercise is fairly prepared, analysed then before implementation decides what performance measurement yard sticks you wanted to go for, for assessing different business attributes.

Performance Measurement

When performance is measured, it improves. When performance is measured and compared, it improves further. When it is measured, compared and appropriately recognised and rewarded, it improves even more drastically.

To obtain desire performance from employees, an organisation must first have a well-defined accountability system. Employee must know what is expected from him. This is accomplished through performance standards. Standards help management and employees more easily to monitor performance and serve as a basic for evaluation. Clarity of goals, feedback on reaching goals, periodical performance review are the subprocesses to be developed in performance standards process.

Managing people has three identified parts of a performance review:

- **Performance planning** – in which you set the goals and objectives and develop plans for achieving these objectives.
- **Coaching** – day-to-day coaching, in which area you work with your people to help them reach their goals.
- **Performance review** – overall evaluation of performance for the specific planning period in which you evaluate progress toward goals.

Our daily business activities function according to certain agreed-upon formulas. This formula when written down explicitly becomes performance standards. Successful management on day-to-day level boils down to one precept: maintain and improve standards. This not means adhering to current technological, managerial, behavioural operating standards: but also improving current processes in order to evaluate current standards to higher level.

6.1 PERFORMANCE STANDARDS

There are two types of standards; one is managerial standards, which are necessary for managing employees for administrative purpose and include administrative, personel rules, policies, guidelines, standard operating manuals, etc. The other is called operational standards. Which have to do with the way people do a job to realise quality, cost, and delivery in product or service? While managerial standards relate to the internal purpose of managing employee; operational standards relate to the external demands to satisfy customers. Following standards is like driving a car. The driver must follow certain rules and regulations and yet, as a result, he gains the freedom to go where he wants to go. Likewise, when employees follow standards and do the job rights, the customer – internal and external are satisfied with the product or service and the company prospers and the employees can look forward to job interest and progression.

Thus, performance standards have key features:

(1) Represent the best, easiest and safety way to do a job. Standards reflect many years of wisdom and know how on the part of employees are doing their jobs.

When management maintains and improves a certain ways of doing something making sure that all the employees follow the same procedure, their standards become the most efficient, safe and cost-effective way of doing the job.

(2) Offer the best way to preserve know-how and expertise. If an employee knows the best way to do the job and leaves without sharing that knowledge, his know-how will also leave. Only by standardising and institutionalising such know-how within the company does stay in the company, regardless of coming and going of its employees.

(3) Provide a way to measure performance with established standards managers can evaluate the performance. Without standards there is no fair way to do this.

(4) Show the relationship between cause and effect. Having no standards or not following standards invariably leads to abnormalities, variability and waste.

(5) Provide a basis for both maintenance and improvement. By following standards means maintenance and upgrading standards. Without standards, we have no way of knowing whether we have made improvement or not.

(6) Provide objectives and indicate training goals, standard can be described as a set of visual signs that show how to do the job. As such standards should communicate in a simple, understandable manner generally in written document form.

(7) Provide a basis for training once all standards are established, the next step is to gain employee to such an extent that it becomes second nature for them to do the job according to the standards.

(8) Create basis for audit or diagnosis of work. Work standards are often presented to employees for periodical presentation on performance showing vital steps and checkpoints – KRA's, job descriptions of employee in their work area. These standards serve as reminders to employees. The primary job of management is to see whether standards are being maintained and at the appropriate time, whether plans to upgrade current standards are being implemented.

(9) Provide a means for preventing recurrence of errors and minimising variability. Management task is to identify, define and standardise key control points to be followed at all time. Often 'A' company turns out to be better than 'B' company in quality, product and service not because 'A' is superior in all aspects of process, product and people, but because 'A' is making concerted and collaborated efforts to ensure that all process are followed as specified in standards. While 'B' company find that one or two processes are not always followed. Thus, standardisation is an integral part of performance management and without standards there can be no way to build performance management and development system.

The performance measurement system is management's tool for evoking behaviour. Management always gets what it asks. Also performance system interacts with reward system. Hence, performance measurement must promote desired behaviour. Because it determines who gets promotion, raises, etc. Employees do response to the performance measurement system. If the system is bad (no standards for measurement), management will get dysfunctional results. Performance appraisal should be criterion based. People should be evaluated against standards and expectations not against each other. All employees should have an opportunity to receive an outstanding rating. Therefore the organisation must set uniform standards and rate everyone performs well, everyone should get 'A', if no one performs well no one should get 'A' this systems promotes cooperation and maximum efforts. Decentralisation, empowerment through distributed authority and measurement system all go together and provide all important results.

Measurements of specific goals or objectives against standards provide these results:

- Focus on – what is important?
- Objectivity – from the comparisons.
- Recognition – of what/where to fix?
- Improvement – on the right things.
- Motivation – to improve the score.
- Decentralisation – when cohesion/control.
- Commitment – from this empowerment and reward process.

You simply won't get results without means to measure, compare, analyse and feedback to those doing the work. All the research on high performance shows that three to five goals are the ideal number of goals, peak performance concentrate on. Remember Pareto 80/20 rule: 80 per cent of the results you want to obtain from people comes from the 20 per cent of their activities. Therefore, you want to limit the number of goals employees have and attempt to identify the few key activities that have the highest impact and yield the greatest results. Once these goals are established and standardise, they should be written down as standards. So that, they can be frequently used to compare actual behaviour. It is therefore, necessary that your performance standards/goals should be SMART.

S – Specific, M – Measurable, A – Attainable, R – Relevant, T – Trackable.

6.2 SETTING – SMART GOALS

- **Goals should be specific** – you just don't say to somebody, "I want you to improve". The area and method of improving must be specifically defined.
- **Goals should be measurable** – an important thing to remember is, "If you can't measure it, you can't manage it". Therefore, the goals have to be observable and measurable.
- **Goals should be attainable** – you need to able to reach your goals and stretch yourself in the process. Difficult but obtainable goals keep individual motivation and behaviour positive to put more efforts to attain the goals.

- **Goals should be relevant** – you want to set goals in areas that are important to the job.
- **Goals should be trackable** – you need to set goals that people's progress be praised if they achieve it. So, there must be some trackable measure. Submitting report on production by every 30th of the month, the chances of receiving it on 30th help to keep track on goal achievement and praising along the way. Thus, goal tracking is maintained by the virtue of 30th date.

6.3 PERFORMANCE – GOAL SETTING EXERCISE

All good performance starts with clear goals. This involves making sure that all employees are clear about three things:

- What they being asked to do – their areas of responsibility.
- What good performance looks like – performance standards by which they will be evaluated.
- What is expected of them in their work – specific terms of output task or goal information to the employees and their commitment to it.

These three simple things pull organisational people back to goals and objectives by asking again and again:

- What are we in business for?
- What are the purposes of this organisation?
- What goals or services are we trying to produce?
- Who is our customer?
- Who are this work and this expenditure necessary?
- What will be the outcome if we succeed or fail?

Human being is purposive being, people live to attain goals. They set them and create them both on their own and on suggestions form others. Organisational goals are collective goals of all individuals. Hence, these must be set with involvement.

Company's Common Goals

Any organisation has some common goals of its business. These are:

(a) **Customer Goals** – our customer goal is become an organisation with whom customer are keen to do business.

(b) **Employee Goals** – is to create an environment where employee can take pride in the organisation and feel responsible to its business.

(c) **Business Goals** – is to increase profit, market presence at a faster rate than competitors in the market where we compete.

(d) **Improvement Goals** – is to reduce price of non-conformance in every work area and commit ourselves to reduce operational cost in every aspect of our business operation.

(e) **Quality Goals** – is to integrate leadership through quality principles, tools and processes in day-to-day management of our all business operations/processes and establish quality of worklife.

These goals communication to one and all in the company help them learn the basics of business and they take those as standards of their conduct, character and codes of their personality at work. They also know that our role in the organisation to move around these goals and we are measured against these standards. Once common business goals are set as standards of performance measurement, they should be kept close to the hands of everyone.

Following some of the instruments/guidelines systematically direct the user in a way increase the probabilities for their successful goal achievement. These instruments are developed by Kelsey Tyson and Drea Zigarmi.

We will briefly discuss each of these instruments/guidelines:

(a) **Setting Goals** – "What is the persons/departments job?" Specifically list the most important activities you want a person/department to accomplish in the next six to twelve months.

(b) **Setting Priorities** – "Which goals are more important?" Rank the priority of achieving goals with specific deadline for each goal.

(c) **Measurable Indicators** – "How will you know if the person is doing the job well?" This should include two or specific variables within the persons control that need to track for changes and improvements.

(d) **Standards of Performance** – "What does the outstanding performance looks like?" There should be minimal acceptable and outstanding levels of performance determined for each goal.

(e) **Incentive and benefits** – "What will the person gain by doing a good job?" These can include such items as increase autonomy, flexi time increased responsibilities or additional money.

(f) **Obstacles to Goal Accomplishment** – "What could get in the way of accomplishing the person's goal?"Consider both factors within the persons control and likely actors beyond persons control.

(g) **Action Steps** - "What steps will the person take to accomplish the goal?" Determine what is the favourable plan for success including the help and support that will be needed from others. Most goals can be successfully accomplished in a variety of ways.

(h) **Praising and Rewards** – "What happen if the goal is accomplished?" Recognition should be planned for both final completion and progress towards final completion. Don't over look one of the simplest yet important and powerful forms of recognition: sincere appreciation.

(i) **Reprimands and Redirection** – "What happens if the goal is not accomplished?" If the employee has the necessary skills to complete the task but does not, the person should be reprimanded. If the employee lacks the necessary skills, redirection is more appropriate. When redirecting goals and actions steps are predetermined and the person tries again.

Goal setting clearly is an activator; behaviour is the performance you want and consequences are what follow behaviour. Hence, managing consequences is important factor in performance management. Positive consequences tend to increase the frequency of positive behaviour-performance.

6.4 PRICE SYSTEM IN PERFORMANCE MEASUREMENT

The price system developed by Robert Lorberd and his associates, consulting firm is a five step productivity performance improvement system, used by various companies to improve their company's performance.

P – Pinpoint:

Where is the current performance not meeting expectations? Where is the biggest discrepancy between the real and ideal level of performance as company sees it. Obviously, if you can't measure it, you can't manage it. Under this system, remember in pinpointing a performance-improvement area that you must be able to measure progress in that area. You have to be able to observe and quantify performance. You must be able to specifically describe the current and desired level of performance and how you will measure improvement as it is made. The five key measurement areas used in many companies are quantity – how many; quality – how good; cost – amount of money; timeliness – on or off schedule and amount of change – the difference between past and present performance. You have to develop measurement format through observation, surveys, interviews or analysis of reports. Select measurements that are reliable, measure is reliable if it measures what you say it measures. Use measurements that are fair and unbiased. Anyone who cares to examine the results, they should be true, factual, realistic and unbiased. Measurement become unfair and biased who those collecting the information have a vested interest in the outcome. Organise measurement so that they can reflect the performance on the smallest work unit. Choose measurements that are stable and not subject to too many outside influence and contingencies.

When pinpointing, priorities areas of improvement those that demand your immediate attention and those that are not quite as pressing. Your criterion for top priority or low priority might be cost impact on company's human resources, degree of difficulty for change, centrality to the company mission or the time the change will take place. These pinpointing enable managers to see and understand where unit performance improvement is most needed. It helps managers to determine effective measurement for evaluating improvement and assist managers in selecting priorities for performance improvements.

R – Record:

Once you have identified a performance area that you want to improve, the next step is record present performance in that area so that you can develop base data for examining performance standards. Hence, start with base line data. If you have no base line, it is difficult to assess the improvements. Record systematically on an ongoing basis – collect data regularly and or at short intervals. Don't allow lengthy amount of time to go between data collection points. Collect the data in consistent manner. The same person collect the data at the same time of the week or month in the same work area, in the same way minimises the errors. Collect data that covers all relevant aspects of the productivity improvement efforts. Make sure your data is accurate. Check figure with data recorded in the past and then display progress prominently. This becomes automatic feedback mechanism that can motivate employees. Graphical presentation also held good.

I – Involve:

Once you have recorded in order to present performance in a pinpointed area you are now ready to involve others. To effectively implement a performance progress, the people who can most influence that area must be involved. The involve stage consist of four steps: inform people: agree on standards and strategy formulation; set goals with individuals that correspond with that goals and establish reward and incentives. The involve step allows employee commitment as how the performance is improved; allows for employee input into the standards and levels of performance; allows for employee understanding as to how their individual goals fit into the goals; emphasis informal and formal incentives to reinforce outstanding performance.

C – Coaching:

Coaching involves the management of consequences by praising progress, reprimanding poor performance, and redirecting the errors of inexperienced people. Coaching requires constant communications and feedback. Consequences must be made clear. Praising, redirection, renegotiation and reprimand on achieving non-achieving of performance.

E – Evaluate:

At predetermined periodic intervals sit down together and evaluate performance. Interaction between the managers and employees will be revived and progress toward goals assessed. The evaluation stage includes an examination of manager's leadership behaviour. Whether continually emphasis and reinforce the change requested and see consequences effectively. Did he allow enough time for the desired improvement to occur. The other benefits of evaluation step are: formalise the exam of project results and the group effort; allows for the further group strategy generation and problem-solving, requires alternative actions if little or no progress has resulted.

Effective performance measurement is an indispensable component in achieving and maintaining organisational performance. Its checkpoints are:

(1) **Assessment/Measurement** – An estimate and determination of significance value of something – people, processes, policies, etc.

(2) **Audit** – A planned independent and documented assessment to determine whether agreed upon goals, objectives or requirements are being met.

(3) **Evaluation** – A systematic and independent exam and evaluation to determine whether task activities and result comply with planned agreement and whether these arrangements are implemented effectively and are suitable to achieve goals.

(4) **Surveillance** – The continuous monitoring of the status of producers, policies, methods, work conditions, product, processes, services, people and analysis of records in relations to stated reference to ensure that requirements or goals of the tasks are being met. Performance measurement based on the price system and their checkpoints help management develop defect free system of performance management.

6.5 GOAL SETTING METHODOLOGY

Getting the best out of people is always hard. It is always an imperfect activity and there is always more to learn and make employee learn. The benefits of getting, the best out of people in business are as rewarding as the penalties are dire. The organisations who ultimately succeed are those who have developed their core competence, skills, style, values and purposive and positive human resource management, which enables them to command respect in market and community at large; their combination of sound intelligence, keen observation and willingness to learn and make learn, with strategic intent improve their performance caring for their employees and organisational requirements is the only root of successful goal setting. It is a key to measure organisational and individual performance, motivation, initiative, ability and attitude. The individual performance, motivation, initiative, ability and attitude. The individual will feel that this is the first time he really knew what is his job and my manager wanted of me and what management support, services made available to me. Obviously, achievement of performance standards will give you, your self-appraisal and to your manager the contribution and commitment you have fulfilled. So, it is management's primary task, responsibility and obligation to his employee to make them aware of goal setting methodology.

Goal Setting Methods

(1) **A goal should be a statement of an output** – It should represent the final consequences of an activity not merely activity. It is acceptable that a goal will be "100 tonnes per day" but not to state that "we will improve production". The former is output, the later is a hoped for activity that is vague.

(2) **A goal should be explicit** – The output that is defined for a goal should be explicit that later on when people are trying to agree on whether or not it was actually achieved, they find easy agreement.

(3) **A goal objective should have some of a time as a part of it** – The tonnage should be defined as being per day output. Without time included the output statement is not a commitment. Why not come for a dinner at seven O'clock, evening on Saturday? To get a commitment the statement of output should be accompanied by some time reference.

(4) **Make your goal of ascending difficulty** – Define first those of regular, routine and ordinary things, which have been done in the past. In such case there is data to back-up the choice of numbers, time, etc., then turn to the problems that need solving for which there may not be experience to use determining the solution date. Finally, the highest and most difficult levels of goals are those that are innovative in nature. Innovative things that do most for the organisational growth.

(5) **Goals are both long-range and short-range** – The long-range goals usually are of two to five years, duration are called strategic goals. The short-range goals are for immediate year and for shorter period are called operating goals. Long-range goals are generally defined by corporate top management. While short-range goals are defined by operating managers, executives.

(6) **When setting goals in the face of uncertainty** – Define them within range, for example the driver who drives on crowded highway may define the goal as "getting office within thirty minutes". This is realism, but experience with weather, traffic and the like makes the range more logical and perfectly scientific. Always ask service managers to define their forecasts and goal within ranges.

(7) **Always examine the part fully before you define the future goals** – The past data becomes the foundation for defining ordinary and reasonable levels barring any unforeseen changes. If you want to change the goal outcomes of the future you must include plans for change in your objectives.

(8) **Goal should always be set face-to-face in discussion** – And not by circulars and letters alone. Goal setting discussion often involves bargaining, resolving, disagreement and getting commitments to change one's behaviour. None of these can be done by correspondence, but require face-to-face discussion.

(9) **Goals starts at the top of the organisation** – If the top management of the organisation can't define corporate or overall organisational purposes, the rest of the people can't help them achieve those goals. Thus, corporate personnel must be the first members of the team to define their goals before other people define theirs. The goals of the organisation flow down; methods for achieving those goals should flow-up.

(10) **Summaries of statement of operating goals should be brief** – Enough to be filed. By disciplining oneself to right goal statements that describe output instead of activities.

(11) **A mistake in goal will produce a mistake in activity** – Bad goals produce bad activity, good goals produce good activity. The effects of choosing a wrong goal or stating it improperly will produce a matching chain of behaviour and activity which naturally follows.

(12) **Goals are most useful when they are stated as indicators** – The most exciting goals and lofty purpose must be converted into some kind of indicators, which can be used to measure performance. Counting managers trained does not ensure quality training. It merely makes such quality possible if nobody was trained quality would be zero.

(13) **Goals can reflect real effectiveness or apparent effectiveness** – Real effectiveness means making a real contribution to corporate strategy, not just being a statistically great performance or organisational hot-shot in operation.

(14) **You can induce good goals from overall organisational performance** – Goal should include the number of assists; the numbers of managers promoted out of unit, building of overall strength and long-run effectiveness not yearly one year or periodic bursts of excellence.

(15) **Try participative goal setting** – The expectations of managers and executives must be met participating them in goal setting exercise. Participative management as a principle deters you from imposing goals. If they participate they will have partnership in achieving those goals.

(16) **Measurement of goals is easy if don't reason to conceal them** – Generally some biased opinion, organisational politics not because results could not measure.

(17) **Make sure that everyone has measurable goals** – Even if they are arbitrarily set. But also be prepared to adjust the goal to keep it SMART – specific, measurable, attainable, relevant and trackable.

(18) **The environmental and the cultural setting are important elements of goal setting** – Goal setting is always done within a context and the context should be included as a part of rationale for a goal. Every problem no matter what its origin is a business problem when you are setting business goals. This includes government legislation, energy crisis, inflation or simply the weather.

(19) **Goals are means of attaining power** – People set goals to assist them in their drive for power and goals produce a diminution of power they won't set or they don't vigorously pursued if they are set. People always resist power flowing away from them and seek power coming toward them through goal setting.

(20) **Low confidence, low morale** – Means low goal achievement, high confidence, high motivation and morale translate into high goal achievement.

(21) **Good goals create the resources to produce them** – People should be informed that no important contribution shall be withheld for lack of funds, for a good goal bump another less worthy goal and employ the lesser funds.

(22) **It is good idea to pick-up a goal to common resources** – The best goals are one's that promise to add value to the resources to be consumed in producing them. Goals that show promise of being profitable will supplant goals, which don't promise such value added or are unclear on what the value might be.

Proper measurement systems are essential. You must keep score, assess and provide feedback to all of the employees. That is how to judge how everything is working. Please remember you can't measure what is not defined. Effectiveness is a matter of team performance, without productivity measurement business has no control. Ultimately what you measure? Productivity and quality of product and service in comparison to goals, history and like activities for over all assessment of organisational performance.

Whether the company is manufacturer or service provider, to be successful its management should be concerned to ensure that:

- Products move smoothly and swiftly through the production cycle.
- Warranty repairs are kept to a minimum and turned round quickly.
- Supplier's delivery performance is constantly monitored.
- Quality standards are continually raised.
- Sales orders, shipments and backlog are kept to a minimum.
- There is overall customer-satisfaction.
- Labour turnover statistics are produced in such a way as to identify managerial weaknesses.
- R&D costs do not escalate.
- The accounting and finance departments really understand the business.

Looking at each of these areas in turn, the following non-exhaustive list of performance measures is relevant. No one indicator should be over-emphasised and no one indicator should reign supreme for long in the corporate consciousness of executives or management gurus.

1. Manufacturing and production Indicators

The sheer volume, variety and complexity of managerial issues surrounding the production process make this area of corporate activity a particularly rich one for non-financial indicators. Performance indicators can be devised for all operational areas.

(a) Non-financial indicators, depending on the exact nature of the production process, might include the following:

- ❖ Indicators deriving from time and motion studies.
- ❖ Production line efficiency.
- ❖ Ability to change the manufacturing schedule when the marketing plan changes.
- ❖ Reliability of component parts of the production line.
- ❖ Production line repair record.
- ❖ Keeping failures of finished goods to a minimum.
- ❖ Ability to produce against the marketing plan.
- ❖ Product life cycle.

(b) Indicators concerned with controlling production quality – right first time:

- ❖ Measurement of scrap.
- ❖ Tests for components, sub-assemblies and finished products.
- ❖ Fault analysis.
- ❖ Most likely reasons for product failures.
- ❖ Actual failure rates against target failure rates.
- ❖ Complaints received against the quality assurance testing programme.
- ❖ Annualised failures as a % of sales value.
- ❖ Failures as a % of units shipped.
- ❖ Various indicators of product/service quality.
- ❖ Various indicators of product/service reliability.

(c) Indicators concerned with the purchasing department's external relationships with its suppliers:

- ❖ Inventory levels and timing of deliveries.
- ❖ Just in time inventory control measurements.
- ❖ Stock turnover ratio.
- ❖ Weeks stocks held.
- ❖ Supplier's delivery performance.
- ❖ Analysis of stock outs.

- ❖ Parts delivery service record.
- ❖ % of total; requests supplied in time.
- ❖ % supplied with faults.

(d) Indicators of sales delivery and service:

- ❖ Shipments vs. first request date.
- ❖ Average number of day's shipments late.
- ❖ Response time between enquiry and first visit.

2. Sales and marketing

- ❖ Measurements based on staying close to the customer.
- ❖ Complaints are manuals.
- ❖ Complaints are packaging/ease of opening.
- ❖ Quality of packaging materials.
- ❖ Customer satisfaction analysis.
- ❖ Price of products comparisons.
- ❖ Check on unsuccessful visit reports.
- ❖ Monitoring repeated lost sales by individual salesman.
- ❖ Sales commission analysis.
- ❖ Monitoring of enquiries and orders.
- ❖ Sales per 100 customers.
- ❖ Strike rate turning enquiries into orders.
- ❖ Analysis of sales by product-line.
- ❖ By geographical area.
- ❖ By individual customer.
- ❖ By salesmen.
- ❖ Matching sales orders against sales shipments – the trend from the mismatch.
- ❖ Backlog of orders analysis.
- ❖ Flash reports on sales.
- ❖ Publication of sales teams performance internally.
- ❖ Analysis of basic salaries and sales commissions.
- ❖ Share of the market against competitors.

- ❖ Share of new projects in the industry.
- ❖ New product/service launch analysis.
- ❖ Time to turn round repairs.
- ❖ Delays in delivering to customers ?(customer goodwill)
- ❖ Value of warranty repairs to sales over the period.

3. People

- ❖ Head count control.
- ❖ Head count by responsibility.
- ❖ Mix of staff analysis.
- ❖ Mix of business vs. staff personnel needs.
- ❖ Skilled vs. nonskilled.
- ❖ Management numbers vs. operations staff.
- ❖ Own labour/outside contractor analysis.
- ❖ Workload activity analysis.
- ❖ Vacancies existing and expected.
- ❖ Labour turnover.
- ❖ Labour turnover vs. local economy.
- ❖ % of overtime worked to total hours worked.
- ❖ Absence from work.
- ❖ Staff morale.
- ❖ Cost of recruitment.
- ❖ Number of applicants per advert.
- ❖ Number of employees per advertising campaign.
- ❖ Staff evaluation techniques.
- ❖ Evaluation of staff development plans.
- ❖ Monitoring of specific departments, example, accounting.
- ❖ Speed of reporting to internal managers vs. HQ
- ❖ Accuracy of reporting as measured by misallocations and mispostings.
- ❖ Queries are what reports mean.

- Monitoring of developments performance long-term.
- Pay and conditions vs. competition.

4. Research and development

- Evaluation vs. basic R&D objectives, strategic objectives and project objectives.
- Product improvement against potential market acceptance.
- R&D against technical achievement criteria, against cost and markets.
- R&D priority vs. other projects.
- R&D vs. competition.
- R&D technical milestones.
- Analysis of market needs over the proposed product/service life of R&D outcome.
- To management audit of R&D projects.
- Major programme milestones.
- Failure rates of prototypes.
- Control by visibility – releases, example, definition release, design release, trial release, manufacturing release, first shipment release. R&D release.

5. Environment

- Workplace environment yardsticks.
- Cleanliness.
- Tidiness.
- Catering facilities vs. competition.
- Other facilities vs. competition.
- Etc.

6. Final note

Many executives will talk freely in terms of quality and standards of "just in time" inventory control, and of other performance measurement yardsticks and may be quite knowledgeable about them, but when questioned as to the exact nature of the non-financial measurements that they actually have in place in the company will be hard-pressed to tell the researcher what the company is in fact measuring on an on-going basis. There is a lot of lip service paid to these measures, as opposed to those of a purely financial nature, which are of the course to a great extent the product of regulation and company law. So, much remains to be done to broadcast the merits of non-financial performance measurement indicators.

EXAMPLES OF PERFORMANCE MEASUREMENTS (A)

Performance Measurement Record Sheet

Measure	Customer Complaints (A)
Purpose	To understand which aspects of performance upset our customer so that we can continually improve our service.
Relates to	The need for business to satisfy its existing customers and to retain their customer in the future.
Target	Maintain a customer complaint ratio under 1% during 2009–2010.
Formula	*Number of customer complaints × 100* Number of customer orders dispatched/executed in the period.
Frequency	To be measured and reviewed monthly
Who measures?	Mr. X Y Z, Gen. Mgr. Q.A.
Source of data	The customer complaint system (Regi. Tel., etc.)
Who acts on the data?	Mr. X Y Z and his team.
What do they do?	Analyze complaint by key process, ensure process owner conduct root cause analysis and complete corrective actions flag, any major trends.
Not and Comments	We need to ensure that all customer complaints are captured by the customer's complaint system and that staff are regularly reminded about the customer complaint procedure.

EXAMPLES OF PERFORMANCE MEASUREMENTS (B)

Performance Measurement Record Sheet

Measure	Process First time yield. (B)
Purpose	To measure the rate of improvement in production efficiency.
Relates to	The needs to reduce waste, minimise rework, control production and reduce costs.
Target	Achieve a first time yield rate of 95% in the end 2009.
Formula	The procedure for $\frac{\text{(Number of goods Produced)}}{\text{(Number of units Processed)}} \times 100$ all Processes.
Frequency	To be measured and reviewed monthly
Who measures?	H O D / Shift I/C.
Source of data	Daily Process report sheets.
Who acts on the data?	Route cause analyse is undertaken and corrective actions are planned, implemented and the impact reviewed. (H.O.D. / Shift I/C).
Note and Comments	Target to be reviewed at the end of the year, we also need to monitor the impact of the operator SPC training.

Chapter 7

PERFORMANCE DEVELOPMENT

Structure:

7.1 Performance Development

7.2 HR and OD

7.3 Performance Appraisal

7.4 Potential Appraisal

7.5 Assessment Centre

7.6 The Critical Mass Techniques

7.7 The Workout

7.8 MBWA

7.9 Employee Counselling

7.10 Mentoring

7.1 PERFORMANCE DEVELOPMENT

Performance development is a process of upgrading employee's knowledge, skill, competencies and bahavioural traits to prepare them for present as well as future jobs and responsibilities. Performance development process is normally applied by three-member team company-wide.

- ❖ A process-owner – the manager who acts as teacher and coach to his subordinates.
- ❖ A representative from HR department – who acts as an enabler or advocate.
- ❖ The employee as a self-directed learner – performer.

In PDP specific goals are set for employees, covering business, personal and professional (development) goals with time limit. To help him achieve these goals, long-range and short range development planning is done. Once employee 'gaps' are identified in the areas of functional, motivational and bahavioural, are made known to an employee through official feedback. This feedback is again the collective result of potential and performance review undertaken by the management. Through this PPR, not just the skills and knowledge required to perform every role activity is assessed but also social skill inventory is also taken to balance his personality at work and thus his career goal path and career planning is designed and developed. After all, professional growth is a shared responsibility between the employee and the management. But ownership rests with individual employee. Performance Development – a psychological contract is not transactional, but long-term in nature and therefore, it is CEO's responsibility to provide an opportunity to an employee with meaningful performance target achievement and consequential rewards.

The key concept in implementing performance development strategy is to fashion an open, creative team-environment in which all people understand company's vision, mission and goals and are motivated to contribute to its success and are able to continually improve business performance and personal growth based on commonly held principle – collective performance. When you affect their pay, promotion, when you tell them that now their pay is dependent on how they perform, that gets their attention. Performance development rests on four principles.

- ❖ Employee's expectation and their satisfaction.
- ❖ Management by facts.
- ❖ Respect for and ownership with people.
- ❖ Plans do check act (PDCA) cycle.

Performance includes number of aspects that taken together are satisfactory or not. The focus is on the outcome. Therefore, performance programme must describe three major elements:

- ❖ Management commitment to improve people, process and practices and thereby their performance.

- ❖ Task performance management at every work activity.
- ❖ Assessment to check conformance to requirements.

Effective implementation of tasks performance and its effective assessment are clearly an indispensable component in achieving and maintaining organisational success.

7.2 HUMAN RESOURCES AND ORGANISATION DEVELOPMENT

In our earlier chapters, we focused on issues and challenges to be faced by manager and managed while working on performance management. When we opt for performance management implementation, we encounter a whole new set of problems. Some of these are chronic; others are related to employee's morale, motivation, attitude, aspiration and so on. These two employee management dilemma sometimes discourages us to try out new concept-performance management. Today, we may be operating on the values and culture of X management theory with little addition of Y management principles and values. Even to say further, we may be operating on the principles, values of Y management theory or expecting to implement Z management theory to our organisation. Our expectations of performance management can't be fulfilled unless we get ourselves clear on management of human resources assumptions. 'Pay me well', 'Treat me well', 'Use me well' are the assumptions of people at work advocated by X, Y and Z theories of organisation. And, for successful implementation of performance management, you have to learn and practice this statement loudly. You can't change the fruits unless you change the roots. You have to change your present thinking into prospective tomorrow. You have to resolve your present dilemma. Stephen R. Covey in his book *"PRINCIPLE – CENTRED – LEADERSHIP"* nicely described the management dilemma, which will help us resolve the classic managerial and organisational dilemmas before implementing performance management.

Resolving Management Dilemmas

- ❖ How can we have a culture characterised by change, flexibility and continuous improvement and still maintain a sense of stability and security?
- ❖ How do we get our people, the culture, aligned with the strategy so that everyone in the organisation is as committed to the strategy as those who formulated it?
- ❖ How do we unleash the creativity, resourcefulness, talent and energy of the vast majority of the present workforce, whose jobs neither require nor required such use?
- ❖ How do we clearly see that the dilemma of whether to play tough hard ball to produce a bottom line or to play soft ball to "be nice" to people is based on a false dichotomy?
- ❖ How do we serve and eat the lunch of champions (feedback) and then the dinner of champions (course correction) within the context of the breakfast of champions (vision)?

- How do we turn a MISSION statement into a constitution – the supreme guiding force of the entire organisation – instead of a bunch of nebulous, meaningless, cynicism – including platitudes?
- How do we create a culture where management treats employees as customers and uses them as local experts?
- How do we create team spirit and harmony among departments and people who have for years been attacking, criticising, contending for scarce resources, playing political games and working from hidden agendas?

As you read these statements, you will gain an understanding of the basic principles of effective organisational performance and leadership and you will be cleared, empowered to resolve these and other management questions by yourself and will follow correct road map with specific milestones of successful performance management.

Effective Knowledge Management

Today, in the post-liberation era, the CEO must turn his organisation into caring corporation. Because employees view their management of today is extremely practical as well as money-minded and expects their contribution to be acknowledged. They accept that if they are working in the company, it is company's responsibility to ensure that their mind is free of worries about their families. Thus, recognising employee's contributions to company and scope for alleviating personal problems that impede their professional performance are the man motivating factors for employees. And, as we move towards a knowledge-based society, the knowledge employee is becoming critical to the organisation. Their innovative and creative attitude, their positive initiative, their originality of customer service and deep understanding of customer – internal and external needs that goes beyond the desired organisational performance level.

Their knowledge that integrates the diverse functions, departments, and operations of the organisation into a single tool for acquiring total performance targets to get an edge over its competitors. The knowledge pool of people will play a momentous role in the organisation of today. Organisations are discovering that their core abilities lie not in a particular product, process or technology but in the knowledge pool and skill of people. They are realising that TQM, Business Process Reengineering, Management Reengineering or Organisational Restructuring plans will not succeed unless the right people with appropriate set of skills are in place to manage these new processes. Hence, CEO must ensure that his and their people's mind sets are reengineered too. In other words, it is people who will make or break the application of these management tools.

People are the movers and shakers of the organisation. It is, therefore, necessary to ensure that the knowledge resource of each individual is applied directly to the tasks they have to perform. Managing people becomes absolutely critical to perform at global standards. Human resources performance creates manpower configurations to boost up the ability of the individuals. And through it all, balances corporate and employee interests by designing performance development plans right from recruitment to retirement. The new challenges of HRM are:

- Attract people with multidimensional experience and skills, matching with the requirements of organisational tasks.
- Induct outsider employees with a new perspective to lead the company.
- Infuse fresh blood at every level of the organisation anticipating future growth plans.
- Develop a culture that attracts people to the company.
- Locate people whose personalities fit the company values.
- Devise methodologies for assessing psychological traits and behavioural dynamics.
- Seek-out unconventional development grounds of talents.
- Design pay and benefits that competes on quality and not quantum.
- Anticipate and find people for positions that do not exist yet.

The company that cares for people and gives them room to grow will be the company that will attract good people. The aim of HRD programmes ought to be releasing tremendous creative power, potential and performance of people by involving them in a meaningful change and development process. And the aims of organisational development process are to gather and diagnose the data to select developmental priorities, values and objectives; to identify and evaluate alternative solutions; to compare results with organisational goals and to monitor the results on continuous basis to shift the organisation from good to better position. HR growth at work is characterised by step-by-step developmental process. When individuals are trained with purpose in performance management, they gradually liberated from old habits and are increasingly motivated and directed from within. And when people in the organisation are thus trained, they find ways to make their style, structure, skills and systems increasingly congruent with their mission, role, goals and objectives. It is then necessary that the HR development should evolve obviously from company's vision, mission and principles. All HRD programmes should attempt to empower, involve people and liberate them to make a quantum leap in total performance.

It is generally experienced through organisations survey literature that the real problem of performance development was that people were not trained; they were not sure what management expect them to do or how to do it. The survey further identified several areas where employees perceived a need for improvement; system effectiveness, organisational climate, work environment, inter-personal and inter-departmental relations, communication, participation etc. The management that is interested in performance management must consider this before adopting change management strategies.

I believe that in most organisations sustained competitive advantage comes from more productive workforce. It may be difficult to some companies, but maintaining competitive advantage is a requirement not an option. No business can survive if customers do not have a compelling reason to buy its goods and services. Hence, creating a source of competitive advantage has become a real challenge. Therefore, it is of prime importance to continually improve the health of goose (Human Resources) rather than exclusively focusing on golden eggs (Profits). People's performance improvement plans enable us to improve capabilities of organisation that drive productive and fruitful changes on a long-term basis.

Does your organisation have a disciplined approach for improving workforce performance? High performance can't be created by training and performance management alone. Each is a legitimate stand-alone part, but performance improvement requires a system based tools, techniques, interventions, models for improving people performance and development.

Following are some of the innovative instruments to bring qualitative and quantitative rigor to the people-development processes.

7.3 PERFORMANCE APPRAISAL MANAGEMENT

Personal or organisational growth at work is an improvement process. To improve, we must start from where we are; not from where we should be or where someone else is. It takes more patience, understanding and courage to increase capacity through hard efforts and discipline to improve. It can't be quick fix or made to order formula. Introspection gives us an accurate understanding of our weaknesses and power to overcome them. Self or organisational introspection guides us on the following vital issues.

- Until we drop unwarranted assumptions about people, organisation and self, we can't expect to bring about lasting improvements in our organisational life.
- We can't magnify our human resources using manipulative management techniques.
- Individual and organisation ought to be guided and governed by set of proven principles.
- While managers must focus on the bottom line, leaders must look to the top line for clear vision.
- Individual and organisational reconditioning is important and careful planning helps us maintain a sense of mutual perspective, purpose and ordered priorities for maintaining consistent performance.

Once reconditioning is confirmed, you have to examine your organisation before implementing proactive performance appraisal. You have to answer the following questions:

- What is the present situation of Performance Appraisal?
- What can management do to improve it?
- What can individual(s) do to improve it?

The management interest in checking its own part in creating condition to encourage executives focusing fresh attention on the organisation of work; they will take fresh look at the questions of what tasks exist and of what is the best possible way to structure them.

Performance appraisal is an evaluation carried out to take a stock of the fulfilment of corporate/departmental/individual objectives through the achievement of company/ departmental/individual goals and means employed to make an evaluation of the overall effectiveness of its programme for management development. Result-oriented performance system is based on:

- ❖ Identifying dimensions of performance (employee's behavioural traits at work and outcome necessary to accomplish the objectives).
- ❖ Identifying standards of performance.
- ❖ Identifying performance measurement system.

Result-oriented appraisal is consistent with the psychological principles that people work better when they have definite goals or objectives which they must meet in specified period. By providing feedback, it helps employees to know where they stand performance-wise. It is a fair method to identify employees SWOT profile. Through this method, management identifies:

- ❖ Employee's core competencies – to slot them into suitable functions where an individual gets motivation and initiative to further enrich him in his job and other peripheral jobs.
- ❖ Employee's core weaknesses – are identified and efforts are made to avoid slotting them in function which can't be compatible.
- ❖ Employee's peripheral competencies and weaknesses are then overcome through training. Encouragement is given to them to take assistance from peer and subordinates when necessary.

Performance appraisal is not carried out with due importance and seriousness; hence, it is generally taken as annual ritual. Subjectively, judgement, bias and prejudice can be eliminated to a greater extent provided satisfactory answers are found to following questions by the management.

(1) Who requires appraisal? – Everyone in the organisation right from CEO to cook.

(2) What needs to be appraised? – Knowledge, skills, attitude, relations, competencies, goal fulfilment, potential traits, etc.

(3) Who should do it? – Immediate superior, peer and subordinates too.

(4) When appraisal is necessary? – On continuous basis.

(5) What is the purpose of appraisal? – To assess critical attributes, strengths, weaknesses and areas of improvement.

(6) What are the methods? – Various depending on company's culture and climate.

The main **OBJECTIVES** of Performance Appraisal are:

- To highlight the strengths and weaknesses and areas of performance improvement.
- To evaluate and compare the performance of an employee in contrast to other executives.
- To identify the development areas of an employee and provide right kind of opportunities.
- To discover the latent and hidden skills, strengths, talents, potential, etc.
- To assess whether an employee is on right jób, right place or not.
- To assess how far an employee can grow in the company taking in capabilities into account.
- What kind of job rotation or career opportunities can be planned.
- Whether an employee can be considered for career progression now, taking all the above into account.

The evaluation of performance appraisal is thus helpful in fulfilling certain key purposes.

Administration: Decision-making, employee development, placement, transfer, promotion, etc.

Motivational: Counselling, self-appraisal, identifying opportunities for personal development.

Developmental: Communication, training and development, involvement.

Performance appraisal is an attempt to think clearly about each person's performance and future prospects against the background of his total situation. It appraises the best aspects of individual work and suggests possible areas for improvement. It provides systematic judgement to back-up salary increases, benefits, promotion and some-times demotion or termination. Performance appraisal is a means of telling employee how he is doing and suggesting needed changes in his behaviour, attitude, skill or job knowledge. It tells him where he stands in the eyes of superior. Thus, it is an integral link in the chain of effective managerial operations. It is all powerful instrument directing individuals, who are ultimately responsible for the performance of the organisation. It is the central and core system of an organisation with linkage to all other HRD systems. It is an evaluation in terms of the individual effort, resources availability, its utilisation, environmental interference, and organisational support.

In performance appraisal system, it is important to ensure that it should not only serve the purpose of a genuine appraisal and be relevant to job performance, but also be directly observable, verifiable and measurable. Proactive and result-oriented performance appraisal system has its own merits:

- Collective performance targets are set by superior and his employees/team, considering his team is knowledgeable and can assess each other.
- The boss is rated by his team's collective performance – upward approach is followed while appraising on performance targets.
- Team-members evaluate the team leader and more harmony can be obtained.
- It helps in taking corrective action in time, grievances at lower levels can be made known and action is taken in time.
- Makes boss more productive and develops leadership qualities among team-members.
- The system is more balanced and allows two-way free interaction and communication.
- Provides opportunities to probe into strength and weaknesses and seeks clarifications where necessary.
- Training needs of employees can be ascertained fairly, accurately and training becomes a continuous process.
- Empowers employee down the line and they work wonderfully and keep employees highly motivated.
- Motivational force initiates goal achievement where role clarity, efficiency, effectiveness and stemming of wastage in emphasised.

Methods of Performance Appraisal

Appraisals are most important to both management and employees. They are the aids to evaluate individual performance, rewards and to develop an employee and plan his job career. An employee should understand that there exist linkages between the performance and potential appraisal and that these together can effect a career progression.

- Self-appraisal, trait appraisal, general assessment and task related appraisal are the parts of performance appraisal.
- Performance appraisals have been extended to incorporate views of peer, subordinates, superiors, internal customers and external customers.
- Keeping promises, setting targets or setting goals or objectives for individual linked with corporate goals is also one of the important methods of performance appraisal assessment.
- Self-appraisal during training, probation, confirmation, periodical potential appraisals and annual record systems are the processes of performance appraisal methods.

❖ The role conversion script based appraisal system is an open system of appraisal where manager and managed discuss their progress report mutually. This is a fair and to some extent proactive performance appraisal system. Based on conversion through script employees development plan is prepared focusing his training and further development.

❖ Measurement of productivity and performance, managerial incentive scheme, and their performance, team performance appraisal, 360 degree appraisal, assessment centres techniques are some of the result of oriented recent methods of performance appraisal based on the philosophy of total performance management.

A – 1 – Pereformance Appraisal at Work

Employees are broadly classified into four categories;

1. **Question Marks:** They neither show any improvement in performance nor do they improve themselves. *They have low potential as well as low performance* (10%) of total work population.
2. **Problem Children:** If not properly taken care, they are problematic. Such employees will either have problem with boss or with job itself. To tap their potential, such employees may be given new job or job locations. *They have high potential but low performance* (5%) of total works population.
3. **Star Performers:** These are race horses of the company and must be kept engaged with assignments all the time and groom them for higher assignments in future. *They have high potential and high performance.*
4. **Solid Citizens:** They are high on skills but limited in capacity to grow beyond present job profile. The company has to look after them constantly. If they were given proper training and suitable self-development plan, these mediocre can be changed to excellent performer. *They have low potential but high performance.*

Through performance review, such employees SWOT analysis is planned and their developmental plan is framed depending on the employee competencies and organisational needs.

PERFORMANCE APPRAISAL

Performance appraisal is very much related to employees "AAKASH" and will indicate whether they are well equipped with:

❖ Professional soundness

❖ Constructive orientation to result

❖ Confidence in human skills

These are the probable bases for self-change and environmental change.

The decade of 2000-2010 is a decade of performance:

- On cost saving
- Work improvement
- Innovations
- Total quality
- Thrust for learning

If business leaders and employees do not adjust to these new realities and continue to love *status-quo* situation, there is every danger of facing business/career interruptions.

EMPLOYEE'S – AAKASH

Employee's work performance can be considered to be a result of his ABILITY, ATTITUDE, KNOWLEDGE, ACTION, SKILL AND HABITS.

The whole personality at work demonstrates all above variable in employees with varying degree – Positive, Negative, Neutral. Anyone acting in absence of one of these variables will fail to achieve the desired performance.

For example: A hotel waiter who is enthused by his work and wants to satisfy his guest-customer in every way; but does not know how to handle a service spoon and fork is likely, make mess of extending his services to a guest.

He has right attitude, but not right ability.

Hence, the synergistic combination of all above variables, acting together in balance will always result in the desired performance.

1. Ability

It is the quality that makes an action possible. Understanding and learning skills, creativity, inter-personal network and other competencies are the abilities to perform the activities at work. Ability is a mental and physical skill. Ability can be blocked at work-place if proper environment is not provided. Ability is just like a bank cheque. If it is encashed, then it has value. If not, it is invalid. Many a time, organisation block individual abilities because of company's culture, values and employee's abilities get invalid.

2. Attitude

It is a settle mode of thinking. Any attitude contains an assessment of whether the object to which it refers is liked or disliked. Attitude is developed through experience. Attitude is affected by company culture, behaviour of management, policies, quality of worklife, etc. Thus, the way in which people see the world of work is influenced by their attitude. Behaviour at work is the manifestation of attitude demonstrated as the individual interacts with the environment and people. From the combination of experience, social conditioning, personality traits, attitude is demonstrated in behaviour.

3. Knowledge

It provides the ability to administer the functions effectively. It is an application and productive use of skills, acquired by an individual over the years. Knowledge is always upgraded by continuous learning. The knowledge, skills of employee comes from education, training, work experience which generates a certain stock of productive capital.

4. Action

Action is a way of communicating with people around you. Any act in the form of communication is called transaction through words, voice, body language; we display our intentions of act, within given situations. Through our action, we demonstrate our behaviour, attitude, thoughts and feelings to others. This defines your traits – whether you are controlling, disciplining, restricting boss/subordinate or whether you are helpful and a caring person. Action can be reactive, positive and proactive.

5. Skills

Skills are the aspects of human behaviour that are learnt and improved with practice. Skills are witnessed and experienced by others and therefore, can be appraised. They can be learnt and their acquisition and development can be established. Skills are used to control behaviour (skills are – Delegation, Team-building, Communication, Negotiation, Self-management, etc.)

6. Habit

Our personality traits; behaviour, attitude, desire are a composite of our habits. We sow a thought, then reap an action, sow an action and reap a habit; repetition of this cycle forms a habit. Habits are consistent and are expressed through our behaviour, desire, feelings and produce effectiveness or ineffectiveness at work. Habits can be learnt and unlearnt. Personality, neatness are the good habits for which individual is appreciated.

What is Performance Review?

- Performance review is an evaluation in terms of individual's efforts, resource availability, its utilisation, environmental interfaces and organisational support.
- Performance review is an attempt to think clearly about each person's performance and future prospects against the background of total situation.
- Performance review provides systematic judgements to back-up salary increase, promotion, professional development and sometimes demotion/termination.
- Performance review is a means of telling an employee how he is doing and suggesting needed change in his behaviour, attitude, skill and job knowledge. It tells him "where he stands" in the eyes of the management.

It is all powerful instrument directing individuals, who are ultimately responsible for the performance of the company.

Why Performance Review?

- To improve the competency level of employee and company.
- To retain and develop HR and to enable them to realise their potential for accomplishing the company's objectives.
- To create healthy working atmosphere that fosters creativity, innovation, involvement and respect to each other.
- To maintain a continuous review based on job attributes, self-appraisal, potential appraisal and work objectives.

Performance Review Objectives

- To develop role clarity to do the right things and avoid wastage of time.
- To enable managers to identify employee development needs.
- To provide positive feedback to employee at work.
- To help decide matters of increment, promotion and training.
- To prepare an employee for performing higher level of jobs by reinforcing the development of qualities required to handle higher level of responsibilities in future.
- To maintain hard core data on individual performance so that appraisal, both positive and negative, is objective.

Performance Rating

- It is always be more important to raise performance than to rate it.
- Consistency of performance assessment is important to employee where they are engaged in similar work.
- Generally, the following are the main options in terms of employee rating.
- Employees are rated against their personal traits, job objectives, their skills and competencies.

Rating Options

- **Highly effective:** Meets all job objectives, behavioural traits, exceeds required standards in a proficient manner. (We called it Very Good-level – I.)
- **Effective:** Achieve required objectives and standards of performance – Meets agreed requirements of job. (We called it Good-level – II.)
- **Fairly effective:** Meets some expectations with varying degree of effectiveness. (We called it Average-level – III.)

- **Ineffective:** This is unacceptable performance level, failing to meet basic objectives and requirements of the job. Demonstrate lack of commitment to performance improvement. (We called it Below Average-level – IV.)

ROLE OF RATERS – Appraiser and Reviewer

- The appraiser/reviewer to assess appraisee (employee in question) on the overall performance and not upon isolated incidents of recent past.
- Each job attribute to be considered independently, uninfluenced of rating given to other factors by you.
- Consider only relevant factors which you have personal opportunity to judge.
- Give feedback of rating to concerned employee regarding his areas of improvements.
- If employee is rated below average, his development plan, through identifying his training needs, coaching must be chalked out or alternative steps be recommended in the format of PRDS.
- Employee appraisal to be carried out periodically in a year for all the employees.

Rating Factors

- Appraiser/reviewer and reviewing Authority will appraise under A B C D rating factors, tick-marking one at the boxes from job attributes. Total job attributes factors are 10 in numbers.
- The normalised rating shall suppose to be:

  a. Very Good – 5%

  b. Good – 30%

  c. Average – 60%

  d. Below Average – 5%

- Once rating by appraiser, reviewer and reviewing authority is completed. Personnel Dept. will normalise the rating of employee and put it up to PRDS team for final approval.

Thus, employee performance appraisal becomes a teamwork task, free from prejudices and subjectivity.

PERFORMANCE MANAGEMENT AND SYSTEM (PMS)

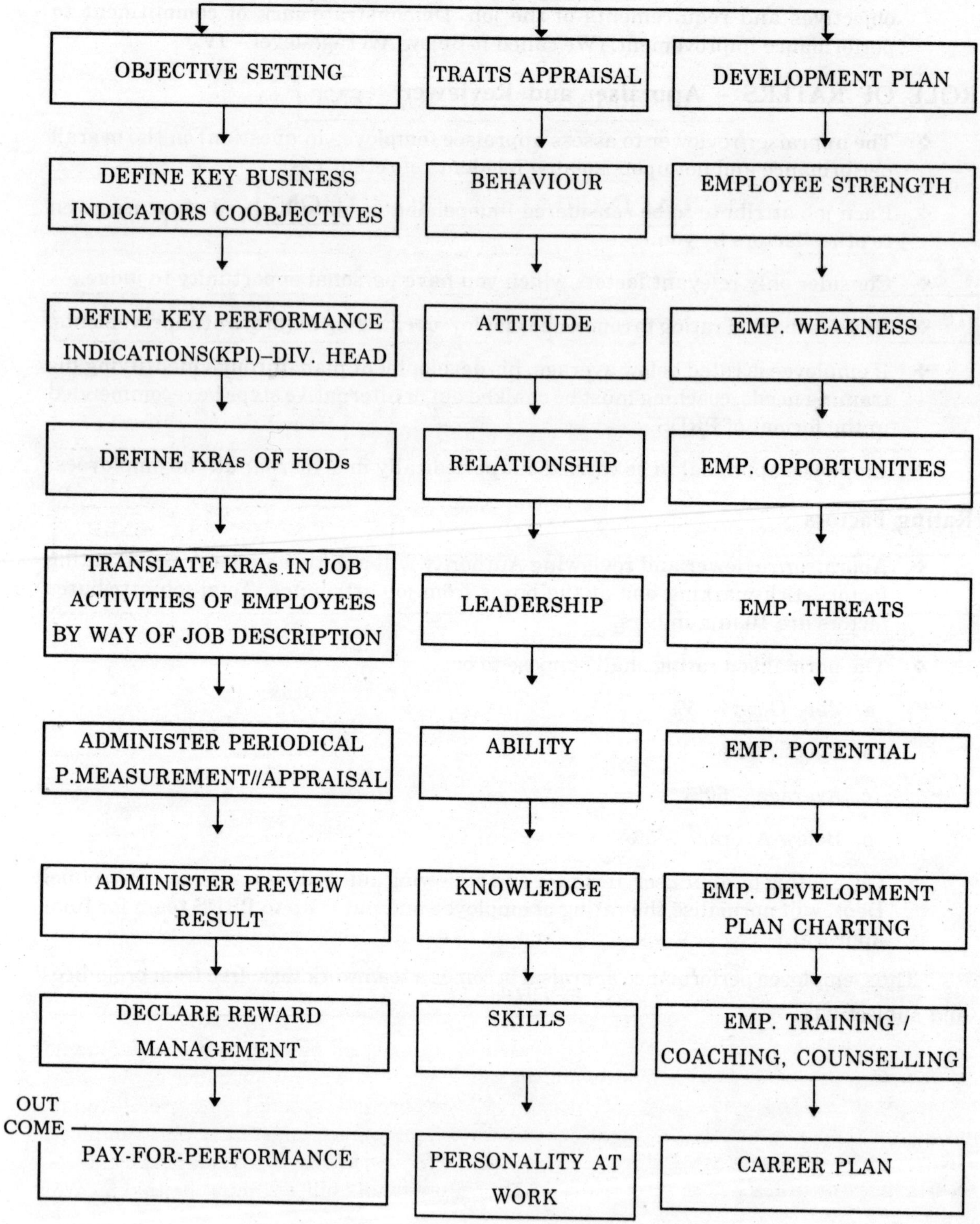

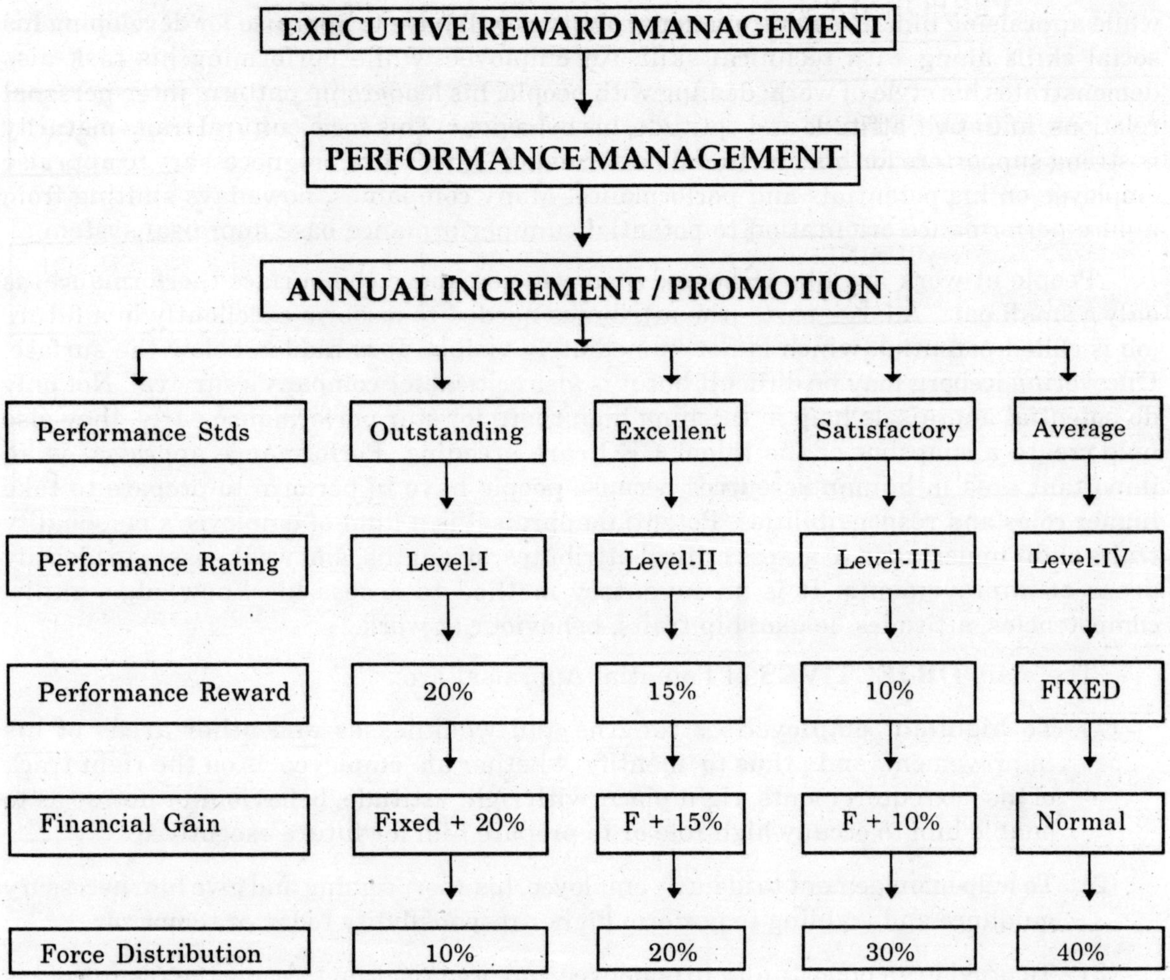

Legend:

Level-I – Stands for outstanding P. Achievement

Level-II – Stands for above normal P. Achievement

Level-III – Stands for Acceptable P. Achievement

Level-IV – Stands for Minimum P. Achievement

7.4 EMPLOYEE'S POTENTIAL APPRAISAL

The employee's potential appraisal system is an integral part of man-management development process and is used for employee's development. The performance appraisal's prime objectives is to identify potential employee for his personal and professional development as desired by the management for achieving organisational performance. The potential employee, who reflects his potentialities not just in his track performance record, but also in his personality traits and non-functional abilities, must be taken care while appraising him. His non-functional abilities will have to appraise for developing his social skills along with technical skill. An employee, while performing his task also demonstrates his style of work, dealing with people, his leadership pattern, inter-personal relations, initiative, attitude and aptitude, his behaviour. This socio-cultural traits maturity is strong supporters for his functional performance. It is, therefore, necessary to appraise employee on his potentials and performance. Many companies, nowadays shifting from a pure performance orientation to potential-cum-performance base appraisal system.

People at work are like icebergs, what you see above the surface (performance) is only a small part. A large part – the attributes needed to perform excellently in a future job is called potential, which is not immediately visible. It is hidden below the surface. Uncovering iceberg may be difficult but it is also critical for company's survival. Not only do potential appraisals help in catching high there for star performance early, they also help create a snapshot of the talent CEO care breeding. Performance appraisal is an important area in human resources because people have to perform to prepare to take higher roles and responsibilities. Potential appraisal is a kind of employee's personality traits audit undertaken to assess critical attributes, strengths, and weaknesses to identify areas of improvements. It is an inventory method to assess his knowledge, skills, competencies, attitudes, leadership traits, behaviour at work.

The main **OBJECTIVES** of Potential Appraisal are:

(1) To highlight employee's strengths and weaknesses and other areas of his improvement and thus to identify whether an employee is on the right track of his job requirements, right place, with right attitude, behaviour or not, so as to enable him to occupy high role or to prepare him for future executive.

(2) To help management to identify employee, his short coming and give him necessary guidance and training to perform higher responsibility today or tomorrow.

(3) To provide an opportunity to employee and organisation to know the results of his assessment and possible improvement areas sc that he gives improved performance at work. Through performance appraisal, he understands himself, his potential, whether matching as per organisation's requirements or not.

(4) To evaluate individual employee's traits, competencies along with performance and then plan his reward and develop him and thus plan his job career path. It helps management to understand its manpower strength to make organisational plan performance-oriented today or in future.

A PROFILE OF POTENTIAL EMPLOYEE

- A high potential employee is a self-assured man about his achievement without getting complacent.
- He perceives himself as a resource rather than issue who needs to be handled by management, peers and subordinates.

- A high potential employee has more of forward-looking agenda and is driven by concern for achievement rather than of petty reward on the way.
- A potential individual is not dogmatic about subspecialisation but is quite open-minded about others view points and contribution. These are the characteristics that make him an attractive worker.
- Identifing potential employee is to observe whether he invest in the subordinate, contribute to process, product and practices.

POTENTIAL APPRAISAL'S BROAD ATTRIBUTES

Employee's potentials are generally assessed on the broad-base attributes.

- **Employee's conceptual effectiveness** – His business vision and orientation, entrepreneurial orientation, sense of reality, etc.
- **Employee's inter-personal effectiveness** – His network relationship and directedness, negotiating power, personal influence, verbal behaviour, inter-actionable skills, etc.
- **Employee's operational effectiveness** – His result-orientation and ownership concepts, individual effectiveness, risk taking, self-control and control on others, etc.
- **Employee's achievement motivation** – His drive to excel, professional ambition, innovation and search for excellence, stability, etc.

Potential appraisal and performance development are the tools for individual as well as organisation is all powerful technique specifically directing individuals who are ultimately responsible for the performance of the organisation. It is the central and core system of organisation development with linkage to all other HRD systems.

7.5 THE ASSESSMENT CENTRE - TECHNIQUE

This tool is an intensive test to evaluate employee's functional expertise, skills in order to check his leadership qualities, ability to innovative, palpating the managerial possibilities that lurks within them and then decide on his promotion, upgradation and career planning.

Method – The employee who has to assess are taken out of workplace and subjected to battery of tests including skill, attitude and functional knowledge and viva voce on functional exercise.

- List out which of the employees to assess.
- Design the battery of tests relevant to his role play (60% basket test and 40% personal interview)

- In basket exercises are given to him for two to three hrs. Tasks, such as accept an invitation and confirm his attendance, reply to an urgent fax message, invite job applicant to an interview, write a report on a visit to plant, give extempore speech, etc.
- This will help interpret employee's organisational skills, grasp of language and his initiative and ability to translate ideas into meaningful communication.
- Another task such as, giving organisational problems for solving it, leave, absenteeism, frequent unrest, strain IR, poor quality or product/services, etc.
- Depending on the category of employees, these tasks/exercises can be changed.

Assessment Tests: Tests of skills – group exercises and individual exercises.

GROUP EXERCISES

- Assigned role exercises used to assess negotiating skills, ability to persuade and ability to compromise.
- Unassigned role exercises used to assess ability to handle uncertainty, changing office and industry environment and stress.
- Team exercises used to assess ability to work in a team and solve problems collectively.
- Selling module – used to assess ability to sell.

Assessors are then ready to test concern employee, based on above six exercises. (Ten marks for each test, 60 marks for six tests are allotted and 40 marks are allotted for personal interviews.)

HOW TO IMPLEMENT IT?

- Identify requirement.
- Incorporate feedback from previous assessment.
- Receive nominations with one page sketch.
- Design programme with venue, time and dates.
- Compose panel (Assessors) depending on the profile of participants.
- Decide combination of group and individual exercise. Finalise sequencing of the mix between activity-oriented and sedentary modules.
- Day-1, 9.30 a.m. briefing assessors for an hour 10.00 a.m. event begins.
- Day-2, exercises.
- Day-3, interviews, candidates disperse, panelists remain to finalise list.

- ❖ Announce results within 15 days of the event.
- ❖ HOD and HR chief get detailed feedback on strength and weaknesses of those who could not make it.
- ❖ HOD and HR chief chalkout an improvement plan for those not selected.
- ❖ Those selected are considered for promotion, etc.

7.6 THE CRITICAL MASS TECHNIQUES

Critical mass technique is a self-sustaining, change producing and chain reaction tool, helping a company involve all its employees, executives, suppliers and clients in defining company's vision, mission, goals and strategies.

Collective brainstorming helps company to become 'one heart and one brain'.

WHY THIS TECHNIQUE IMPLEMENTATION?

Individual/employee now look upon his employment with a company as an opportunity to test his knowledge and apply it to the work. Today, professionals are much more demanding than they have been in the past. They possess the capabilities to determine their performance. Realising the importance of people in the new people in the new paradigm of business, the company must utilise their knowledge, skills, and core competencies to make company competitive in product and services activities to establish global presence.

It is, therefore, necessary for CEO to involve them in the company affairs freely as possible.

The critical technique is build around the premise that if all your employees are involved in decision-making, problem-solving, they can inform/absorb information/company realities that will make them more of the larger of the company. It shows the power of groups in energising people into action.

HOW TO INITIATE CRITICAL MASS TECHNIQUE?

To facilitate organisational change process and business paradigm shift, this following formula to be kept in mind. (Dannemiller's Rationale Formula)

Where:

D= Dissatisfaction with the present situation.

V= Vision for future possibilities.

F= First steps required to attain the vision ***has to be greater than "R"***

R= Resistance to change.

Needless to say, if any one is missing, the company will be unable to change, (Resistance of course, is an omnipresent as people are)

HOW TO IMPLEMENT CMT?

A – Leadership alignment: Design team of 20-25 people of cross-functional nature, including supplier, client and consultant.

- **Environment Analysis** – Realities, trends, competition (for change envisaged)
- **External Stakeholder** – Customers, suppliers, investors.
- **Internal Stakeholder** – Top management, CEO, Executive, Workers.

B – Form a Mission: Vision, values and guiding principles.

C – Strategic Goals: Key thrust areas of business, strategic areas, and objectives. Direction plan for next three years.

D – Strategic Business Objectives: Expected results, turnover, sales, expansion diversification, HRD, etc., and details on what, when, how to achieve above plans.

E – Implementation plan: Redesign and then plan, do,, check and act plan.

F – Evaluation: Results inspections.

DESIGNING TEAM

- Purpose, agenda and norm or design team.
- Personal introduction.
- Information and issues data base.
- Desired outcome.
- Purpose or event/meet.
- List of participants.
- Brainstorming.
- Detailed agenda for three days.
- Review by leadership team.

TEAM FUNCTION

Based on D-P-P-E modes, necessary company data shall be collected.

D= Data on the organisation.

P= Purpose of the exercise.

P= To formulate plan for the actions necessary to achieve purpose.

E= Evaluation – effectiveness of the plan.

TEAM PARTICIPANTS

Consultant, employees of various departments, functional heads, union leader, make 3-4 groups, having 5-10 strength in each group.

CRITICAL MASS FUNCTION AT WORK: 3 DAYS SESSION

Day One:

1- CEO spells out purpose of the event.

- Group facilitator is chosen.
- Reporter prepares report

2- Environmental analysis session: each group discusses company's threat, chart it out on flipchart. This is pasted on wall for voting to be made by the participants.

This is followed by participant's background introduction, their contribution and frustration.

Then, Senior management leader describes the environment in which company operates.

3- Organisational diagnosis is carried out, of the masses agree on change.

4- Tasks/topics on problem-solving, decision-making leadership, career development and teamwork are assigned to each table group.

Day Two:

Shareholders, union leaders and other company stakeholders raise issues vital to them based on operational functional issues receive and send back open communication on how to resolve issues relating to internal/external organisational conflicts. Then rethink on organisation strategies and review draft vision and suggesting changes to it by voting.

Day Three:

CEO explains rationale behind the revised draft of the corporate mission evolved by the participants and gets consent of participants on organisations futuring – objectives are displayed on walls by way of posters – focus plan detailing how each person and group can work differently to drive the company towards its new strategic goals and aim of critical mass is informed to all.

7.7 THE WORKOUT TECHNIQUE FOR CHANGE MANAGEMENT

MERITS

- ❖ It is a tool that brings out the best ideas from your workers, staff, and executives to improve work methods, culture and climate in the company.

- ❖ These suggestions or solutions to problems are institutionalised in our company.
- ❖ Thus, knit your workforce into motivated mass of loyalist with commitment to bring improvement to the company.
- ❖ It is one of the best planned efforts to alter people's behaviour attitude and skills to bring positive cultural value change revolution in the company.
- ❖ They feel involved in organisational development, hence to some extent act as change agent of company.

WHY THE WORKOUT?

(1) **Every company** – is crammed with employes who have some ideas lying dormant about improving the way they do their work.

(2) **Layers of company** – executive structure and redtapism act as barrier between this found of innovation and the decision-makers at the top.

(3) **The result** – the complaints flew fast and furious from bottom, middle level employees, and top management session on problem-solving got little accomplished.

- Senior management shows disinterest in fulfilling employees need.
- The company's objectives make sense but execution stand and employee says if this is the best company, then why I go home feeling so miserable?
- Traditional modes of communication – seminars, meetings, circulars, and memos can't turn away the barriers between ideas and decision-making.

To avoid this, workout technique implementation allow employees at every level to speak the minds fearlessly with the assurance that their complaints would be addressed and their ideas implemented if found good enough.

WORKOUT – PILLARS

It is a mechanism to change minds – rests on four vital qualities, which are basic objectives of these techniques.

1. Employees feel comfortable thrashing out issues not only with their immediate bosses, but also with senior and top managers. It powers them to speak freely as possible-without jeopardising employment career.
2. Those closes to the work are more knowledgeable about it then their superiors and its decision-making is handed over to them, they will feel more responsible for their job than before.
3. Workout tool is used to identify unnecessary work, policies, procedures, practices, methods; reports thus work on the line of critical review appraisal system and detector.

4. The workout techniques helps the company to define and faster positive interactions, inter-relations and human relations at work, where best practices are implemented across the company, departments, units and functions without any barriers.
5. By applying this technique, the company tells its workers that both the problems and solutions are theirs but not the managements.

WORKOUT SEQUENCE

- Departmental managers, workers gather together.
- They define, discuss and dissect the major problems they face at workplace.
- Appoint coordinator responsible for guiding the suggestions that emerged out for implementation.
- Brainstorming session to start and solution to the problem be listed.
- Implementation responsibility rests with team.
- Before implementation discuss it with Senior management.

HOW TO CONDUCT A WORKOUT?

Choose problem to discuss – from team – choose coordinator for implementing suggestions – let team meet for brainstorming for solution – set meeting with team and Senior management who will give decision "yes/no" – hold additional meetings and implement suggestion.

WHAT IS ACHIEVED THROUGH WORKOUT?

Build trust – empower employees – eliminate unnecessary work – share values across the company – make job process quicker and faster – bring conduct and honesty to behaviour – new culture establishes.

AREAS OF PROBLEM FOR WORKOUT

Rework, repairs, wastages, rejections – housekeeping, safety, firefighting, strain departmental relations, communication, obsolete policies, success stories, excellence in work can be route through workout technique.

7.8 MBWA – MANAGEMENT BY WANDERING AROUND

A successful manager will have good rapport with his employees. The people will be comfortable in talking with the leader – manager. There is nothing wrong with complainer if he tells you face-to-face what they observe during their plant morning round. Talk to them as they know more about the shop floor situation than anybody. Always remember in talking to employees, the most important thing to do is to listen. You will never know what is going on in their mind unless you can hear them. You must lead the man. It is easier to lead than to push. If employees won't say to a manager what they say to each other, the organisation is already in deep trouble. Listen them, in such caes, one could plan an organisational psychologist in one's own workforce. No one likes to have someone spy on them. Eliminate fear of spying and encourage two-way communications. The manager who wanders around learns more about himself and his company from employees looks for signs and symptoms that reveal organisational culture. Look at your company from customers point. Talk to employees. Good listener should not have to disguise him or herself to get honest feedback. Clear, face-to-face communications are essential for harmonious and effective working relationship. It adds to develop person as well as organisation's performance of work. Talking to them on the spot, praising or reprimanding on reinforcing behaviour that is moving an employee closer to the performance goal may it be productivity or discipline goal. Catch people doing something right, when you do, you immediately and specifically share your feeling with them. One-minute praising is the most powerful activity a manager can do. In fact, it is the key to training people and making winner of everyone working for you and you are ready to obtaining desired performance.

MBWA translates your theory of desired behaviour modification into the more memorable techniques of catching people doing things right. MBWA focuses on three effective concepts derived from behaviour modification principles. Goal setting, praising and reprimanding, which are necessary in total performance achievement. MBWA conveys the necessity of direct participation by managers, not distant order giving.

Too many managers deal in a world of papers, not people. Go out, get out of office and talk to people on shop floor/office face-to-face, if that is what it takes to make the company work. Most creative, constructive ideas come from discussions with employees, from problem-solving suggestions with supervisors, from talking to workers who have identified a difficulty or proposed a better method from listening to your workforce/sales force.

MBWA is a social skill; technique demands clear interactions, inter-relations, involvement and understanding to achieve common commitments-performance. Human organisation of the company is not populated only with "standard individuals", i.e., MD, CEO, manager, workers but also with socio-psychological and personal values, opinion people brought at workplace and social structure aimed through their interactions. People interact daily plant round; departmental meetings, training sessions, safety meeting, morning greeting. They also occasionally interact during social occasions such as annual get-together, sports meet, farewell functions, birth/marriage day party, etc. These interactions cultivate a sense of direct participation, involvement and feeling of being a member of a team. Inter-mingling with people give them a sense of being head self-expression, recognition. MBWA approach tells you, step-by-step to unleash the enormous power your employees have and how to capitalise on their feedback, skills, knowledge and behaviour. MBWA gives you and your people a chance to discuss their problems freely and help find out mutual solution on the spot. It offers to unleash their creativity and capacity for innovation. MBWA set them all free from feeling of inequality; they feel as if they are empowered to solve their problems themselves. Obviously, you will see that these employees are mighty forces that can drive organisation to the new height of performance.

7.9 EMPLOYEE COUNSELLING

With increased realisation of the need to develop human resources for organisational effectiveness, employee counselling is becoming focal area of attention. Many managers tend to think that employee counselling involves specialised skills, which only behaviour scientists possess. This is not true. Counselling employee for better performance and development certainly requires some skills, but it requires more of attitude than skills. Any manager interested in the development of his subordinates can be effective counsellor.

In most inter-personal relationships, counselling takes place. To counsel means to help, to advice. People at work keep counselling others without realising that they are participating in a counselling process. Managers counsel employees when they see that the employee facing problems and need their intervention. They counsel employees while appraising them and while promoting. They counsel employees while inducting them into job. They counsel while in meeting or in training sessions.

Thus, counselling process involves the following:

- An understanding of the employee, his background, personality, knowledge, skills, environment, problem issues, where he is operating.
- An understanding of employee's potential for development, opportunities for development and mechanism to utilise these opportunities or create new opportunities or increase his potential, etc.
- A concern for development of the employee with an underlying, belief that employee development always helps organisational effectiveness.
- Sharing the concerns, communicating or advising skilfully in an open climate of understanding and mutual respect and helping the employee's plans, actions, for future development.
- Reviewing development from time-to-time together with the employee.

Employee counselling is a continuous process initiated through a consciously planned interview setting and continued all through the year, reviewing from time-to-time. Employee counselling requires attending, listening, responding a concern for others, respect, integration and action. Employee counselling takes place in two ways.

1. Reactive Counselling

Reactive counselling is done in response to a problem faced by an employee or when the employee himself is a problem. In this process, an attempt is directed towards helping the employee tackle the problem situation. However, the primary objective of reactive counselling is not development but solving the problem. Some insightful managers have an ability to use such problem situations to help the employee's development and have the focus. This counselling can be used right from employee's development and have the focus. This counselling can be used right from employee's personal problem-solving situations to performance problem-solving solutions.

2. Proactive Counseling

In proactive counselling, there may be no problem situation, but the counselling is aimed at helping the employee realise his strengths, potentialities, knowledge, skills and attitudes; needing improvement. It helps him workout a plan of action to develop his strengths and help him carryout such an action plan. The employee and his superior-counsellor initiate objective of the proactive counselling together. The objective of the proactive counselling is to help the employee's development. As everyone has to plan his own development at work, the counsellor (superior) through understanding of the employee and situation helps the employee develop a plan for self-development for his organisational effectiveness. The most important achievement of counselling can be planned development of the employee at desired level. This provides an opportunity explore for the employee along with his superior his own psychological field, future organisational opportunities, gaps, etc., and the action plan is made more towards the goals in self-development. Thus, the employee learns, develops and sets directions for his growth and then with the help of counsellor implement plan of action, reviews it periodically with his superiors.

Through employee counselling can be achieved

- Most useful and valid information to plan employee development realistically for the future career plan, job enrichment, multi-skilling, performance targets, etc.
- A professional and warm climate between the superior and the employee.
- Team spirit and clear understanding of organisational goals and superior's expectations.
- Openness and empathy that would insulate future frustrations.
- An opportunity to clarify expectations and obligations.
- Satisfaction of being heard and understood.
- Ability to give and receive feedback and help better understanding of the problems, aspirations, style of work, etc., an opportunity to share one's own problems and issues.

Managers who are generally responsible to develop employee performance have to advise and guide their employees and work. Guiding plays a significant role in managing employee performance. Guiding has three phases: Identification of performance goals; Achievement of these goals within given time; Evaluation and follow-up of goal achievement.

The manager must offer appropriate guidance to the employees so that he can achieve his performance. Thus, the manager has three roles to play in offering in guidance through counselling:

- He has to be concerned with developing his people and the work environment in which they function. He has to establish and maintain an atmosphere of mutual trust and listen and respond empathetically to employees.
- He must ensure that an individual's personal goals and the organisational goals are clear and they overlap more than conflict. The grievance of both sides should be objectively considered and resolved by him.
- The manager should use the resources and capabilities he has to help the employee establish better goals or decisions. He should offer structure and reassurance to help the employee to achieve these goals and define specific strategies while working with employees.

7.10 MENTORING – GROOMING PROCESS FOR AN EXECUTIVE

Mentoring has grown out of formal learning technique like behaviour modelling, in the corporate context. It is the process whereby a senior manager acts as friend, philosopher, guide and guru to new recruits as well as potential employees. It is practiced like formal methods of job description, orientation, indoctrination through which individual is absorbed and adopted in organisational culture. It is a socialisation process by which organisation shapes the attitudes, thoughts and behaviour of the employees. It also occurs when an employee encounters others at work, watches, and questions or is advised by them on acceptable pattern of organisational behaviour.

A special form of socialisation occurs when an employee "adopts" or being adopted and guided by others. The mentor is often older, respected employee, who is willing to commit his time and energy, to assist a new or potential employee to move up the corporate ladder. In effect, the mentor serves as role model to help employee gain valuable data on role to play and roles to avoid. Mentoring is a human resource development tool include coaching, grooming and to some extent succession planning and developmental planning for career management. Mentoring is invaluable for growing self-confidence and empowers manager, who can operate under stress while reaiming their quality standards and values for the company.

It helps a vital in smoothing the creases arising from cultural diversity, which bring together a group of people with varying expectations, beliefs and methods by offering individual's path through what appears to be a bewildering array of systems and processes.

Mentoring create an enabling system, which helps the mentee to absorb organisational culture, values quickly and forged ties with customers – internal as well as external. It also synergises with the core values of company, customers, integrity, performance, people, and policy, growing out performance. It also perceives in the culture of empowerment, support and reinforcement that is being done during the process of mentoring. It thus helps on combating executive stress, improves emotional intelligence and reinforces our identity as a learning organisation. Mentoring is essentially acted as role methods to subordinates while grooming the latter for leadership. The mentoring technique can be translated into tool of employee career development to map the career path of each employee. The objective is to prepare manager of tomorrow for their future role-play. Mentoring model can be developed in the following manner:

(1) Profiling mentee and deciding on the match for effective behaviour modelling. (One day personality test and workshop and allotment of mentor).

(2) Familiarising mentees with corporate functions and smoother initiation. (Five-day induction of corporate values and first mentor-mentee meeting.)

(3) Avoidance on mentor – mentee role conflict and forging closer ties with mentees. (Role clarity workshop for mentors and weekly meeting with mentee within the first month.)

(4) Extending the concept to the peer-level. (Fortnightly mentor-mentee meetings and assigning of buddies.)

(5) Reinforcing the formal and informal learning. (Need-based meetings, supplemented by phone calls, e-mail, etc.)

(6) Revisiting the process to generate feedback. (Review of the process by mentor and mentee.)

(7) Crystallising the feedback for corrective action. (Formal presentation by the mentee on mentoring achievement.)

Thus, one-to-one coaching can be developed and may be given as performance target for employee development.

OBJECTIVE OF MENTORSHIP

(a) To provide the new entrants with an insight into the organisation and their role in the situation for promotee, it is to prepare him for future role, imparting him cross-functional activities.

(b) Mentorship can be role models in terms of both career success and personality attributes needed for organisational success.

(c) It is a communication device to acquaint an executive with the different roles that he is expected to play in the form of human conduct not a depersonalised training process. For the knowledge at low levels, the mentorship is expected to ensure smoother initiation and cultivate a sense of ownership and for new hires, the benefit is quick acclimatisation. For performer, the idea is to supplement the existing skill base and provide a different perspective for stretch tasks.

PROFILE OF MENTOR

A mentor is usually a Senior manager who has spent more than five years with the company and can act as a role model in terms of behaviour and approach to work. Generally, he is from functions other than the mentee's own. The match is always cross-functional to add the skill base and provide interaction with different functional streams. It is like, historically, what Chanakya was to Chandra Gupta Mourya and mythologically, what Krishna was to Arjuna. This one-to-one training tool is nowadays, used in various companies to upgrade their executive's skills, attitudes, knowledge to the desired level of company within timebound period, of course it is continuous process to be followed by the organisation at all levels.

Mentorship is a process wherein mentor to mentee executive/employee inducts him through the rites of organisational rituals to sustain successful organisational life. From job content to personal counselling, from business manners to individual performance expectations, mentor teaches him lessons on organisational expectations and conforms him to follow the same as his grooming process. Through mentorship on the job training is imparted in short time. Thus, cuts through system led organisational lines by ensuring individual attention to problems, which usually results in quick action on providing solutions. Meaningful advice on resolving dilemmas and useful tips on getting the best out of the systems of the company is prime purpose of mentorship of course, this makes the systems of the company is prime purpose of mentorship of course, and this makes the learning flexible rather than structured. Mentorship makes it happen in the areas of career development of employee, cross-functional executive preparation for tomorrow. It paves developmental path for individual and organisation for achieving total performance mutually.

Chapter 8

WORKPLACE PERFORMANCE IMPROVEMENTS

Structure:

8.1 Introduction

8.2 Quality Circle Management by Participation

8.3 Kaizen – A Continuous Improvement Process

8.4 Innovation and Innovativeness

8.5 Employee Coaching

8.6 Teamwork

8.7 Personal Assessment, Positive Thinking and Positive Attitude

8.1 INTRODUCTION

"If you don't listen well, you cannot involve people. If you don't listen, they know you think they are unimportant."

ARE WE LISTENING AND INVOLVING OUR EMPLOYEES?

Doubtful to reply:

It is observed that only 34% of organisations listen to their employees while 66% organisations don't listen to their employees. Because the supposition is prevalent the world over that there would be no problem in production/service department, if only our employee would do their job in the way they were taught. (Do as I say approach). The result is: The employees are handicapped by the system and the system belongs to management (and we are the management). Thus, if you put a good person into bad system the system will win most of the time. Deming a Quality Guru takes it further this way: Most trouble and most possibilities for improvement belong to the system, which is controlled by the management. Centralisation of decision-making, love for *status quo* operating systems, are the culprits discourage employees involvement. Juran – Quality Guru points out that: Objectives research has regularly shown that about 80% to 90% of the damages done by poor quality are traceable to managerial action.

Our old thinking trap us into old pattern of doing the things, no longer fit in the new circumstances created by competitive economy. The new economy with enrichment of QMS, TQM, BPR interventions empowering people to manage themselves.

This new paradigm puts PEOPLE at the centre of the business and replaces rigid, *status quo* hierarchies of old-age management with NEW NETWORK OF RELATIONSHIP MANAGEMENT STRUCTURE emphasising INTER-CONNECTEDNESS OF ACTIVITIES.

And majority of continuous improvement efforts owe much of their success to effective employee involvement and empowerment.

- Involvement means winning the hearts and minds of your associates – superiors, subordinate and colleagues.
- If management solves employee involvement problems, employees solve internal and external problems and develop win-win attitude toward work and people.
- The magic of employee involvement is that it allows individuals to discover their own potential and to put that potential to work in creative ways and people develop in themselves pride in self-discipline workmanship, self-respect, self-reliance and a heightened sense of responsibility.
- When people are involved in the problems, they become significantly and sincerely commit to come up with solutions to the problems.

- By getting other people involved in the problem, managers release some of the natural driving forces already in people. When management external driving forces (growth, cost-cutting) are synchronised with employees internal drives and motivations, we can create synergic problem-solving teams for achieving highest production, productivity and efficiency.

EMPOWERMENT

Any process that provides greater autonomy to employees through the sharing of relevant information and the provision of control over factors affecting job performance. Empowerment helps remove conditions that cause powerlessness while enhancing employee feelings of self-efficiency. Empowerment authorises employees to cope with situations and enable them to take control of problems as they arise.

BROAD APPROACHES TO EMPLOYEE EMPOWERMENT

(1) Helping employee achieve job mastery (giving proper training, coaching and guided experience that will result in initial successes).

(2) Providing successful role models (allowing them to observe peers who already perform successfully on the job).

(3) Using social reinforcement and persuasions (giving praise, encouragement and verbal feedback designed to raise self-confidence).

(4) Allowing more control (giving employee freedom to do it yourself to learn complexities in the jobs.)

(5) Giving emotional support (providing reduction of stress and anxiety through better role definition, task assistance and honest caring).

Using these approaches by managers, employee begins to believe that they are competent and valued and their jobs have meaning and overall impact on performance.

FOUR CONDITIONS OF EMPOWERMENT

(1) Win-Win Agreement:

a. Specify desired results to achieve.

b. Set guidelines and communicate.

c. Identify available resources.

d. Define accountability – Hold them accountable and evaluate the results by way of measurement, observation and discernment.

e. Determine the consequences – Reach an understanding of what follows when the desired results are achieved, not achieved. Positive consequences may include financial, psychic, reward, recognition, appreciation, advancement, added responsibility. Negative consequences may range from reprimand, no encouragement or termination.

2. Self-Management:

Use your own good judgement and do what you think is appropriate. Win-win is a human resource principle recognises that people are capable of self-direction and self-control and can govern themselves to do whatever is necessary within the guidelines to achieve the desired results.

3. Helpful Structure and Systems:

Unless expectations are clarified and commitments made upfront, people can expect performance evaluation to be difficult, you must have objectivity base appraisal system well supported by helpful built-in structure, form, procedure and system. When people know what is expected, evaluation will be more accurate, more complete and more honest. There must be a system and understanding of what results are expected and what criteria are used to assess employee's performance.

4. Accountability:

Standards of performance to execute when to give progress report, feedback on performance is a must.

People in organisation are like diamonds, have a basic value. But it is only after they have been polished and that the world will understand their real values. Company values, culture is a bank of "Shared Values"; is the manifestation of how people see themselves, their company, and co-employees. Organisational culture represents organisation vision, mission put together understood and implemented by all level of organisation. Employee as an individual in the employment is an entrepreneur to add more value in your job. You must expand your knowledge, skill and ability to give more to the company.

To do this asks yourself:

(A) How can I be worth more to the company?

(B) How can I help it to achieve more in less time?

(C) Are there some ways that I could help cut cost and increase quality, productivity, efficiency?

(D) What new system could I develop?

(E) What new product/service development could I use that would allow the company to produce its products and services more effectively?

If the organisation can help people to do more with less, then we truly are empowering people. They will take the organisation at the peak of performance, excellence. They will create innovative organisation. Work improvement is nothing but outcome of involvement, participation and empowerment.

For innovation and efficient companies it is necessary to adopt new and different approaches assuming work and people. The hard aspects of organizing people must be combined with soft aspects of values, visioning new way of thinking, doing a new means of influencing behaviour at work. Attracting, managing and nurturing knowledge worker is the single most critical issue with the new people management. People are crucial to every work operation, because best products, best price and best services are created by the people. Hence, there must be greater involvement and empowerment given to people. When you share your care is the basic mantra for involvement, empowerment and participative management.

People make it happen. Employee involvement, empowerment and teamwork coupled with continuous training are extremely important to realising work improvements and that is called performance improvement. To convert performance improvement into action, organisation must have specific areas, objectives in which it desires to seek improvements. For example, a product fails too often during acceptance testing and the objective is to reduce test failure by 50%. The finance department is habitually late paying account payable and the objective is to assure all payments are made in less than 30 days. Each of such problems provides the framework of an action plan for the organisation to realise work improvements. The work improvement concept focuses on finding shortfall and sources of variability in product, people, processes, practices, policies and procedures that detract from a desired output and then improving the things to eliminate undesirable results or outputs. All such action plans, programmes, projects are carried out by people in the organisation, who are the owner, researcher and programmer of their jobs. Employees are the people who are responsible for converting every organisational input into desirable output. May it be manufacturing, finance, human resources or services? Obviously, then it involves defining and identifying employee needs and expectations. Organisation and individual commitments for improvement is necessary for overall performance improvement of the organisation.

Once we decide employee's improvement plans, we are open for implementing foundations of improvements, educating and empowering them to eliminate errors, wrong doing, they will do wonders to the organisation. They will generate internal profit to the organisation by arresting cost of doing the wrong things. High performing organisations know that each employee has the best vantage point to identify and recommend improvement to the work, giving necessary information, involvement and education. Such organisations install a framework of training and development for their employee's improvement on continuous basis. Success comes about when all employees can continually; clearly and fully describe their changing job needs and the work done within the business. For this, generally three things are to be done. First, a new set of values must permeate the business, from boardroom to security gate. These values must results in an insistence that improvement no longer be a stand-alone issue, but be completely linked with the purpose, vision, strategies and business objectives of the organisation. Second, everyone must be given right training, tools and skills to do work-place improvements correctly. Third, improvement must be a win for everyone. Employees must see their win in a greater job satisfaction resulting from better performance. They must also see their win in receiving training in new skills that are applicable not just on the job, but at personal level as well. Organisation will win through increase profits which will enable long-term capital investment and perpetuation of business and finally, shareholders must gain their win through enhanced stock performance and dividends. Such mind-set must be developed among all concerned that causes them to recognise and truly believe that improvements by individual is not for himself only, but it is for all in the organisation. They should believe that collective performance improvement is also a corporate performance improvement. Such feeling of improvements comes from continuous training and development of people in the organisation and they then fully meet business objectives, the needs of organisation and individuals now and into future, with continual improvement in efficiency and effectiveness. This chapter on workplace improvements describes philosophies, tools, techniques and initiatives focusing individuals and teams that can help solve organisational problems to meet business objectives in an efficient manner.

8.2 QUALITY CIRCLE MANAGEMENT BY PARTICIPATION

Every one of us has a great reserve of capabilities, abilities and time. But if a person perceives that working harder is great threat to him, he will work less, thus using less of his brain power. On the other hand, if a person sees working cooperatively, can improve communication and quality, cut waste and also eventually give more job satisfaction and enjoyment. He will work more effectively and will use more of his untapped brain power. It has reality that has profited both the company and its people. This is the basic foundation of quality circle. Production/office employees who know their jobs better than anyone else are the real manufacturing/service cost reducers. Involve their mind as well as their hands as they are the most valuable partners in cutting waste at workplace.

Our forefathers were fine craftsmen were committed to quality,products/services and used to work in a team. They taught us that team of skilled workers, motivated and with the opportunity to contribute can turn product of highest excellence. Today, our managements has to recommit themselves to the spirit of our forefathers.

- People want to do better and will, provided they are given authority to participate.
- If people doing the job are involved and desire to improve the ways things are done, they may prove to be a superior source of improvements.

Virtually, all employees of the company do feel some degree of identification/ownership with their job/company. If the relationship is healthy, the employees feeling of ownership/ proprietorship is far stronger than those of the other associates of the company (shareholders/stockholders) "*WE ALL ARE IN THIS TOGATHER*" reinforces quality team concepts.

Quality Circle contributes to the improvement of the quality of worklife, but their primary purpose is to improve quality of product/productivity. Quality circle (QC) is a people-building philosophy – with this sincere desire, the management can help their employees to grow and develop through QC and for this management commitment to develop employee's technical skills along with social skills is a must.

Productivity can be improved not only by using new technology, qualified people, but also by tapping human brain power and working together. The aim of management is to turnout mediocre men excellent performers. People and their brains are the most precious resources; the management must improve productivity, not at the expense of people, but at the expense of wasted time, lost motion, unnecessary work and product of poor quality.

QUALITY CIRCLES – KEY ELEMENTS

(1) **It is a people empowering process** – With management's sincere commitment, if people are involved, liberalise and empower, they will produce best results skill-wise, best-of-the-breed, core competence can be nurtured at shop floor level through introduction of QC.

(2) **It is a voluntary programme** – Formation of QC is completely free of fear and favour. No formal circular, notice, meeting will fruitful unless employee's initiative is taken into consideration.

(3) **Members help each other to develop themselves** – Since all members are part of QC equally able to understand and use the technologies, procedures and practices. Thus, they help each others development. It is only leaders job to see that "it happens".

(4) **Everyone's participation** – Being voluntary/participative programme, therefore, the leader must see that more interested persons have a chance to say what is on his mind.

(5) **Projects are circle efforts** – It is a collective wisdom developed by various individuals. Everything done in a circle is a team effort. The circle as a whole should receive recognition for any achievement it has accomplished.

(6) **Training is provided to employee and management** –

(7) **Creativity is encouraged** – A non-threatening environment for ideas must be created. People will not risk suggesting a half-developed idea if they feel may be ridiculed or rejected. From seemingly build ideas, often comes with practical solutions.

(8) **Projects are related to members work** – The projects which QC undertake need to have something to do with their work – not the work of others or non-work related subjects. Members are expert at what they do, but not at what other people do.

(9) **Management has to be supportive** – Unless someone in management is willing to give QC some-time, some advice and some commitment in the beginning, QC will not have the encouragement they need to grow and get mature.

(10) **Reduction of the "WE" and "THEY" mentality** – Each of us strive to make his job more creative and meaningful. QC when used correctly, help company to reduce that "WE" and they mentality of employees, since everyone is a winner in the race and management encourages to participate in problem-solving process.

QUALITY CIRCLE – OBJECTIVES

(1) Self-development – Training and Education.

(2) Mutual Development.

(3) Improvement in quality – Problems-solving by quality improvement.

(4) Improvement in communication and attitude – open minded.

(5) Waste reduction – helping each other with understanding.

(6) Job satisfaction – people feel happy and take pride in work.

(7) Cost reduction – Value analysis concept encouraged.

(8) Improvement in productivity – Reduction in cost and elimination of reject pays.

(9) Safety improvement – New changes implementation.

(10) Problem-solving opportunities – Thinking together for common problem.

(11) Team-building – Feeling of togetherness.

(12) Link all levels of management and workers together to achieve success.

(13) Get people more involved and interested in their work – Who are made known at all level.

(14) Improve participation – Cohesiveness and unity with harmony.

(15) Reduce absenteeism and grievances – Reduced personal problems.

QUALITY CIRCLE AT WORK

(1) Executive committee – The top management people who approves QC policies and programmes. This committee perform the following functions:

- ❖ Attend QC meeting frequently.
- ❖ Understand principles and techniques of quality circles.
- ❖ Suggests problems from time-to-time.
- ❖ Promotes QC programmes in level of top and middle management.
- ❖ Promotes benefits and advantages of QC.
- ❖ MD's, VP's, Directors are the persons/members of this committee.

(2) Operating/steering committee – Consists of works manager, plant managers, HR managers and circle leaders. The operating committee is really another informal QC which oversees the QC programme to ensure proper implementation of circle projects and to promote QC activities.

(3) Quality improvement committee – Every department head is a member; this monitors the actual functioning of QC programme.

(4) Quality improvement committee – Department level.

(5) Quality circle starts.

In brief, operating team perform following key functions:

a. It is responsible for preparing objectives for the plant.

b. Meets with facilitator.

c. Promotes QCs throughout the organisation.

d. Attends meetings and constantly reviews the progress.

e. Keeps programme interesting and fun for members.

f. Publicises the programme.

g. Follow-up the completed projects.

h. Reviews training programme.

i. Obtain training material and adds news material to enhance the knowledge of the members.

ORGANISATION STRUCTURE OF QUALITY CIRCLE

(A) Small group of people usually four to ten, who do similar work voluntarily meet regularly to identify and analysis cause of problems in their area, recommend their solutions to management and wherever possible, implement the solution approved by the management.

(B) **Role of QC leader** – A staff advisor to his department circle show interest, get involved in circle activities, promote and encourage the concept (circle).

- ❖ Provide liaison contacts and feedback on request in a timely manner. Encourage new employee to join circle.

(C) **Quality circle leader** – is chosen by circle members. Hence, responsible for the operation of the circle.

(D) **Quality circle facilitator/coordinator is**

- ❖ Responsible for the over all QC programmes.
- ❖ Trains leaders and members – Maintain records, coordinates circle operations – interface between circles and company, organisation and department.
- ❖ Work closely with steering company.
- ❖ Attend circle meeting and organise leader's meetings.

QUALITY CIRCLE – TECHNIQUES OF DATA COLLECTIONS

(A) Collection of data through *Statistical Methods*. In order to make effective use of quantitative data in making decisions, it is necessary to have systematic methods of organisation, summarising and analysing the facts. These methods are called statistical methods. Basic steps in applying statistical methods:

- ❖ Defining the problem.
- ❖ Collecting relevant information.
- ❖ Investigation.
- ❖ Analysing the data and
- ❖ Presentation of the findings.
- ❖ Problem-solving methods.
- ❖ Techniques of data collection and analysis – check sheet, graphs, histograms, control charts, sampling, etc.

(B) **Brain Storming:**

1. Brainstorming is a technique for generating the greatest possible number of solutions to a problem for evolution and development.
2. The problem is well addressed and understood by all.
3. All suggestions are recorded, equal opportunity to express ideas to all, suggestions are encouraged.
4. Brainstorming is used because it is a proven effective step in generating a maximum number of solutions to problems.
5. Most employees are aware of problems affecting the quality of their work and usually think about the solutions. With this general assumptions, "well, if you knew to solve the problem, why did not you, tell us?" Answer: "No one asked me?"
6. In brainstorming, we are asking for your ideas so that we can apply the right solution to the right problems with a minimum of efforts and time so that we can reduce scrap, improve quality and enhance overall works performance.
7. Brainstorming brings out the ideas trapped in people's minds.
8. It recognises that certain conditions exist, and that people can participate in a creative process that is self-fulfilling and makes use of the company's most valuable asset. The ideas and minds of the employees – those people actually doing the work day-in and day-out.
9. Brain-storming is one step in an organised approach to the problem-solving.
10. It is generally used when individual efforts do not yield satisfactory results.

11. Rules for brainstorming: Criticism is ruled out:

   (a) Free wheeling is welcomed.

   (b) Improvements are sought.

   (c) Pareto analysis/cause and effect diagram – To recognise important causes, to compare operational procedures, to find major solutions, to figure out what to do and to improve the process this Pareto analysis technique is used after brainstorming.

   Causes/reasons collected through sample data, historical and brainstorming are classified in four major areas of the process. Man, Machine, Material, Method.

   (d) Action Plan – After Pareto analysis, action plan to attack immediate causes is decided and solutions are presented.

   (e) Presentation – To peers, subordinates and superiors.

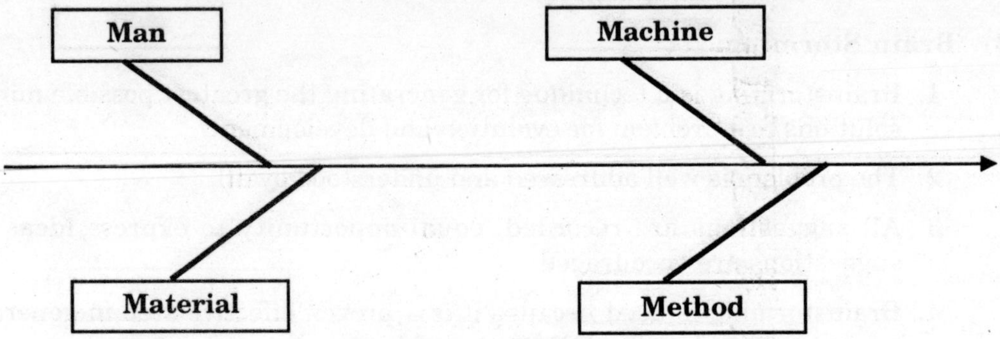

FISH BONE DIAGRAM

PRESENTATION OF Q C PROJECT

(1) Time - 20-30 minutes, minutes including opening and closing comments of the leader.

(2) All members are introduced by the leader and the leader closes the session by answering any question.

(3) All members (QC) participate in the presentation.

(4) All information gathered is used during the presentation, such as histograms, Pareto diagram and cause and effect diagrams.

(5) Cost saving and other supporting information is also discussed.

(6) The outline should be prepared for presentation.

(7) Good organisation of programme is essential.

(8) All guests, steering co-members and other dept. heads should be invited.

TEN STEPS TO A SUCCESSFUL MANAGEMENT PRESENTATION

(1) Have a schedule and try to start and end on time.

(2) Use a large enough room with plenty of seating.

(3) Have a chairperson or coordinator present so that the meeting is under control.

(4) Use an agenda with subject and speakers outlines; leave the room for taking notes.

(5) Use visual aids such as slides, charts, graphs, etc.

(6) Do not discredit other department or people.

(7) Use positive points as accomplishments.

(8) Invite all interested parties.

(9) Do not ask for additional funding or people.

(10) Do not ask for on the spot decisions.

8.3 KAIZEN – A CONTINUOUS IMPROVEMENT PROCESS

For all business practices there are three major activities directly related to earning profit: developing, producing and selling. Without these activities no business organisation can exist. Secondly, in a broader sense, there are two basic approaches to do business first, applying the latest high-cost technology, such as state-of-the-art technologies and other tools, inventing a great deal of money. The second is use of common sense tools, checklist, techniques and human skills that do not cost much money. Putting common sense into practice and improve the work activities is the subject-matter of Kaizen. Kaizen involves every body, starting from the CEO in the organisation for planning and working together for business success. Kaizen can achieve significant improvement *vis-a-vis* performance and prepares the organisation for truly high performing organisation.

Gemba Kaizen is a Japanese concept and practice. Gemba means *workplace*, Kai means *change* and Zen means *improvement*. In short Gemba Kaizen means workplace improvements. Most of the people do want to make improvements all the time but our systems discourage them. It is very rare to find an individual, who does not think of improvement. Improvement requires involvement. True involvement is only when an individual makes a creative contribution in doing his work and is busy to finding out his own ways to do it better and better, "When you share you care" is the basic of involvement. And continuous improvement comes when we work together with common purpose. Gemba Kaizen provides the use of a common sense, low-cost approach to managing workplace – the place where value is added collectively. Small improvements, on continual basis gradually accumulated, lead to significant quality improvement, cost benefits and productivity improvements and ultimately total performance improvement. These are three major activities under Kaizen – standardisation, the 5-S and elimination of waste (Muda).

Productivity performance improves when less input produces the same output, or when output increases with the same input. Input refers to human resources, utilities, and material while output refers to products, yield, added value and services. When everyone in the organisation works toward this goal, there is a positive impact on cost-effectiveness. It is proved that to realise performance improvement in quality, cost and delivery simultaneously by employing various management systems, the organisation may improve overall performance to make it more profitable than it has been in the past. Keeping this is mind Kaizen – a common sense, low-cost and continuous improvement approach, every management must implement. The brief introduction of Kaizen will help you to imbibe and implement it at your workplace.

KAIZEN – WHAT IT IS?

- It is simple, more practical and sometimes zero investment tool to solve workplace problem.
- It is cost reducing and cost saving programme which generate internal profit to the company and gives freedom to employee to use his skill, knowledge and competency to solve the problem at his level.
- It is do-it-yourself project assignments on cost reduction, waste elimination and shop-floor housekeeping.
- It provides an opportunity to implement low-cost improvements on continuous basis using common/sense into practice.
- Gemba Kaizen is an umbrella approach cover housekeeping, 5-S, Muda – waste-elimination and standardisation of workplace practices.
- If properly applied Gemba Kaizen can improve quality, reduce cost and meet customer's delivery requirements without any significant investment.

HOUSE OF GEMBA KAIZEN MANAGEMENT

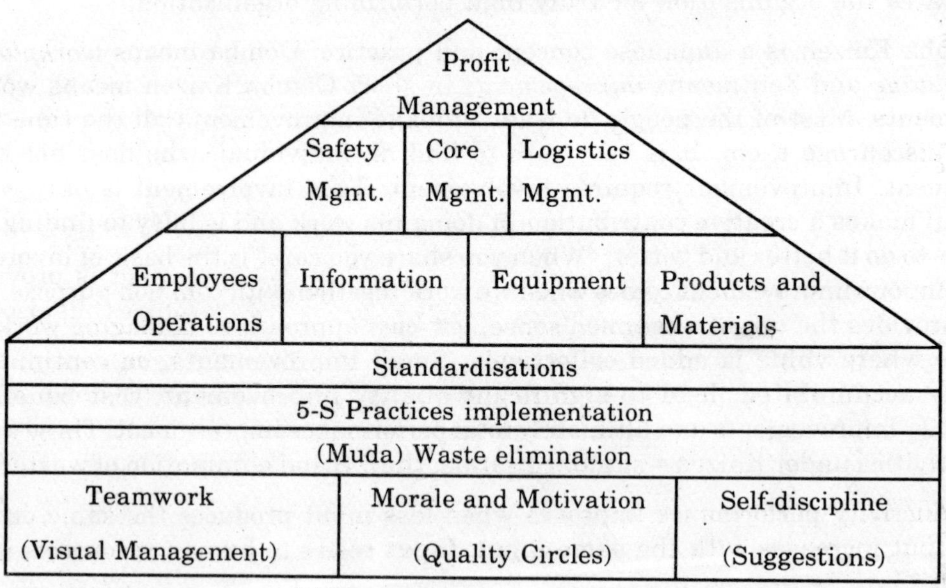

ANALYSIS OF *STATUS QUO* SITUATION

- ❖ Absence of 5-S in workplace indicates inefficiency in our work operation/service by way of poor quality, high cost and high waste.
- ❖ Absence of waste elimination (Muda) indicates insufficient self-discipline on account of quality, cost and delivery.
- ❖ Absence of standardisation on account of efficient use of men, material, money and methods create abnormalities in day-to-day working and produces non-quality products and services.

(I) **5-S ACTIVITIES:** It is a science as well as art of

- ❖ Stratification management ⟶ (segregation) ⟶ Seiri
- ❖ Functional storage and elimination ⟶ (set in order) ⟶ Seiton
- ❖ Cleaning and Housekeeping ⟶ (super clean) ⟶ Seiso
- ❖ Visual management ⟶ (Standardisation) ⟶ Shitsuke
- ❖ Habit formation and discipline ⟶ (System discipline) ⟶ Seiketsu

1. **SEIRI** – Means distinguish between necessary and unnecessary items and discard the letter.
2. **SEITON** – Arrange remaining after seiri in an orderly manner.
3. **SEISO** – Keep machines and working environment clean.
4. **SHITSUKE** – Build self-discipline and make habit of engaging in 5-S by establishing standards.
5. **SEIKETSU** – Implement and sustain standardisation in every activity you are doing.

(II) **WASTE (MUDA) ELIMINATION**: Anything or any activity that does not add value is a waste:

- ❖ When an employee is coming late he is adding no value to the company. Loss of non-working hours may cost money loss. It is a sheer waste of company's money.
- ❖ When marketing department or any other service department is providing its services inefficiently, the company is not wasting its own resources but also stealing the valued customer's time. It is a waste.
- ❖ When maintenance engineer is not attending machine break down efficiently within time, he is not adding value. He is wasting company's money. The value is added when he is attending break down right the first time. He is reducing lost production time, efficiently saving company's money and eliminating waste in way of saving loss production value.

Such and similar work activities if arrested, we can save average 20% company's revenue and can generate internal profit.

GENERAL WASTEFUL AREAS AT WORKPLACE

(1) **Waste in Production:** Low production, productivity, yield, excess break down, excess material consumption, poor quality and poor human skill and knowledge, etc.

(2) **Waste in Time:** Wasting time, slow workin-progress, hold ups, late ppc programme, delayed materials supply, delayed shipments, documentation, absenteeism, late coming, too many meetings, etc.

(3) **Other Related Wastes are:** Waste in transport, waste in processing, waste in inventory (excess storage of materials and equipments), waste in movement, waste in rejection, waste in arranging work, waste in expenses, waste in indirect labour deployment, waste in human resources management, waste in equipment.

Avoiding (Muda) *waste*, (Muri) *excess* and (Mura) *unevenness* in our work activities, saves our time, effort and money and ultimately brings profit to the company. These are the most cost-effective techniques under Gemba Kaizen.

(III) **STANDARDISATION:** Daily operational activities in each process, practice and procedure when written down explicitly becomes workplace standards. In absence of standards, abnormalities occur at plant causing rejection, rework, repairs, rescheduling, reconciling, redoing the rejects, machine down time, missing production and delivery targets, excess customer complaints, employees late coming, early going all these contribute to wasting company's money and generate poor quality of products and services. Whenever problem arises, people go in fire-fighting approach. Non-standardisation activity cost money to the company. No standard means sub-standard.

At workplace, we operate two types of standards: MANAGERIAL AND OPERATIONAL

- **Managerial Standards:** Are necessary for managing people for administrative purposes and includes rules, regulations, guidelines, policy, procedures, practices, and systems in production, computers, personnel, finance, logistics and other work activities.

- **Operational Standards:** Are to do with way people do jobs to realise quality, cost and delivery (QCD). These are generally related to the external demands to achieve QCD to satisfy customers.

Hence, establishing standards is the safest, easiest, most cost-effective and productive way for company to assure quality for internal and external customers.

- Standards offer the best way to preserve know-how and expertise.

- Standards provide a way to measurements of performance (budget, annual plan, etc.)

- Standards establish relationship between cause and effect.

- Provide basis for maintenance and improvement in activities.
- Provide objectives and indicates goals.
- Provide basis for training (training needs identification).
- Create basis for audit (measurement and quantification).
- Provide a means for preventing recurrence of error and minimising variations.

It is management task to identify, define and standardize key control points at each process and make certain that such control points will be followed at all the time. standardisation is an integral part of performance improvements: Standard Operating Procedures/Practices (SOP), Department manual, personnel manual, QS manuals are the product of standardisation.

For standardising any activity one may practice SDCA, PDCA, EPDCA or FADE cycles.

SDCA – Standardise-do-check-act in Gemba Kaizen terminology, manager must seek out root causes of non-quality, take action to remedy the situation and then change the work procedure to eliminate the problem. As long as our standards are within control, have no abnormalities that mean we are working as per standards. The next step is to adjust the *status quo* and raise standards. You may follow PDCA – plan-do-check-act cycle. In both the cycles act refers to standardising and stabilising the job. Thus standardisation becomes inseparable part of everybody's job.

BASIC RULES FOR PRACTISING GEMBA KAIZEN

(1) Discard conventional, rigid thinking about production, process and people.

(2) Think how to do it, not why it can't be done.

(3) Do not make excuses, start by questioning current practices.

(4) Do not seek perfection. 50% right way target achievement is right to start with.

(5) Correct mistake at once.

(6) Ask 'why' five times and seek root cause.

(7) Seek wisdom of ten people rather than the knowledge of one.

(8) Remember that opportunities for Kaizen are infinite.

The ability to lead and exhibit patience in order to achieve dramatic, long-term improvement only comes from understanding the concept that sustainable improvements in results comes from long-term improvement in our workplace activities.

A. What is good Kaizen?

(1) Whatever you feel happy and proud of improving performance, is a good Kaizen.

(2) Self-initiated work activities are placed higher in the improvement category as compared to work done on the instructions of superiors.

(3) One of the objectives of Kaizen is to stimulate team spirit. Therefore, improvements done by collaborating with others are considered superior and hence rated higher than improvement carried out alone.

(4) If you have carried out an experiment to effect some improvement you may present it as an improvement in your Kaizen meeting, irrespective of the success or failure of the experiment.

B. How to prepare your Kaizen write-up?

1. At the top right corner of the first page, please write your: name, team no., department.

2. The following format has been found to be concise and easy to understand.

   Existing situation

   Changes made

   Resulting improvement

C. How to conduct yourself a Kaizen meeting?

(1) You may speak about your improvement for a period of five-six minutes. Adherence to timing is vital.

(2) Explain the improvements in easily understandable terms to all there present.

(3) You may present your improvement in any way or through any medium you choose: (OHP, LCD, Slides, etc.)

(4) When one person is speaking during the Kaizen meeting, all other participants including the evaluator will listen to the speaker, without disturbing him/her and without passing evaluative comments.

GUIDELINES FOR KAIZEN EVALUATOR

(A) Conducting meeting:

(1) The very presence of the evaluator ensures a sense of seriousness and order in the Kaizen meeting.

(2) Please ensure adherence to timings by the individual speaker.

(3) Any questions asked can be only for clarification and not for cross-questioning.

(4) The evaluator should not pass any evaluative remarks like "Good job, well done".

(5) The key to successful introduction and maintenance of Kaizen is in the evaluator's hand. That key is the listening ability.

EVALUATING THE IMPROVEMENTS

(1) The evaluation can be done on two aspects of improvement.

(a) How much time the participant has spent on carrying out the improvement. This is purely judgemental. More time spent of making improvement deserves higher rating.

(b) Improvement in the method employed to carry out the work. The emphasis should be on process quality, rather than on the actual results. An improved method of doing things deserves a high rating, irrespective of the results.

In short, Kaizen-continuous work improvements approach simply involve attention to work details and common sense ways of working smarter. If taken together by all people at workplace it can make a big difference in terms of improved performance. Kaizen is a way of life. It is an attitude and spirit that prevails at all times in the company. Through this there is a continual interaction and dialogue between management and employees as they work together to help set and meet standards and then develop new and better standards and you will find improvement has no end. Instilling a sense of mission and pride is an integral part of management responsibility for Kaizen. It requires commitment of employees. Employees must be inspired to fulfil their roles, to feel proud of their jobs, and to appreciate the contribution they make to their company.

The above narrated three major Kaizen activities: standardisation, the 5-S and the elimination of waste contribute to successful workplace performance improvement. These three activities are easy to understand and implement and do not require sophisticated knowledge or technology. Anybody – manger, supervisor, shop-floor/office employee can readily introduce these common sense, low-cost activities. But building the self-discipline is necessary to maintain them: once management and employees understand the implication of these three pillars (standardisation, 5-0S and elimination of waste) they become excited at the prospect of the tremendous benefits these activities can bring to workplace.

8.4 INNOVATION AND INNOVATIVENESS

The outstanding creative thinker in any field differs from other men in degree, not in kind. Innovation means not merely introducing novelties but making of changes to something already established. Innovation is an act that strives to produce small improvements on what is accepted today. Innovation requires a certain amount of humility. We have to build upon others contributions and allow our own to be build upon by others in turn. Innovation is not getting new thoughts but how to get old ones out. The greatest difficulty in the world is not for people to accept ideas, but to make them forget about old ideas. Therefore, if you change yourself, you will trigger off change about you. Develop an atmosphere of trust and warmth, a supportive and constructive climate where individuals are encouraged to think of themselves.

Innovation means:

- ❖ Change in an old custom, rule, method.
- ❖ New practices implementation.
- ❖ Bring in novelty in work areas.

It is an act of removing *statusth quo* situation for betterment of the company.

Innovation occurs when an employee/organisation learns to do something "it did not know how to do before" or "learns not to do something that it formerly did".

Innovation can include:

- ❖ Any improvement due to change in an old procedure/system/practice.
- ❖ Productivity and work improvement projects.
- ❖ Quality success stories, 5-S practices.
- ❖ Prevention of non-confidence by root cause elimination.
- ❖ New idea implementation for cost reduction.

Innovation does not mean Invention:

- ❖ Invention means discovering something altogether new, which did not existing.
- ❖ Innovation means rediscovering the new and fruitful ways/ideas of doing the things.
- ❖ Innovation can be in any field of work, manufacturing, quality, maintenance, commercial, personnel, etc.
- ❖ Innovation is an act that endows resource (men, material, method, and money) with a new capacity to create wealth.

Once upon a time bauxite mineral oil were nuisance to the mankind, as they were troublesome to agriculture. Today, they are resources due to their innovative uses. Innovation that way indeed creates a resource out of nuisance.

Why Innovation is Important?

For the decades, companies have devoted their energies to managing supply side of business right from manufacturing, distribution and product pricing. They have made enormous improvements in production and productivity, market share. But opportunities and ideas to drive incremental growth are drying up.

Increasingly the companies will have to focus on the new ideas by way of innovation.

External as well as internal revenue enhancement is the ticket for innovation. While relative cost must remain under control and cost be kept to a minimum. It is innovator in the long haul, who will reap the rewards.

Innovative and creative thinkers are different from the rest of us. They do not do different things, they do the thing differently.

- They see what we overlook.
- They turn the ideas into what others can't.
- They lead us on a path of discovery, rediscovery and reinvention.

Majority ideas come from people at work, as they are professional service-providers and receivers.

- Make people vital centres of intellectual capital accumulations, rather than the prime source of bureaucratic system followed under centralised governance.
- Wealth in the new era flows directly from innovation, not optimisation only. That is wealth is not gained by perfecting the known, but by perfectly seizing the unknown – new ideas, rules, methods, etc.

We have to remember that all our existing product capacity, product market and services have short life/limited capacity due to new technology explosion. If the company has to survive, it has to keep pace with the technology advancement conducted with innovative uses of technology to better the results. Hence, innovations are important.

Can Innovation be Planned?

Yes. Systematic innovation consists in the purposeful and organised search for a change and in the systematic analysis of the opportunities. Systematic innovation needs innovative opportunities, which need monitoring of sources.

(1) Unexpected events: Unexpected success or failure in work activities gives an opportunity for an innovation.

(2) Incongruity: It is a discrepancy between what is and what ought to be.

(3) Process need: Need is a source of innovation.

(4) Change in perception: How we see the same situation, half-full glass or half-empty glass. Our observation into situation may give an opportunity for innovation.

(5) New knowledge: New knowledge in every field brings opportunities for innovation.

(6) Climate for innovation: (Management responsibility)

   a. Systematic policy of abandoning outdated systems, practices, products, etc.

   b. Regular business activities X-ray to check how products and services need innovation.

   c. Measuring innovative performance by proper feedback, systematic review and recognition.

(7) Innovation is conceptual and perpetual.

a. Go out to look, to ask and to listen.

b. Meet customers and users to see what they need.

c. Expect only simple innovations.

What have we to do for creating innovations?

- Chart all your daily activities, services, procedures, products, etc.
- Write since when it is *status quo*, situation.
- Review for innovation.
- Plan for innovation.
- Create new things or modify it for better results.
- The problem is never how to get new innovative thoughts into our minds, but how to get old ones out is our problem.
- The greatest difficulty in the world of work is not for people to accept new ideas, but to make them forget about old ones.
- Hence, the best things a manager can do for his employees are to allow them to discover their own greatness.
- If I don't do something, nothing is going to get better.
- Cutting jobs is hardwork (downsizing). Jobs are genius (multiskilling). Turn every job into improvement project.
- Finally, whatever made you successful in the past will not necessarily make successful in the future. Therefore, start thinking of new idea implementation. You will create innovative organisation collectively.

INNOVATOR'S PROFILE

- For innovator, innovation, renovation signifies the rebirth of things, which are more efficient and acceptable.
- For them, change is viewed as good and new is viewed as better than old.
- For them, good, better and best never let it rest till their good is better and better is best. Their innovative mind-set forces them to view their jobs in a different ways.
- As long as an employee continues to learn and produce new ideas and insights and incorporate them into their work, they provide a lasting source of competitive advantage.

- Experimentation acts as a form of learning less costly and more useful than sophisticated market research or careful start planning.
- New ideas do not get off the ground because they were never given a chance until it is brought to fruition.
- Every new idea has innovative value, convert it into money-saving, time-saving device.
- Be open to new ideas. The person who stands still may avoid stubbing his toe, but he will not make much progress.

WHAT MAKES A COMPANY – AN INNOVATOR

Innovative companies have some or all, of the following characteristics;

- They are the best in their industry.
- They grow faster and more profitably than their competitors.
- They hire and retain the best people.
- They respond quickly to changing market conditions.
- They are not satisfied with the *status quo*, they continually upgrade facilities, processes and skills.
- Innovative companies continuously encourage and empower their employee's problem-solving skills by "Do it right yourselves projects".
- They test new ideas in their business.
- They make customer satisfaction an obsession.
- They do not compromise their quality standards.
- They work with vision, mission and strategies to make the company world-class.

The best thing a leader can do for his company is to allow its employees to discover and rediscover their own greatness (knowledge, skill and competitiveness) for renewal of the company on continuous basis. (They adopt 5% technology and 95% psychology and attitude approach).

CONTINUOUS WORK IMPROVEMENT PROCESS

THE COST OF IGNORING GOOD IDEAS

Typically, managers are sometimes unable to solve the problem themselves. But unwilling to ask others for their ideas. They are trapped themselves. They assume sole responsibility for generating ideas and solving problems.

People, who process the work in general, have better ideas than those of in the office/ shop-floor. Just give them chance to present their ideas and their collective improvements shall be enormous.

The goals of improvement process should be:

- ❖ Generate profit from employee's ideas.
- ❖ Promote a sense of involvement.
- ❖ Develop an entrepreneurial attitude among employees.
- ❖ Support the corporate plans that enhance the quality of work life/product and service.

OUR AIM IS TO CREATE INVENTOR AND INNOVATORS

- ❖ An inventor creates for profit.
- ❖ An innovator creates for self-satisfaction and pride in job performance.

Thus, you unlock the power of ideas by educating employees, giving them an opportunity to develop their skills, creativity and attitudes.

When people put their mind to it, there is no limit to the novel ideas they can create.

Points to be consider:

- ❖ Everyone has valid ideas, regardless of their level in the organisation, their experience and their education.
- ❖ A planned, defined programme on new ideas generates huge money saving and service commitment.
- ❖ Ideas from grassroot employees hold tremendous money and service potential.

Innovation does not consist of the introduction of some flashy new product for the mere sake of having new one to sell. The product or service must have a market; it must be able to help people to live better material in some way.

A company that intends to stay in business can make no decisions about innovation without a plan that answers the following questions:

- ❖ What materials will be required, at what cost?
- ❖ What will be the method of production?
- ❖ What new people will have to be hired?
- ❖ What changes in equipment will be required?
- ❖ What new skills will be required, and for how many people?
- ❖ How will current employees be trained in these new skills?

- How will supervisors be trained?
- What will be the cost of production?
- What will be the cost of marketing?
- What will be the cost and methods of service?
- How will the customer use the product or service?
- How will the company know if the customer is satisfied?

As obvious as these questions seem, it is amazing how many companies forge ahead without answers to them.

By its very nature, innovation requires faith in the future. It cannot possibly succeed, Dr. Deeming says, "Unless top management has declared unshakable commitment to quality and productivity".

- It is the ability of a company to innovate continuously.
- Innovation is one of the hardest rules of the game to master because it applies sense of being able to ensure breakthrough by using intuitive and initiative.
- The challenge is "How do you get a whole organisation to think outside the box".
- Innovation leads to quantum changes in a step-by-step improvement process as it is based on fundamental of TQM tenet.
- Innovation need not always be radical change in a big way. It might just as well be spawned through small continuous improvements that cumulate to provide breakthrough overtimes.

How one can build a culture for fostering continuousv innovation?

Stephen M. Shapiro, one of the authors on innovation observes: "An innovative culture is like a jazz band".

"An innovative business model requires no less than, having good jazz scores (**operating model and process**), played by good jazz musicians (**employee**), play high quality instruments (**technology**), in the right way, so that the audience (**customer**) enjoys the performance. Central to all this is innovation."

- Innovation demands a bold and imaginative approach. It requires vision, it requires commitment to say good bye to *status quo* situation, which is outdated.
- A business can thrive on innovation and is the acid test of managerial performance.
- Successful innovation is the most reliable measure of employee and managerial competence.
- Technological innovation is easy to understand.
- The jet engine was a great innovation.

- The Xerox copier is a major innovation.
- Mobile phone is amazing innovation.
- Thus, innovation is possible in every business activity, production, marketing, industrial relations, HRD, replacing old, somewhat outdated policies, procedures and practices or system with new one is always innovation.
- Innovation paves the way for progress and prosperity to the company and its people.
- Company without the innovative spirit will stagnate and eventually go out of business.
- It is, therefore, the manager must create confidence among his own people that the company is constantly planning for the positive future.
- 5-S, quality teams, self-managed teams and other work improvement interventions are instrumental in creating innovation.

8.5 EMPLOYEE COACHING

"All the coaching in the world will fall short if the behaviour you expect is not honoured and recognised"

– S. Bartlett

Everyone can develop the skills, the personal techniques, and the attitude to successfully coach other people. You can learn how to improve your coaching skills and become a person who inspires others to give 100% result. If you want to be a coach what is your attitude about being a coach? Do you really understand the need to be an effective coach? Do you grasp how important it is to be a good coach? These fact findings shape your attitude about being a coach, because people act on what they believe or value. You only succeed when people are communicating, not just from the top down but in complete interchanges. Communication comes from fighting of 'my ego' and listening. Highly successful and innovative leaders have tapped in to an unlimited resource – their people and they by learning the secrets of coaching skills made it happen. You as a manager, is it not your role much like that of a coach? Your team-members all have different talents and skill level; they are people with strengths, short coming and personal lives that sometimes affect their ability to perform at work. And regardless of how difficult it may be at times, you as a team leader responsible for winning with that special mix of people for keeping your people inspired, motivated and working together toward team goals. The greatest coaches are those who know how to motivate others to succeed, stay focused, believe in themselves and overcome disappointment. Coach inspires others to aim higher, work harder and enjoy doing it. Henry Kissinger once said "Leaders take their people from where they are to where they have never been before". That is what your role as coach will help you to take your people from where they are (limited) to where they have never been before (unlimited). Therefore, you as a leader and coach must keep in mind three critical facts.

COACH: Three critical facts for you.

(1) Leader's responsibility is getting things done through people. Your job is to work through people who works for you. That is how you will get results from your people. When you do everything yourself, you are just a technician, when you get things done through others, that is when you become a leader or coach.

(2) You need your people more than they need you – because the only way you are going to get result is through them. You can't do every job; only your people can get everything done.

(3) You get paid for what your people do not for what you do. It is true that the people who work for you are helping you get results, then what they are doing, you get paid for. Thus, no other investment will pay higher dividends than an investment in your people. Winning coach use to inspire their people to excel.

The most enlightening fact about leadership is worthless until someone decides to use them, to actually apply this truth in your job setting. And that happens only when leader/ coacher believe their potential values, as a result of their actions. So, let us consider the values of successful coacher.

VALUES OF GOOD COACH

(1) Clarity – A strong sense of direction and purpose make sure people are communicated clearly, if not people start to fail or do nothing.

(2) Supportiveness – A commitment to stand with and behind team-members. Providing the help people need, giving understanding and encouragement shows that you are standing behind people. It is important to communicate your intention to be supportive.

(3) Confidence-building – A personal commitment to build and sustain the self-image of each team-member – review with people the keys to successes and praise the commitment to excellence behind every victory. Publish/advertise team accomplishment periodically. It provides performance exposure for team-members within and beyond the team environment.

(4) Mutuality – A true partnership orientation – mutuality means sharing a vision of common goals. To make sure your team goals are mutual, shared by every member; explain your goals in details. Why is this goal for the team? How will it benefit individual members what steps must be taken to achieve the goal? When? What reward can we expect when the goal is achieved? This type of coaching will make that the goal achievement is mutual. Without goals mutuality is impossible.

(5) Perspective – An unflappable focus on the entire business enterprise – understanding from inside out "is getting inside a person and seeing things from his perspective" said by George Kelly. To understand someone from the inside out, you have to ask: How is your new life? Anything I could do to make it easier for you. These kinds of get involved can ultimately reveal who your team-members really are.

(6) **Risk** – The encouragement of effort that reduces punishment for mistakes and encourages learning in all things – risk is letting team-members to know it is can to fail. The only way you can grow it by taking risks. Failure is not terminal, as long as everyone learns from it. Establish a clear, unthreatening way to deal with errors, a way that starts with the individual.

(7) **Patience** – A view of time and performance that equitably balances learning and business demands – as a coach, you should know that time and patience are the keys to preventing from simply reacting. A coach can and should avoid knee jerks responses to unexpected situations. Evaluate the situation objectively; identify alternative solutions; get respected opinions and input; implement your chosen response and assess result and alter your approach as needed. The best coach don't react, they act. They use patience to their advantage.

(8) **Involvement** – A genuine commitment to allow team-members to control their work-involvement means caring for someone enough to attempt to understand his experiences. It is finding out what is going on with your people. It is being interested enough to find out the significant facts about family background, hardship, ambition, drive as well as what type of person the employee is: shy, outgoing, easy to please, suspicious, etc.

(9) **Confidentability** – An ability to protect the information of team business-Confidentability results when people demonstrate the rare ability to keep quiet. It takes discipline to stop yourself and not give away confidence. The moment you betray a confidence, trust is lost. And once you lose an employees trust, it is almost impossible to get it back.

(10) **Respect** – A commitment to value and see the treasure within your people. Respect involves coach/manages perceived attitude toward the individual he leads. You may respect your people highly, but if they don't perceive that value …… if this contradicted by your failure to share goals, your willingness to become involved, your inability to exercise patience, you communicate disrespect. How far do you think a team can go together if its members feel the coach disdains them? If you answered 'nowhere', you are right!

Successful coach passes above values and skills plus character and personality traits that make them effective. You must learn to incorporate these values to get yourself as skilful coach. "Good coach is not necessarily a winner but a person who is a good teacher …. who does not abuse his players, who gets the most from the players and who works within the framework of the rules." **(Dan Devine)**

SKILLS OF HIGH PERFORMING COACH

Knowing what must be done is the essential first step toward doing it. Success is not established by how high we climb as coach, but by how many people we take with us to climb. Coach is often unaware of the impact his values have on other people's lives. The truth is, everyday you imprint your values upon your team-members. Hence, ask yourself this: what kind of values and attitudes do I communicate to the team I lead? An attitude of supportiveness, confidence, commitment, mutuality, patience and involvement? To answer these questions, it is often helpful to identify where your attitudes come from. Your parents, teachers, friends, siblings, spouse, boss, subordinate were probably, who helped you become who you are today. They probably inspired your taught or corrected you. They were also the people who taught you understood cause and effect, imparted desire for knowledge, helped and corrected you when need be. They were the people touched your inner chords and helped you develop skills. Remember those people who especially inspired, taught and corrected you, and the attitudes they had that you admired. Are these attitudes you communicate to others daily. Your personality traits of today are the by-products of their positive attitudes they demonstrated while you were a child, young and adult. They challenged you to go "above and beyond". Obviously, no coach has ever had the perfect team. The difference between the success and failure of any team is how well the coach understands its members and motivates them. To make this happen, a coach must possess following skills:

(1) **People reflect their views of life:** Please understand there are people who have negative, pessimistic, grumbling and complaining attitudes. You can predict exactly how they view their life negatively. If people are happy and see problems as challenges, you can pretty well count on that people having a positive outlook of life. Hence, you need to understand the philosophies/attitudes the people work for you. You as a coach never understand what makes people tick unless you spend time with them. You have to get close enough to understand the person's attitude or action. Helping people develop positive perspective is essential, but be honest in your methods.

(2) **Individuality should be valued and explored:** People have capabilities and creative minds. When you tailor this tool to your specific needs, go for their talent inventory. Working together will naturally reveal more about the talents and potentials of your entire team. People who excel in their performance ideally be involved in planning, scheduling, etc. Those who are creative be involved in concept development. In short, let your people express their individuality with the project framework. You will find your people morale will increase dramatically.

(3) **Lack of motivation often reflects discouragement:** Some people are not motivated; it is because they are discouraged, not because they are lazy or stupid. Find out why they are discouraged. If you identify that, then be creative in your encouragement. The motivation you were missing can suddenly begin to surface. Apply RAP to find out your peoples problems and perspectives. Review the past, analyse the present and plan the future. With this approach, you and your people can focus on a review the past performance contrasted with present performance and then look together to an improved future. As a coach this will help you keeping track of where and what progress is made by the team.

(4) **Consequences determine performance:** If some people are constantly performed unsatisfactorily, examine the consequences of their behaviour. The consequences negative or positive, must fit the behaviour in order to change it and they must be implemented and consistently.

(5) **People treated responsibly take responsibility:** People in team who are viewed as responsible for their actions tend to take responsibility. When someone gives you responsibility, you tend to rise to the level of trust. As you give them responsibility they will rise to it. They will develop pride, self-respect and loyalty.

ROLE OF A COACH

You as a coach of the people what will you do before, during and after the project you have undertaken. Critical to your ability to function effectively in the coaching role, are your willingness and ability to become involved with your people/team and develop trust, confidently, honesty, and support to team people. Encourage free communication and reward performance clarifies expectation and verifies understanding. Motivate and inspire them and provide the challenge to look beyond the tasks at hand to new horizons. Tell your people the truth, even if it hurts. Many coaches believe that the game is won or lost before the actual competition. Ideas work best when you do. Hence, you do and practice your coach role this way:

1. **Communicate your involvement with people:** Coach involvement in team activities are perceived by its members as "caring". Tom Peter's MBWA, teaches simply being with the members of your team means getting out from, asking them question about people, project. How are people doing can you help. Is there something you can do to improve a process? Management By Walking Around (MBWA) involves you with your team. The more you involve, they feel they involved with your goals. Once you start getting involved with the people, you will find the next step to filling the coaching role comes very naturally.

2. **Develop trust among people:** Every team-members should be convinced you are the right coach for the team........ even if your decisions are not always popular: without trust a team may win occasionally, but when the pressure is on when performance really counts victories without trust become less the rule and more the exception. Trust is built on confidentiality, honesty, support and reward. Encourage for communication freedom. When your team trust you with personal or professional news and expect you to hear them with objectivity, understanding and compassion, you are a coach who will be able to count on the extra mile from your people.

3. **Clarify expectation and verify understanding:** Best working team does not guarantee success unless the plan is communicated and understood by its members. Victories can't happen without clear, purposeful direction from coach and consistent team-members comprehension. Therefore, it is necessary to communicate in terms, team-members can understand. (Policy, procedure and practice to follow.)

4. **Verify teams understanding:** When you put up your plan to team, clarify your expectations by reviewing it to team-members and you verify the teams understanding. You may ask questions to members. Make it sure that freedom exists among team-members. "Is there anything that might still be a little unclear about what I have said?" Such questions can encourage members to search their understanding and verbalise any doubts that may exist especially when the coach asks it in an agreeable voice.

5. **Affirm the team:** Once you have established a trusting mutual relationship, you are ready to turn your attention to affirming team-members in their best efforts to improve performance. No team-member works well for long without a compliment and no coach compliments people if his view of an employee is always negative. Like rewarding employees, affirming or complimenting them on efforts and attitude must be the nature of winning coach.

6. **Motivate and inspire the team:** Your job as a coach means helping the people catch a vision for victory in every task. It means energising them. You must have willingness to be involved with your people, to earn their trust by being real and by respecting their points of view, to keep the lines of communication clear and to affirm their efforts to be the best they can be. As a coach, you will provide challenge to look beyond the tasks at hand to new horizons.

8.6 TEAM WORK

Someone said that the membership of a club (group) is made up of four kinds of bones. They are WISH BONES, who spend their time wishing someone else would do the work. There are JAW BONES, who do all talking but little else. Next comes the KNUCLE BONES, who knock everything that everyone else tried to do. And finally, there are BACK BONES, who get under the load and do the work.

If you simply throw people together and deal with them as a group you may destroy the possibility of them building. Individuals need both, knowledge in order to commit to a team, and also the opportunity to express their feelings. If the team leader handles these individual's requirements well, he will have the strong foundation for team-building. Putting people together gives people opportunities to develop, to overcome weaknesses in thinking or social cycle and increase their competence as individuals through working within team.

Team-building is a human process involving human feeling, attitudes and actions. It is something that people have to accomplish among themselves. There is no substitute for human beings making a mutual commitment to try to work together more effectively.

SOME DIMENSIONS OF TEAM-BUILDING

Any team has a basic activity and goal. People in the team to make decisions about variety of matters: defining goals, developing strategy, giving/taking assignments to persons, allocating resources, cutting, expanding resources for various functions, preparing budgets, setting schedules and deadlines and so on. It is important for a team to understand that the quality and acceptance of team's decisions can have an immense impact on many other people at workplace. Members of a team must together, perform a set of interlocking tasks in order to accomplish an end results, products, service or activity. The evidence is that people who trust one another can work together productively and effectively on a team. In fact, the building of trust should be a key goal for any team. Trust is the glue that keeps team-members together. Most of the research and writing on human factors clearly points out that there are three component forces that seriously affect human performance. The three components are culture, systems and individual.

THREE COMPONENTS OF TEAM BINDING

Unless teamwork and collaboration are part of the organisation's culture, the organisation's systems and the individual's arsenal of skills and knowledge, the organisation will probably unable to sustain a process of high involvement and participation at all levels in the organisation.

1. Culture – This component is the most powerful, is often difficult to detect, and it is the most difficult to change culture of any organisation which represents the basic shared values and assumptions held by the people. Culture defines what things are right or wrong, what matters are important, how troubleshooting is done and how people are expected to see the whole organisation. It is critical to the work team that the shared culture emphasise that teamwork is essential and that people at all levels get into trouble if they do not collaborate with others and respond readily as a member of the total team.

2. Systems – Functions of the team in the organisation are carried out on the basis of agreed-on-methods. These integrated agreements or systems regulate almost all aspects of the organisation's life. It is critical that the systematic aspects of the organisation be in agreement with the broader, shared cultural orientations.

3. Individuals – Inside the fabric of the culture and systems of the organisation are people, with power and influence. Most of these people spend considerable time orienting their people to the demands of the culture and the systems. People are to function effectively and consistently with the most popular aspects of the culture or the systems, they must have appropriate knowledge and skills.

The organisation world today is extremely complex, and it appears that those organisations that can create diverse, creative, effective teams will have the advantage. These organisations will work to keep the culture, systems and individuals consistently congruent.

WHY TEAMS ARE REQUIRED?

(1) Teams are helpful to solve problems. In this context it plays two roles: one is to support individual as they do their work and the other is to solve problems to improve how the work is done together.

(2) People need to feel a sense of belonging and teams help to fulfil this need. It is a formal vehicle to address the workplace problems and find out solutions for the well-being of workplace collectively.

(3) Teams are not only necessary to solve complex problems and effectively implement solutions, but the problem-solving process itself reinforces teamwork. The methodology of solving problems establishes a standard or a goal and a purpose for getting there.

(4) Teams are most effective and efficient than the sum of individuals and that when they are given the skills and systems of problem-solving, the sky is the limit when the teamand process come together the balance between creativity and discipline is achieved. By having teams in work processes that rely on facts and consensus, are able to weld the ideas that have a better chance to make an impact and create improvements.

(5) The most important role of terms is in developing team-members, maintaining discipline needed for following standardised work processes and continually improving it.

(6) Without the team functioning systems will collapse and improvement will stop in its tracks. Teaching people to work together cooperatively both within the team and across the teams to solve problems, with new and improved version is the basic objective of team formation.

(7) Without formal and informal support it is impossible for individuals to develop to their potential in the people value systems. Hence, people supporting formal and informal teams are necessary at workplace. Particularly, mix of formal and informal team-member's practices reflect norms and values about supporting team-members in a physically and psychologically safe environment. The strong belief in objective problem-solving that focuses on improving systems instead of blaming individuals underlies a good deal of work improvements.

(8) To sustain the individuals, team-members and working team in their coordinated efforts to add value, every opportunity to solve work problems, in support with each other helps everyone to contribute value-added-work. The emphasis of team formation is to encourage participation, keeping with the values and actively supporting the commitment to continuous improvements.

BUILDING BLOCKS FOR TEAM

Workplace is a happy place to be, people enjoy themselves wherever possible. This enjoyment is conducive to goal achievement, nor barrier to it. People get satisfaction from their working lives and to some extent meet their needs and aspirations. Therefore, the wise team leader does not intervene unnecessarily. The leader's presence is felt, but often the team runs itself.

Henry Ford an industrialist once said "coming together is a beginning, keeping together is progress, and working together is success". These characteristics are also seen in team-building. The team may be an organisation, division, department, section or any working team. Generally, teams are building on following blocks:

- **Design a Team** – Develop a mission. Team needs purpose. They need to know why they are being set-up and what they must achieve.
- **Clarify Roles, Boundaries and Expectation** – The clearer it is the quicker team people will get going and the fewer the conflicts.
- **Plan to Transfer Responsibility** – Develop a mile stone chart to promote the orderly transfer of tasks to the team.
- **Determine Team Structure** – Decide whether the team should be cross functional or a collection of people doing similar tasks.
- **Understand the purpose of the Team** – Be clear about what to expect from the team.
- **Selecting Team-members** – Develop a profile sheet for each member and position in the team. Select the team leader. Encourage participation-understand culture, systems and individuals, give constructive feedback, enjoy promoting people.
- **Starting the Team Meeting** – Explain purpose, indicate goals, its measurement criterion, strategy, for performance improvement, negotiate ground rules of team discipline, confirm agreement to rules, identify skills of members to see how they complement each other, increase delegation of responsibilities, and meet periodically to ensure the momentum does not stop.
- **Measure Critical Success Indicators** – Such as quality, timeliness, cost-effectiveness. Set team rather than individual goals for key indicators. Provide regular feedback on team performance. If performance declines do not look for victims. Involve the team in problem-solving. Find out why performance is dropped and ask for ideas on how to improve.
- **Develop Team Action Plan** – For improvement involve all in the process, develop a list of actions with specific dates for implementation. Ask members to take responsibility.
- **Encourages the Development of a Team** – Allow to develop their own ceremonies for recognition, arrange informal get-together for promoting a sense of belonging.
- **Remove Poor Performers** – Poor performers and negative attitude people spoils the team spirit. They will sap the energy of the team and cause dissension.

Maintaining performance at high level for the benefit of the organisation is essential. You can sustain and even improve performance if you look into the above team-building blocks.

WORK IMPROVEMENT TEAMS (WITS)

Performance improvement comes from solving the problems that exist in an organisation. Since different kinds of organisation identify their problems differently, each must have tools appropriate to its needs. Performance Improvement Teams (PIT), Work Improvement Teams (WIT), or Self-managed Teams (SMT) are the appropriate tools for solving the organisational performance problems. These teams are from manufacturing and service areas to identify and analyse their problems differently. For example manufacturing teams identify their problem areas by a process of comparison of discrete products against standard norms on identified the problems can be solved.

Service teams identify their problem areas by a process of analysing the work they do, to find out where customer needs are being met or could be met more efficiently and effectively. Of course, flexibility in problem-solving process shall ensure that the varying needs of each team in the company are met. And hence successful planning and coordination rest on a common language the team understood. They need to speak a common language to ensure that each individual understands the direction or the team and can participate in the activities needed to achieve the terms objectives. A common language generates team success in a number of ways.

- A common language gives a team the capability to communicate within self and logically deal with the issue at hand.
- A common language provides a means for the team to effectively present conclusion and recommendations to management. The management will understand the process that the team went through and can relate the recommendations to the step up that process.
- A common language generates communication between team working on different issues perhaps in different parts of the company. This creates a cross-flow of ideas and strengthens each team. It also allows for the flexibility to restructure teams as new needs arise, using any company employee in the process. Such self-managed teams develop the capability to continually improve the products and services in the organisation on account of process analysis, problem identification, and their analytical, innovative, reporting skills are superb, as they have common language on improvement projects.

Work improvement projects enable an organisation to understand and satisfy ever-changing customer requirements through better process that provide excellent goods and services. It also enables an enterprise to stay ahead of the competition through continual promotion of innovative ideas for better products, services and technologies, continuous performance improvement of processes, practices and people has been proven to improve market share, reduce cost, improve effectiveness and enhance company profit and customer satisfaction. The organisation, team or individual that believes in total performance challenge that lies ahead in greater than any, it has faced to date, will adopt the philosophy of continuous improvement.

To improve organisation's performance of all work processes, quality, productivity, human relations, people development, teamwork between individuals and functional areas must be encouraged. A successful team must use:

- Participative approach to goals, objectives and vision setting.
- Allow open sharing of ideas.
- Encourage open communication among team-members.
- Provide team reward and recognition.
- Define mission of each team with focused aim to improve every task of the organisation.
- A team consensus of the goals team with forced aim to improve every task of the organisation.
- A team consensus on the goals should be obtained and the goals then be implemented.

HOW TEAMWORK?

The role and responsibilities of the team, team leader and team-members are described here as guidelines to help continuous improvement teams, may it be self-managed teams, quality circles teams, task force, small group, Kaizen team, or quality improvement team.

1. Define the division of the team – objective horizon.
2. Form a team and select team leader, facilitator.
3. Get the team started on specific problem.
4. Let the team determines its own agenda on improvement.
5. Team focuses on specific problem and issues.
6. Team develops alternate solutions for improvement.
7. Team implements preferred solution.
8. Team audit results and follow-up.
9. Again select new problem for improvement.

Based on above guidelines team working can be decided and they allotted improvement project in different areas of the organisation. The general areas of improvement projects may be quality improvement of product, services, practices, procedures, cost reduction, waste eliminations, productive maintenance, safety standards, housekeeping, human relations, customer services and satisfaction, management development or organisation development, business process reengineering or ISO-9000. All teams workout their working procedures for managing their tasks. They meet CEO at the periodical intervals to brief progress achieved and present their achievement to the management. It helps them check whether their proceedings are on right direction.

The self-managed teams can deliver results that to the management structure often cannot. The only pre-requisite: leave teams free to improvise on methods since that is the most powerful reason for using them, but set clear rules of behaviour and discipline. After that just watch your employees transform themselves into top performing individuals. Such teams-building by involvement and participation have become the way of worklife. These multifunctional teams, if properly sponsored, trained and facilitated, spring forth regularly, deliver remarkable results free of bureaucracy and senior management intervention. Involvement and participation can be talked about and can be encouraged. But the acid test is in the execution. Team-building is the ideal vehicle to practise what we preach.

SELF-MANAGEMENT OF TEAM

Self-managed teams manage their activities themselves, this way:

❖ Form a team	Six to eight cross-functional members (preferably).
❖ Set targets	Analyse current business conditions of company, department, section and division.
❖ Plan the activity	Assign every member a role.
❖ Analyse problems	Identify causes.
❖ Find solution	Consult the leader/manager, if necessary.
❖ Put solution into action	Ensure unity of purpose.
❖ Validate result	Is the solutions permanent?
❖ Register achievement	Acknowledge results as target.

HOW SELF-MANAGED TEAMS (SMTs) ARE BUILT

SMT can be senior level or at shop-floor level, they must have defined road map to achieve their goals. Hence, there should be built-in phase manner activities.

Phase – I

1. Identify key areas, brainstorm whether teams are necessary to manage these business processes or projects.
2. Workout how many teams the company needs. Workout the number of people per team. (make eight – ten)
3. Short list the high performers in the company and screen them with the help of interactions.
4. Draw up a final list of team-members and perform transactional analysis to ready them for change.

Phase - II

5. Rearrange short listed team-members in to clustered groups and initiative sharing of information.
6. Initiative programmes on business appreciation.
7. Involve senior management in preparations of the challenges and strategies for improvement.
8. Identify specialist/leader in various teams for making presentation to their peers on the key business elements in their areas.

Phase – III

9. Make the team go through managerial and leadership skill-building exercises.
10. Encourage informal interaction to make members comfortable with each other.
11. Involve everyone in presentation building skills. This is important for effective team functioning.
12. Seek feedback from each member on other team-mates.

Phase – IV

13. When the team-members have reached adequate comfort levels with each other, start the evaluation process.
14. Lay stress on self-evaluation and colleague-evaluation.
15. Ask the members to perform a cost-benefit analysis of the team-building exercise and seek their recommendations for final team composition.
16. Draw-up final teams based on the recommendations and launch them.

8.7 PERSONAL ASSESSMENT, POSITIVE THINKING AND POSITIVE ATTITUDE

In today's changing and revolutionised world of work, employees, executives and professionals are in a dilemma, as they build their professional career. They are sometimes lured by 100% salary jump, training abroad, fast promotions. But the end-result is generally discouraging. It is because we, as individuals never go seriously into our personal assessment. As a result, we choose wrong road and destiny or someone else will. "It is, therefore, necessary and also helpful to assess yourself before taking any assignment in the organisations."

❖ **Know where you want to go:** Job opportunities and risks are numerous in career advancement, what is important is that each of us make a considered decision of where one wants to reach ultimately. Think yourself and then act.

- **Define success in your terms:** It is critical for individual to define what their parameters of success are. One can't say a hermit sitting in isolated hill of Himalaya is unsuccessful. One can't say professor in a university does not live in the real world because he gives his life to teach thousands of pupils and is content to live in a small house, without car, in a corner of the campus. One can't say a manager in Indian company getting less salary than his colleague in multinational company living abroad is not successful. Today's life is full of peer pressure and trapping of success is defined by others. Looking at your skills, what you want to contribute and what is important to you in life means taking ownership for your life and defining success in your term is absolutely your choice.

- **Be willing to learn and adapt to new ways:** Continually reinvent/rediscover yourself and adapt to situations and circumstances as they happen. With the myriad organisations now operating in the corporate environment with diverse culture, values, beliefs and working styles. Once having made a choice to work with an organisation to get closer to your own goal, be sure that you have built the capability to innovate and learn. This is critical because changes are rapid and there is no time to first dip your toes in the water to learn to swim, it is not just important, it is critical for survival.

- **Think contribution – not just tasks and activities:** "Making a difference" is the name of the game. There are thousands job positions in the job market each day. What set you apart? What are you willing to contribute, what legacy or lasting contribution do you want to make is rest with you. It require us to align ourselves with the organisation we work with, not the organisation work for. Your employability and ongoing marketability is based on what you can truly give, getting in return the fruits of success as you have defined.

- **Be result driven:** Have a touch of the practical. Not everything should be speculation, you must also act. The wisest are easiest to deceive. They may know extraordinary things, but they know nothing of lives ordinary necessities. So, let the wise have a touch of the practical. Know, how to get things done. It may not be the highest things in life, but it is the most necessary.

- **Continuously develop yourself as resource:** Learning and adapting to new ways of functioning is the unfailing work to develop yourself as a resource in terms of your skill and capabilities. The efficiency bar is being raised daily and unless we learn new skills and battle with our own inadequacies, you will never be able to reach to your full potential. There is a constant tussle between specialisation and generalisation. Important is do we have new skills that are required in the marketplace and what are you doing to develop these skills. Your future employability is entirely in your hand.

- **Build your network and be known for what you do:** In competitive environment, it is important not just to do but also to communicate what you have done and what you are capable of. Build your own network in the organisation and outside. Build your reputation and keep it. Let people know how you are developing yourself as a resource and keep working on it without letting yourself rest on past laurels.

The secret of self-correction is simply to gain a normal view and that is always slanted on the positive side of thinking. You will radiate courage and magnetism; regain confidence by simple process of positive thinking and self-conditioning.

You can radically improve your life and opportunities by doing one small thing – having the courage to be yourself. It may seem that you are the one who always has to make the allowances and changes to accommodate others. So, never mind, as boss of your own life, you can do it, you can make all the changes necessary, you can grow and develop and solve your own problems. You have a wide choice of courses of action plan open to you. Keep trying them out in different circumstances. Practice, and make it a habit of life. Most people would agree that you get more from life when you think positively than when you think negatively. That is why human behaviour is sometimes so baffling. Make a decision now! Choose positive thinking and be happier with your life.

POSITIVE THINKING

Following successful results, you will see if you have positive thinking power.

- Always picture success no matter how badly things seem to be going at the moment.
- Whenever a negative thought concerning your personal power comes to mind, deliberatively voice a positive thought to cancel it out.
- Do not build-up obstacles in your imagination Depreciate every obstacle minimise them. Difficulties must be studied and efficiently dealt with to be eliminated.
- Do not be awestruck by other people and try to copy them. Nobody can be you as efficiently as you can.
- Make a true estimate of your own ability. Do not become egoistical but develop wholesome self-respect. Believe in your own God related powers.
- Believe in you and receive power from invisible source of power.

Thus, prayerise, picturise and actualise. Pray-rise means make a daily system of creative and positive things of the side. Picturise is a basic factor in human psychology is the realisable wish. The man who assumes success tends to have success. Actualise that which you have prayerised and picturised and actualised according to the pattern of your basic realisable wish. You will feel full of realisation. One of the deepest drives of human nature is the desire, to be appreciated. The longing to be linked, to be held in esteem, to be a sought after person is fundamental in human being.

Again, getting people to like you, you must have a set of positive manners:

- Be comfortable person, so there is no strain on you.

- Acquire the quality of relaxed easy-goingness so that things do not ruffle you.
- Don't be egostical. Guard against the impression that you know it all. Be natural and normally humble.
- Cultivate the quality of being interesting so that people will to be with you and get something of stimulating values from their association with you.
- Study to get scratchy element out of your personality.
- Drain-off your grievances. Sincerely attempt to heal honesty. Every misunderstanding you have will disappear.
- Never miss an opportunity to say a word of congratulations upon anyone's achievement or express sympathy in sorrow or disappointment.
- Give strength to people and they will give you affection to you.
- The power of positive thinking is practical technique of successful living that works at work.

Your thinking, manners and attitude and philosophy of life will show in your job as a service-giver and so a positive, constructive, creative approach is always important in your private life too.

POSITIVE ATTITUDE AND WORK CULTURE

Attitude is nothing but a settle way of thinking and feeling about person, process, action and other things.

An employee is exposed to several situations, experiences in his worklife, as a result, he develops certain attitudes which exerts powerful influence on his behaviour and this directly affects his understanding, perception and judgement.

Perception is the intake of information; received from the environment, the background of the persons, past experiences, expectations and interests.

WHY DO PEOPLE FORM ATTITUDE?

- Attitude allows them to express their fundamental values of judgement, feelings and thinking about people, company policies, etc.
- Help them adjust to their environment by providing a certain amount of predictability.
- Protect their self-esteem by making it possible for them to avoid unpleasant truth about themselves.
- Help them understand the world around them by organising and simplifying a very complex input from their environment.
- Make it easier for them to get along with people who have a similar attitude.

HOW ATTITUDES ARE FORMED?

Attitudes are formed by family influence, cultural background and influence by society, neighbours, colleagues and superiors.

We form and develop our attitude either from direct experience or from other people.

- ❖ The influence of culture plays dominant role in the formation of development of attitudes in persons.
- ❖ Inter-personal relations are developed when two people are attitudinally similar and have an opportunity to interact, they psychologically reward each others.

ATTITUDE – POSITIVE OR NEGATIVE

- ❖ A person with high level of job satisfaction holds positive attitudes towards the job. A dissatisfied person with his job holds negative attitude.
- ❖ Individuals who express high involvement in their jobs are likely to be more productive and less likely to be dissatisfied frustrated.
- ❖ This depends on working conditions, relations with others, growth prospects, salary and benefits.
- ❖ Positive attitude would mean that the employee would highly committed to the organisation and would perform well. Attitude and productivity or efficiency is thus connected to each other.

Some examples

- ❖ Once one MD of a shoe factory deputed two of his marketing managers to Africa to identify market potential for their shoe product.
- ❖ One manager sent back a fax stating that nobody here wears shoes, there is absolutely no market for our product. (Negative)

The other manager sent a fax stating that nobody wears shoes, market potential therefore, is abundant. Let us get started before our competitors come here. (Positive)

They are having divergent conclusions of the same market because of differences in attitude and market perceptions by them.

- ❖ First, a *Dy. Manager* tells his subordinate that they are below average performers.
- ❖ Second, a *Manager* tells them they are average performers.
- ❖ Third, *AGM* kept on repeating to them that they are really above average and intelligent.

When we go for uniform results of production review, we found that the same subordinates achieved highest productivity.

The above types of attitude of each one are based on their thinking of their subordinates in different way:

- ❖ Employee's attitude, motivation, his joy from work rests with the person to whom he directly reports. Thus, your immediate boss is the critical factor in the whole process of developing your attitude at work – positive or negative.

Fit between person's talent and his task is the best way to motivate people for positive work culture.

The positive thinking gets positive results. The negative thinking, expectations get negative results.

Attitude is a power factor in patient's healing process. For example a group of people from a department had a headache. A famous doctor gave them a capsule ensuring them of the fast relief. It was found that majority people felt better even though the capsule was a dummy one.

See how positive thinking gets positive results. Positive attitudes improve positive thinking at work.

If you continuously tell yourself that you are good at work, you will automatically expand your capabilities, abilities, etc.

Attitudes and habits tend to go together. Change one and you automatically change the other.

If you want to be a winner, you have got to change attitude – think – positive.

- ❖ Winners do not do different things. They do things differently.
- ❖ One of the biggest stumbling blocks to our given attitude is not the company culture, nor lack of career growth opportunities, but the major obstacle is "WE".

You have to decide whether you are a 'winner' or a 'loser'.

People with positive attitude have certain personality traits that are easy to recognise. They are caring, confident and patient and humble. They have high expectations of themselves and others. They anticipate positive change.

- ❖ Having positive outlook we increase productivity.
- ❖ Foster team spirit and teamwork.
- ❖ Solve problem.
- ❖ Improve quality.
- ❖ Make congenial atmosphere.
- ❖ Foster better relationships with employees, customers, etc.

Hence, your attitude is more important than your aptitude. Attitude decides your Altitude.

We can't tailor-make the situation of life but we can tailormake the attitude to fit them before they arise. We can alter our lives by altering our attitude.

HOW CAN WE CHANGE OUR ATTITUDES?

- Think of improvement in personal life, habits, behaviour, mannerisms, etc.
- Relations with neighbours, colleagues, superiors.
- In work methods procedures and practices in interaction – personal, departmental, etc.

In order to bring attitudinal changes in individual, it is better to analyse his function and then adapt to right method. The method would vary depending on the individual and the attitude requiring change.

- Willingness and sustain environment that better the performance of people. (performance management and reward system)
- Structure the organisation to permit effective and innovative ideas of people to rise above the demands of day-to-day working. (work involvement and empowerment)
- Clearly define a strategic focus for people to develop their innovative efforts realistically in ways that will pay-off in person or of rated responsibility, efficiency and productivity. (Defining Key Result Areas (KRAs) and job descriptions, role and goal management)
- Assist in implementing the good ideas of people. (recognition, appreciation and success stories)

If efforts are properly channelised to institutionalise above, the results in attitudinal change among people will result in effectiveness of the organisation.

Positive attitude of people and organisation are the foundation stones of POSITIVE WORK CULTURE.

Positive work culture can be built on:

- Teamwork – togetherness.
- Proper use of resources for effective performance.
- Waste control, cost, time, money, energy, etc.
- Doing right things, the right time.
- Careful scheduling of activities.
- Set time-limit for tasks at hand.
- Delegate when feasible.

Persons who perform efficiency and effectively on the job help establish positive work culture in them in their department and in their organisation.

Positive management or manager never blames circumstances, conditions for their behaviour. Their behaviour is a product of their own conscious choice based on values, rather than a product of their conditions. Proactive leaders are value driven and if their value is to produce good, quality work, it is not a function of whether the weather is conducive to it or not. Proactive leaders though sometimes influence by external environment, but their response to the situation is always value based. Proactive leader's productivity is a part of their organisational culture. Sometime, they may be dormant but they are there. They provide their people clear, undistorted reflection of their social mirror – image in society. I am what I am today because of the choice I made yesterday. No one can hurt me without my consent is the basic directive principle of positive and assertive leader in proactive management culture.

Chapter 9

REWARD MANAGEMENT AND PERFORMANCE

The development of reward management policies, structures and practices are always under pinned by assumptions about how people can best be motivated to deliver high levels of performance. These assumptions may not be articulated scientifically, but the reward philosophies and policies of an organisation can be no better than the motivational theories and belief upon which they are based.

The performance measurement, review of individual, organisation and team level must have a balanced approach. What you measure is what you get. Performance review may generate rating which influence variable pay decisions. Thus, the developmental nature of performance management is a significant and complementary process to the remuneration, compensation strategies and ultimately reward management practices.

Generally, there are four factors that particularly drive the practices of reward management forward: the dynamics of the job market, the employment environment, legislative framework and disparate shortage of certain skills. But on-going upheaval within the organisations has changed the nature of many jobs and also transformed the employment environment resulting into more flexible and adaptive remuneration practices. We are seeing tremendous growth in performance related pay policies, encompassing rewards for pay for performance, competency development and team-base pay, skill-base pay, profit sharing, gain sharing, etc. All this have given further consideration 'fit-for-purpose' reward strategies. Reward policies and practices can play a major part in change programmes, helping achieve strategic goals, which sets the direction and decides how reward management can best provide support that is required. We have described various approaches available from which a choice can be made and their advantages as they appear to us.

It is however, still necessary to set clear short – and – longer-term objectives about what is to be achieved by reward management. Some attempt must also be made to define critical success factors and performance measures and it is of course, essential to monitor and evaluate progress in the light of these success factors and measures.

Reward management is about the development, implementation, maintenance, communication and evaluation of reward process. These processes deal with the assessment of job values, the design and management of pay structures, performance management, paying for performance, the employee pension and benefits, gain sharing, incentive, employee stock option, etc., and the relevant management of reward procedures. Importantly, reward management is also concerned with the development of appropriate organisational culture, climate, core values and increasing motivation and commitment of employees. Reward management covers both financial and non-financial rewards.

Reward management and remuneration strategies main objectives are:

(1) To support the achievement of the organisation's strategic and short-term objectives to ensure that it has the skilled, competent and committed human resources it needs.

(2) To drive and support desired behaviour of people by indicating what sort of behaviour will be rewarded and how this will be done through performance-measurement.

(3) To encourage value-added performance by focusing performance pay and gain sharing schemes.

(4) To promote continuous development through skill base pay scheme for effective performance-management.

(5) To compete in employment market by paying competitive rates which attracts and retain good-quality people.

(6) To motivate all members of the organisation through the judicious use of a combination of financial and non-financial rewards.

(7) Promote teamwork through the use of team pay.

(8) To achieve fairness and equity by rewarding people consistently according to their competence, contribution and performance.

Therefore, compensation must inextricably be tied to people, their performance and organisational vision and values that their performance support. It is an important tool for communicating and rewarding the achievement of new performance goals.

Managing reward is largely about managing expectations – what employees expect from the employers in turn for their contribution and what employers expect from their employees in turn for their pay and the opportunity to work and develop their skills. Expectations are built into the employment relationship. Employee to provide skill, knowledge, efforts to employer, in turn for which the employer provides the employee a salary/wage.

The organisations business objectives and its plans for achieving those will provide the basis for developing pay strategies and policies. The resulting business performance and or the financial circumstances of the organisation will influence the amount it can afford to pay and its pay policies on such matters as how it wants to relate pay to performance and market rates. Sometimes, reward strategy is characterised by diversity and conditioned both by the legacy of the part and the realities of the present.

How reward strategy contributes to the achievement of corporate goals or collective performance is very important to examine because:

The business strategy specifies what the company wants to accomplish, how it wants to behave, and the kinds of performance and performance levels it must demonstrate to be effective. Thus, reward systems in turn, help to drive performance by influencing individuals and organisational behaviours.

REWARD POLICIES

The reward policies will be concerned with:

(1) **The level of rewards:** Policies on pay levels refer to number of grades that should exist in the pay hierarchy. Whether the organisation is intended to plan high average, medium average, below average rate of pay as per assessment of individual skill, knowledge, competencies.

(2) **Market rate:** Any organisation that has to attract and retain employees who are much in demand and where market rate are high may to a degree, have to sacrifice its ideals of internal equity to the realism of the job market.

(3) **Relating rewards to business performance:** This refers to the link between business performance and pay. Pay will vary according to results. Such policies will include gain sharing or profit sharing schemes to operate.

(4) **Contingent reward:** This policy needs to determine whether or not the organisation wants to pay for performance, skill or competence and if so how much and under what circumstances, for example production incentives, production bonuses, special increments, etc., of course such payment should not be less than 10% and preferably more 30% of basic pay. It can be used for individual team or for overall organisational performance.

(5) **Flexibility:** Reward policies should operate flexibility in response to changing conditions and or on the score of total operating performance.

(6) **Communicating to employees:** It is particularly important to explain the basis of pay-for-performance scheme and also to convey to employee how their total pay packet and other benefits is made up.

(7) **Transparency:** Without transparency employees will believe that the organisation has something to hide, often with reason. The organisation must spell out its reward policies and practices and the values that underpin them. Transparency is achieved through involvement and communication.

In conclusion, by linking business and reward strategy, the essential point emerged out is that business strategy sets out what business have to do – how they must perform, behave to be effective. Reward management processes help to drive performance by influencing individual and therefore, organisational behaviour. Reward practices may be broad but they have to be explicit. They have to state, in effect, this is what the business intends to do, and this, therefore, is how reward policies and processes can help the business to do it. The reward strategy must support the implementation of corporate transformation programmes; help to achieve cultural change focus attention on the things that matter if the business is to succeed. Getting people to buy into performance management is a matter of ownership. Both the parties must feel that this is their process not something which has been forced upon them by third party.

Chapter 10

SUPPLEMENTARY READINGS

Structure:

10.1 Changing Workplace Basics

10.2 Quality Management

10.3 Skill and Their Primary Attributes

10.4 Emotional Intelligence

10.5 Learning Organisation

10.6 Work Excellence and World-class Companies

10.7 Training and Development of People

10.8 SDC – 65 - Science of Discipline and Creativity

10.1 CHANGING WORKPLACE BASICS

For Organisation

Every civilisation has its own ideology – a kit of powerful culture, assumptions that structures its view of reality and justifies its operations. "Pay-me-well", "Treat-me-well" and "Use-me-well" organisational culture assumptions of human resources has its standing of that time ideologies and they justified their management of people relevant to that time. The scientific management, has focused upon the basic physical activities involved in production and is typified by time and method study, while human relations movement, is more concerned with the grand organisational problems. Contemporary development in management and organisation theory draws more on the bahavioural sciences. Its approach draws more on emotional intelligence, social intelligence and social ecology of the organisation. In this new economy, far reaching business changes have been experienced, where knowledge is considered most vital. So, people are crucial to every work operation. All corporate strengths are dependent on people. The organisation is built on an effective business philosophy, vision and mission not merely on organisational systems. It is believed that it is only human resources take the organisation at desired competence. It encourages people to learn to produce the result they desire and nurture creative and innovative patterns of collective sharing and learning. This ever-learning, ever-evolving, ever-innovative, ever-competitive organisation of tomorrow will wrest advantages by marrying the development of every single employee to organisational performance by creating and implementing the new people management. Creating new people management means recruiting people with appropriate knowledge, skills; creating a corporate culture for individual excellence and providing training and developing their assigned roles by appraising and rewarding them for meeting corporate goals.

Organisation succeeds largely because its culture offers employee a stable social setting in which they get hearing and draws support to cope with and build the other social relations in their lives. Tradition, climate and values that set a pattern of activities, opinions, and actions instill their pattern in their employees by their examples and pass it down to succeeding generation employees. With this base of values, management begins to look carefully at its approaches to managing people. Company culture is a total of the inherited ideas, beliefs, values and knowledge which constitute the standard that shared bases of social action. These sets of share values affect organisational behaviour at work. Organisational culture thus plays a critical role in socialising its employees in the social systems of the organisation. Therefore, organisation brings not mere changes in how people be managed but also bring changes in their attitudes, learning, skill development and personality traits.

Learning begins when an employee make the kind of contact with people and things. This kind of contracts with people within the organisation, start with Back-to-Basics approach. Their process of learning starts from observation to problem-solving, involves a set of activities, which is termed as 'learning cycle'. What has been learned then must be incorporated into work activities at workplace, behaviour, attitude, opinion, values.

This gradually represents collective culture and attitude termed as organisational behaviour. Engaged in knowledge, skill and self-development – as an individual and as an organisation we are transforming not only learning environment, but also our organisation. Collective learning involves both anticipation and participation. Through 'anticipation', individuals or organisation consider trends of learning and make plans. Through 'anticipatory learning' the future may enter into our worklife as a friend. 'Participation' involves more than the formal sharing of decisions, it is an attitude characterised by cooperation, dialogue and empathy. Without participation, anticipation becomes futile; and participation without anticipation can be misguided. Anticipation encourages solidarity in time, participation creates solidarity in workplace. The informatted organisation is a learning institute and one of its principal purposes is the expansion of knowledge, skill, core competencies not for it but for those employees working with the organisation. Knowledge has now become the real capital of the developing economy. Such collective learning must start with a question, a problem to be solved, a challenge to be met collectively. Ideas or theories can never be enough; they have to be tested in reality. The wheel of learning cannot be left to chance or to CEO relaxing in a reclining arm chair.

Why are these changes occurring in the workplace? Because they have to occur. Faced with the Liberalisation, Privatisation and Globalisation (LPG) it became evident that customer demands better quality, service, product and innovations at workplace by employees. Business leaders have to run their companies in a global, boundary less market place. As a result, increasingly, the focus is turning to the contribution of people as the ultimate key to the success of an enterprise. With this focus, changes in corporate philosophy, policies and practices are aiming at enhancing the ability of employees to perform, participate and share in the operation. The new style of motivating people has replaced the old style of carrot and stick approach to motivation. Today's organisations are guiding their manager's new styles of motivation employees. Those are like: Empower people through involvement. Assume that employees can and will do extraordinary things if organisational barriers to performance are removed. Be frank and open about the company's business strategies and direction and make sure everyone understands company is trying to accomplish. Trust employees to do the right things. Assume that given enough and right information and self-control, employee will act in the best interest of the company and presumably in their own best interest. Create a unique culture and indoctrinate employee from the start of that culture. Make sure everyone knows how to behave consistent with the company's cultural norms. If someone does not in concert with the values, express your disappointment and encourage him to change or leave. The results of such organisational atmosphere, where employees are cared, challenged, urged and expected to be creative, to think individually to take risks to make significant contributions. For the demands of new workplace, this like organisation is right fit. On the other hand, new workplace will demand more from every employee more than before. It will also give more responsibility, autonomy, self-control to employees. Obviously, in such changing values of new workplace, individual will have to redefine his personal management for self-development to match the organisational requirements.

It is therefore, management's challenge is to structure, link and blend human and productivity and organisational performance.

FOR INDIVIDUALS

If we wanted to change the situation, we first have to change ourselves. And to change ourselves effectively, we have to change our perception, assumption about things or persons. We have to rechange our personality and character ethics in a positive way. The character ethics taught us basic principles of effective living and we can only experience true success and enduring happiness as we learn and integrate these principles into our basic character. Personality ethics have two paths: one of human and public relationships techniques and other is positive mental attitude. Your attitude will determine you altitude. Smiling wins more friends than frowning. Success becomes more a function of personality of public image, attitudes, behaviour, skills that lubricate the process of human interaction. Into the hands of every individual has given a marvelous power for good or evil – the silent, unconscious, unseen influence of his life. This is simply the constant radiation of what man really is, not what he pretends to be. We all know that map is not the territory. It is simply an explanation of certain aspects of the territory. Each of us has many maps in our heads which are divided into two categories: map of the way things are, or realities and map of the way things should be. We interpret everything we experience. We simply assume that the way we see things in the way they really are and our attitudes and behaviours grow out of these assumptions. These assumptions are called our perceptions. Though you see the same object, your perceptions are different than me; you look it in different angle than me.

Same is the case with our understanding of people at workplace. Different things we see differently as per our perceptions. When with all differences we work together to manage our human resources to get desired result or sometimes get bad results. To reach an agreement on such matters deal with win-win situations and solutions. Enhance your trust in others to build-up strong relationships. Relationship is like bank account. We make deposit in bank to build-up reserve from which we can make withdrawal when we need it. If withdrawals are overdrawn, the bank cautions us to take care of our reserve and advised us "You can't withdraw unless you deposit further". An emotional bank account is a metaphor that describes the amount of trust that is build-up in a relationship. If you make deposits into an emotional bank account with others through courtesy, kindness, honesty and commitment, you will build-up a reserve of positive human relations at work. You will feel safe with other human beings in the organisation. This is what true personal management is.

Getting hired and surviving in the new workplace will require more and different skills from employees than ever before. No longer will it be sufficient to be good in a narrowly defined technical specialty. No longer will the path to advancement be assured by carrying favour with influential bosses. The new workplace will be more democratic. Key to success will be acceptance by one's peer. And to gain such acceptance, employees will have to demonstrate their various social skills like leadership, team-building, problem solving and communication skills, etc. The most important thing in a new workplace, employee will have to bring to his solid basic education and the willingness and ability to keep learning new skills.

Skill at work whether social, soft, personal skills are called social skills, people skills or human skills. Many a times these are used interchangeably denoting the same meaning. To avoid confusion, I termed them all as social skills. It is surveyed that 80% of the man-management problems are related due to lack of social skills at work. Inter-personal relations, group relations, departmental relations, superior-subordinate relations, leaders-follower's relations and lastly manager-managed relations are related to social skills demonstrated at workplace. And only 20% problems are related to technical skills or other databased techniques used at workplace. Social skills, the foundation skills can consistently make or break improvements. Over the years, it is found that social skills are best built on a foundation of these basic principles:

- Focus on the work process, issues and behaviour, not on person.
- Maintain the self-confidence and self-esteem of others.
- Maintain strong partnerships with your internal and external customers and suppliers.
- Take initiative to improve work processes, partnership and related process skills.
- Lead by example.

Skills acquisition, application and developments are more than just knowing what skills looks like. Skills are developed primarily through practice and feedback. These skills are fundamental to all categories of people and more critical to supervisory and managerial levels. Putting an untrained person on the job to work with trained persons shall be unreceptive, unsupportive or inconsistent to the environment, shall waste everyone's time. Even worse, it may demotivate and frustrate individuals in the group. Therefore, skill development is necessary. Personal skills like ability to communicate, effective planning, negotiating, conflict resolution, building relationships, etc., are skills must be possessed by an individuals before entering into work situation. Understanding of these and such skills is grounded on these Basic Principles:

- **Work efficiently:** Use all available resources to get the job done. Know the expected results of each new task, assemble necessary materials before starting a task, accept change and help new procedure work smoothly.
- **Communicate clearly:** Help others especially the quiet ones speak up, provide facts and ideas, help keep meeting focused on the topic and purpose, ask others for their reaction to the information given.
- **Provide positive mutual support:** Let others know when they have done good job, make people feel good about their work, show interest in the ideas and opinions of others, share ideas with others.
- **Seek and accept help when needed:** Ask for help as soon as he or she need it, allow others to help get the job done better, keep others informed of what is going on, let others know about problems and conflicts early.

❖ **Constructively channel emotions:** Keep control of own anger and disappointment, avoid letting own emotion get in the way of teaching results on the job, deal with negative situations in a positive way.

These are some of the basic principles of skills required for personal management and self-developments. What are the key social skills for self-development at workplace, we have incorporated in the succeeding chapters of this book.

10.2 QUALITY MANAGEMENT

Individual builds an organisation. His personal tendencies are carried within to the organisation. He continues to look for quick fixes – more productivity, more profit and as a result, he neglects quality parameters on all fronts and gradually develop acute, painful systems and try to deal with these chronic habit patterns built-up into day-to-day operations. Chronic individual problems become chronic organisational problems as he encourages instant gratification and quick solutions and create more deep, difficult problems to the company without going into problem-solving process. It is observed that such managed companies exhibit these problems:

Problem-1:

No shared vision and values – Either the company has no mission or there is no deep understanding of and commitment to the mission at all level of the company.

Problem-2:

No strategic road map – Having no well-defined, well thought road map to follow nor strategy is well developed, effectively expressed company mission, the company fails to meet the wants, needs and realities of customers and employees and other manufacturing processes and as a result the company creates acute operational problems.

Problem-3:

Poor alignment – Bad alignment between structures, shared values, between vision and system, structure of the company is poorly served, operated without proper reinforcement path.

Problem-4:

Wrong style – The management philosophy is either in congruent with shared vision and values or the style inconsistently embodies the vision and values of the company mission.

Problem-5:

Poor skills – Style does not match skills or employees lack the skills they need to use with appropriate vision, objectives or goals.

Problem-6:

Low trust – Executives, staff and other employees have low trust, a depleted emotional bank account, and that low trust results in closed communication, little problem-solving, poor cooperation and teamwork.

Problem-7:

No self-integrity – Values do not equal habits, there is no correlation between what I value, believe and what I do. Without a clear statement of values, our habits overpower all the activities at the workplace.

These are some of the vivid problem areas of any unquality organisation. To understand precisely, the problems of unquality organisation, it is better to review diagnosis of a trouble company researched and experienced by Philip Crosby.

DIGNOSIS OF A TROUBLED COMPANY

Crosby's diagnosis of a troubled company

Crosby sees a troubled company as a patient in need of a quality vaccine. Trouble with quality inside always results in trouble with the customers outside. Customer dissatisfaction with the end-product or service may be the final and most obvious symptom of a diseased company, but there are also other symptoms, the appearance of which always indicates trouble with quality. One symptom is usually the consequence of another, something that perhaps facilitates their simultaneous cure. Some of the main symptoms are listed below, and their interrelationship is obvious:

(1) The company has an extensive field service for reworking and corrective actions. But service under guarantee and readjustment or reworking of the product the customer has already bought may be the main cause of losing the customer forever. Investing heavily in such a service is an admission that faulty output is evitable and should always be expected as a way of life; an admission that no process can ever be defect-free. Another version of these symptoms is the presence of an extensive programme of mass inspection. Of course, the reason for the extensive inspection or field reworking service is usually the presence of the next symptom.

(2) The outgoing product normally deviates from the customer's requirements. In many situations, non-conformance is so heavily embodied in the company culture that it has become the norm. Defects are seen as a necessary evil, tackled only by mass inspection or the reworking service. But this is something that normally costs much more than the effort required for preventing defects arising in the first place. Deviation from the desired target is usually the result of ignorance about quality standards, which brings us to the third symptom.

(3) Management does not provide a clear performance standard, so the employees develop their own. It is management's responsibility to provide the conditions in which quality can flourish, and to establish a culture where continuous

improvement is the standard. If this is not done, the workforce defines its own standards, based, justifiably, on the current capability of the processes. But in the absence of a quality ethos and of a management commitment, these processes will always function below their potential, something that will drive employees, through no fault of their own, to commit themselves to a specific level of incompetence! The absence of management commitment and involvement is always apparent from the next symptoms.

(4) Management denies that it is the cause of the problem. Managers tend to blame the workers in order to hide their inability to improve the system. As Deming and Juran state, more than 80% of the problems are traceable to the system, which it is the management's responsibility to take care of. Denial of this responsibility invariably means that management causes and will continue to cause the majority of the problems. Costly fire-fighting then becomes their only line of action, something that gives rise to the fifth symptom.

(5) Management does not know the price of non-conformance. A determination of the cost of quality at this stage could alleviate this symptom. It might reveal how it costs to the company to do things wrong, to fire-fight, to mass inspect, to rework and reinsert. It might reveal the usefulness of prevention and of proper training; training on the appropriate tools for achieving quality, first time, everytime. As long as management prefers to remain ignorant about the costs of non-conformance, extensive field service will always be necessary; which brings us back to symptom.

The above symptoms are indicative of a company that always has problems with quality. Crosby also recognises inter-related symptoms which characterise a company with a poor track record in the quality improvement effort, the most obvious of which are as follows:

(1) The improvement effort is aimed at the lower level of the organisation, as though senior management should not be responsible for and are not serious about quality.

(2) The effort is called a programme rather than a process. This gives the impression of something temporary, soon to be replaced by something else, rather than the impression of the never-ending which requires constant attention.

(3) There are many temporary activities, uncoordinated form above, which always result in cynicism and self-defeating admission of the fact that defects are inevitable, and that the economics of quality require errors.

(4) There is an apparent management of non-involvement in the quality effort, which result in an ignorance of what tools are required and of how long one needs to allow for the process of quality improvement to have an effect. This in turn causes management to become impatient from results, and to proceed with spontaneous actions for short-term solutions which do more harm than good.

Crosby believes that, in the majority of cases, performance reviews are not truthful, usually painting a better picture than people actually deserve, something that shows lack of integrity, an important ingredient of the quality vaccine.

But the main principle shared by Crosby and Deming is the responsibility of management. Crosby believes that the administration of the quality serum requires three distinct management actions or attitudes, as follows:

(1) **Determination** – Awareness that the management needs to take the lead in the new economic age. The times of cheap energy, low labour rates, captive markets and expensive materials are gone.

(2) **Education** – For the managers, who should themselves become the educators and modern leaders, rather than mere supervisors?

(3) **Implementation** – Concentrating on the effort of creating a hassle-free and motivating working environment, providing adequate guidance on the never-ending road to quality improvement, and involving everybody.

CROSBY'S ABSOLUTES FOR QUALITY MANAGEMENT

Unquality problems of the company are curable if we follow the philosophy of Philip Crosby.

Quality management today is a sea of confusion where people are searching for right set of initial and executives make charismatic speeches on the subject that they do not really understand. Concept and efforts of quality management's construction being diluted through superficial programmes and techniques. Everyone seems to be aware of the value of installing prevention management as a way of life; many are trying to short-cut the concepts. Wanting to find a short cut shows that you do not really understand the subject in the first place. For instance, majority people determinedly interwined quality control and quality management. Quality control is based on statistical actions and techniques that contains the non-conformancès of processes by applying a series of screen and sieves. In contrast, quality management is committed to running the whole operation based on prevention, so that there is nothing to sieve out. Quality control is mostly run by employees/ technicians, quality management, by management.

Quality control was developed for the purpose of containing non-conformances within a process by statistical means. Work was measured as it went along and was possible to tell from a few samples if that particular part of the operation was under control. Statistical process control is still an effective way of running a manufacturing process, but it is hardly a management system. SPC's weakness is the assumption that the process can never be totally effective at all times, and therefore, errors are to be expected. This produces the concept known as Acceptable Quality Level (AQL). P. Crosby created zero defects is for the purpose of getting rid of acceptable quality levels. Do exactly as we agreed to do rather than spending a lot of mine and money keeping at the old-fashioned concepts would not produce results of this type, so the pendulum began to swing towards quality management.

Quality management involves with top management. The persons who make-up the company are the main source of good or bad management for that company. Their priorities determine what the employees, suppliers and customers will have to do for performance of the company. If their performance objectives are well thought out on the basis of strategies and policies, then success could be just around the corner. In conclusion, P. Crosby advised that "An organisation must be managed completely with a foundation of zero defects as its operating philosophy". Further, he says "In the 21st century we may well be back to managing people who are coping with a technology that has a mind of its own. This time, however, the people will be utilised for their minds and fingers, rather than their backs and hands." Therefore, successful managements will be those who can establish and implement the proper vision, obtaining the best performance of people in the whole organisational processes. They will have to battle to install zero defects – quality management systems.

Philip Crosby's aim, of course, to prevent or cure the illness of low quality performance in the organisation. The belief that a properly planned and executed quality initiative can and should produce immediate measurable results. It is not easy. It does not happen without change, and sometimes considerable change, especially in the attitudes of senior and middle management men. But it is possible. More important, it is necessary for success in world-wide competition. Quality management is an investment, not an expense. It will provide lasting dividends to the visionary leaders who make the tough choices and move forward toward total quality management in their organisations. This logically asks the organisation and its people to transform them to perform like quality organisation.

TRANSFORMATION PROCESS

Most of the organisational systems, process, practices and policies evolved over a long time, you can't transform them overnight. It requires considerable time, effort and mind-set to replace old ways of doing the things. Lack of management commitment is usually blamed for failure to meet desired performance of the company. But this is an overly simplistic explanation.

Changing management culture, employee's behaviour and attitudes within an organisation is a difficult process. Change never comes easily and it will not happen just because the CEO is committed to a new approach. Secondly, managers may be motivated to encourage teamwork, participation and good communication with employees. But unfortunately the corporate culture imposed on them which they in turn pass on to others, negates these good intentions. If the environment to be changed and the hassles burdening management to be reduced, there is then time for clear two-way communication. The real change comes when managers realise that cooperation and communication will reduce aggravation all-round and make their jobs more satisfying. Specific actions by management in partnership will people are needed to ensure that the environment truly changes.

The process of change thus will be better understood when realisation grows that although the present culture was not achieved by careful planning, neither did it happen by accident. It has been created steadily overtime by the way things are done in the company, by the way objectives are set, by the way people measured, managed, by the way functional or departmental specialisations have grown. That is by steadily doing things differently, such change will be achieved more quickly to emerge the desired culture.

Sometimes, despite all the investment, support and efforts, many organisations get their improvement plan crashed, ground to a halt or slowly sank in the mud. It soon became clear that the senior executives were not focused on and strongly supporting the implementation effort. Many times, it was simply because executives did not know what to do, how to do it. In other cases, the executive team was not ready to support the deployment process and it could never proceed. Managing organisational change is like this rocket example. "The first thing you hear in the lift of a rocket is ignition. Then there is lot of flame and fury and for a while nothing moves. The most tenuous part of the lift-off is when the rocket first slowly start to move." That is how change in the organisations. You have to generate a lot of energy at first; nothing will happen and will become very frustrated. Then when you do begin to see few changes, you can't relax. That is when the guiding system really needs to be put in place. Thus, transformation process calls for huge and sweeping changes in every nook and cranny of the organisation and there is no pet formula to pull out when the organisation hits the wall- cultural change.

As said by Peter Drucker, "Every enterprise requires commitment to common goals and shared values. Without such commitment there is no enterprise, there is only mob ________. Managements first job is to think through, set and exemplify those objectives, values and goals."

In short, generally, people in the organisation will not simply convert from old ways to new ways of organisation. With steady, gradual process of transformation, it will make them easy to absorb change. It will then be easier to develop human resources into common wealth of support for quality transformation. Following are some of the basic guidelines we have framed for carrying out organisational transformation:

(1) The objective of transformation must be consistent throughout the company. Consistency in methods and means must be maintained to achieve the objectives.

(2) When the leaders of the company announce a change to which they expect everyone to conform, they themselves must undergo change. Their change must be a clear demonstration to everyone.

(3) Seek the active support of critical mass. In the process of change, some will resist it, most will be undecided and in wait and watch mode. These movers and shakers are critical mass. With their support, a proposed change will have good opportunity to prove itself.

(4) People don't resist change, they resist being changed. People need to feel change. Hence, their needs, fears, desires and concerns must be listened to, responded to. Their active involvement will bury their instinct of being changed.

(5) When possible, change should be planned and treated like courtship – with a mixture of gradualism and surprises.

(6) Effort to implement change should be anchored. Anchoring means the individuals or groups directly involved in improvement activities should be surrounded by a network of others involved in similar activities. There must be services that offer support and guidance to the innovators otherwise, they will feel isolated.

(7) The more comprehensive and widespread the proposed change, the more absolute is the need for deep understanding and active leadership of top managers, efforts for change may flourish for a while, but it will not last, without proper leadership change shall be passive, shallow and tentative.

(8) Regularly meet with group of employees, listen to their reactions and suggestions, and follow-up immediately when possible.

(9) Managers should set an example of constant improvements and recognise those employees who are constantly trying to improve the systems. This will reduce their fear, barrier and encourage pride in one's work, workgroup and consequently, entire company.

(10) The transformation process is a complex and difficult undertaking. The way to go about it is not in the manager of the bulldozer, rather you can accomplish it in the manner of the weevil, patiently and persistently.

QUALITY MANAGEMENT THROUGH ZERO DEFECTS

By now we understood that uquality or troubled company can be transformed if organisational leaders adapt distinct management action, attitudes and a bone deep commitment to make it happen – a quality company. Philip Crosby in his book *"Quality without Tears"* has prescribed four absolutes of quality and its implementation process followed by fourteen steps. His quality treatment largely sounds like a doctor's prescription. The aim is, of course, to prevent or cure the illness of low quality. In this caption we will outline the main four absolutes and fourteen steps for making the company quality managed the company.

FOUR ABSOLUTES OF QUALITY

I[st] Absolute:

The definition of quality is *conformance to requirement*, not goodness. The definition of quality can never make any sense unless it is based on exactly what the customer wants. A product is a quality product only when it conforms to the customer's requirement. Of course, these requirements should be made known the workforce, which should be provided with adequate tool to achieve them. Consequently, the management has the following three tasks to perform:

(1) Establish the requirements to be met and communicate them to the employees.

(2) Provide the appropriate tools and techniques and the necessary training tools and techniques, and the necessary training in them.

(3) Provide continuous support and encouragement.

IInd Absolute:

The system of *quality is prevention* – The secret of success is to study the process and perform some sort of risk analysis, that is, identify opportunities for error. Something can then be done so that the error is avoided. Contingency plans can also be drawn up, so that if a problem materialises, the damage is controlled and restricted to the minimum possible.

A company which relies on mass inspection of the final output to improve quality is doomed to stagnation. The only prerequisite of prevention is an understanding of the process; implementation of SPC can provide the understanding need. One can then immediately know what to do to prevent rather than inspect, appraise or test.

IIIrd Absolute:

The performance *standard is zero defects* – It is important that a feeling of determination exists throughout the company to do things first time, on time, every time. Determination, coupled with a system of management which provides the communication needed and the tools for prevention, can succeed in making zero defects (ZD) a reality. However, it is important that the concept of ZD is not seen as a motivation programme, but only as a management performance standards, simply indicating that there is no room for imperfection, complacency or the attitude that 'that's close enough'! Crosby admits that many managers misunderstood the concept of ZD and used it as a slogan, imposing an asrbitrary target on the workforce. As Deming emphasises, unless the right conditions are created and the techniques are provided to reach this target, such a treatment of this concept can only create anxiety, frustration and mistrust towards management.

But error-free products are possible, and Japanese industry has proved it. It is not, therefore, unreasonable to expect a level of zero defects, and the quality tools for achieving it do exist. For example; the technique advocated by Taguchi regards the mere satisfaction of specification limits as not good enough; this is because any deviation from the target, however small, causes a loss to society and will keep causing it until zero deviation (or ZD) is accomplished.

IVth Absolute:

The measurement of quality is the *price of non-conformance* – In order to attract the attention of senior management; quality has to be measured in financial terms. This is how quality can become a management function, and not just a technical one. If one measures the cost consequences involved in doing things wrong (due to rejects, reworking, warranty costs, etc.), these can very well represent 20-40% of the total operating costs. This is the price of non-conformance (PONC), mainly the result of not doing things right first time.

When a rough calculation of the PONC is done initially, it can be so alarmingly high that it will surely prompt top management to do something about quality. What will become apparent is the need for professional quality functions, prevention efforts and quality education. The cost of these efforts is the Price of Conformance (POC) – money well spent.

CROSBY's FOURTEEN STEPS FOR QUALITY IMPROVEMENT

The quality improvement process is never ending. To keep the momentum going, the appropriate culture and attitude about quality have to be embedded throughout the organisation. Crosby has laid down fourteen steps to assist in the establishment of a quality ethic. The order is not too important, as most of the steps can run in parallel. However, it is evident that steps 1 to 6 have to be made by management and should naturally come first.

Step 1: Management Commitment

Senior management has to demonstrate a commitment to quality. This is the only way to convince the workforce that management is not only serious about quality, but also prepared to be involved in the process. A corporate policy on quality should be issued. This needs to be clear and unambiguous, and should ideally be based on the important premise of defect-free delivery of products and services, on time. Quality should be the first item on the agenda of all management meetings, and in all the activities that top managers are involved with. Management commitment should continuously be demonstrated and tested until it can be assumed.

Step 2: The Quality Improvement Team

A team needs to be set up to guide the process of quality improvement. This team will require a definite direction and leadership, and should have clear access to top management. The idea is not to use this team for corrective actions or firefighting. Its main initial task will be to change the attitudes and practices of those who run the company; also to set up the educational activities required, and subsequently to coordinate and support the whole effort. In short, the quality improvement team will assist in the changing of the system to enable quality to flourish.

Step 3: Measurement

To avoid frustration and hassle, one needs a clear method of measurement. Every part of any activity, its input, process work and output, lends itself to measurement. The type of measurement can be easily decided upon, by the people associated with the particular activity. Once this decision is taken, a level of reference is created, reasonable can be made. There is no other way to communicate in definite terms.

Step 4: The Cost of Quality

Calculating how much poor quality is costing the company can be beneficial in getting management's attention, in providing an incentive for improvement, in setting up priorities and in showing up trends. But Crosby himself admits that the whole concept of the cost of quality, if it is not handled properly, can be counterproductive and can actually cause more trouble rather than save money. This opinion is also shared by Deming, who actually believes that the most important cost figures are incalculable anyway. Nevertheless, Crosby believes that the quality costs need to be identified objectively, pulled together and fed into the regular management process formally, and treated as a positive rather than a threatening item. Only then can the concept serve as a good stimulus for the quality improvement process itself.

Step 5: Quality Awareness

An adequate system of communication is vital for a company. Through this, awareness about quality should spread throughout the organisation and be adapted to the company's culture. People should be continuously reminded about the management commitment to quality, the associated policies and the training facilitates on offer. Crosby is not against slogans or posters about 'Zero defects' or 'Do it right first time' as a reminder to the workforce of the importance of quality; something that Deming strongly disagrees with.

Step 6: Corrective Action

The main purpose of corrective action should be to prevent errors of identify and eliminate causes of problems forever. Unfortunately, many companies regard corrective action as an activity composed of reworking, firefighting or replacement of the non-conforming item with a conforming one. But such an activity is always non-value-added. Corrective activities need to be based on analysis of past data so that the causes of problems are determined and taken care of permanently.

Step 7: Zero Defects Planning

Proper planning is required for the concept of ZD to become properly embedded in the company culture. It will have to start with a ZD commitment on the part of top management. This is the only way that the concept will be taken seriously and recognised as a dignified ideal.

Step 8: Employee Education

An investment in quality education can result in quantum leaps in improvement. A proper education system requires time and money, class-work and assignments, explanatory videos and workshops, homework and team discussions in order to personalise the subject to the company concerned. Crosby summarises the entire education process in what he calls 'the six Cs':

- Comprehension (understanding of what is necessary, abandonment of the old way of thinking and of outdated practices).
- Commitment (management-led dedication to cultural change.)
- Competence (methodical and scientific implementation of the improvement process).
- Communication (complete cooperation throughout the production process, including suppliers and customers).
- Correction (elimination of all causes of problems and prevention of new ones arising).
- Continuance (never-ending effort for improvement).

Step 9: Zero Defects Day

Another point of difference with Deming's teachings is the matter of zero defects day. Crosby recommends that a ZD day is planned to reward serious efforts, and is celebrated at least annually with speakers representing senior management, the customers, the unions and even the city or region. This will then act as a reminder of the importance of quality and as a demonstration of the commitment towards the ZD principle. Deming opposes unsubstantiated ZD campaigns and exhortations as counterproductive; if a ZD day is part of a quality effort which last only for a single day, without being supported by any quality action in the rest of the year, it will only make the workforce question management's sincerity, and create a negative atmosphere of indifference.

Step 10: Goal Setting

Goal setting is the immediate consequence of measurement. There is no point in measuring something unless there is a target to be met. When it comes to quality, the ultimate goal is that of zero defects, and all intermediate goals should move in that direction. Of course, Deming would argue that arbitrary targets do not serve any purpose whatsoever.

Step 11: Error Cause Removal

The permanent removal of the causes of error requires a team effort. Adequate means of communication will ensure the sharing of the necessary information, which can help not only in the identification of the common sources of error and their permanent elimination, but also in the prevention of the same problems arising in the future.

Step 12: Recognition

Crosby considers recognition as a necessary reference point and as a guideline to help the improvement efforts in the right direction. The recognition process needs to be planned carefully and developed gradually; it should not be rushed. When a 'Beacon of Quality' is awarded to somebody who deserves it, it does not have to be in monetary terms. It can act as an incentive to others and an example to emulate.

Step 13: Quality Council

All quality professionals can be brought together in one group under the name of the quality council. These will be the people who will define the mission, vision, values and policies necessary for managing the improvement process. They can learn from each other, and their coordinated expertise can be more effective in supporting the quality improvement teams in their efforts towards the elimination of hassle and the achievement of zero defects.

Step 14: Do it all Over Again

The process of learning, participating, experimenting with new methods and improving should never end. Quality improvement has to become the culture of the company, and this can only happen if the efforts are a continuous one. The process can then gain speed and permanence. The momentum should never be allowed to slow down. Continuous re-education and involvement, actively supported by top management, are the keys in making quality attainment an enduring way of life.

A FINAL WORD FROM CROSBY

Every ingredient involved in setting up a permanent system to eliminate hassle and to cause quality improvement requires special attention. When management respects the rights of the customer exactly the way it respects the rights of the banks and stockholders, then quality will happen all the time. When honouring the right of the employees to be free of hassle is considered as important as increasing sales, then hassle will be eliminated.

What needs to be done first, is to educate people and at the same time to formalise the management commitment, the measurement and the awareness. Quality is to be first among equals, and it should be first on the agenda.

Quality will never cease to be a major problem until management believes that there is absolutely no reason that we should ever deliver a nonconforming product or service to our customers. The producing of defect-free products and services on time, is mostly caused by the minds of those who hold the strings. If something you want to happen is not happening, follow the string back to its origin. It might terminate in the office of someone you know. Perhaps even yourself!

In conclusion, error free performance does not start with any new statistical methods or problem-solving techniques alone. It starts with each person having a through understanding of the job, right attitude and confidence and with the make it happen attitude. Right from the CEO to grassroot employee everyone handles some or others jobs on day-to-day basis. His daily job handling with purposeful observation gives him various ideas to manage the job in a errorfree manner. Catching his some ideas for betterment of the job, job place, products, and services is the essence of zero defects philosophy. If permitted to present his improved ideas for implementation, will give him a sense of involvement and participation and will inculcate feeling of ownership with his job and will prove himself an excellent performer by creating and presenting success stories of his improved performance.

Zero defects is kind of performance improvement device to achieve performance as per the conformance to desired performance. Alternatively, this will also help reduce the cost of doing wrong thing (rework of any type in process, practice, product, services). Taking a view that employees have useful thoughts, ideas lying dormant in their mind, can be trapped once freedom is given to them. Their thinking, creativity, innovativeness, suggestion, ideas can be studied, analysed and interpreted for making existing working systems defect free. If implemented successfully, every individual in the organisation will transform himself to perform to achieve desired performance and thus all employees performance put together shall be total performance of the organisation.

10.3 SKILLS AND THEIR PRIMARY ATTRIBUTES

It is well demonstrated that human abilities make-up the greater part of the ingredients for excellence at work. Whether you work in a large or small organisation of any type, you are evaluated in terms of your abilities, competencies and skills, though you may not know it thoroughly. If you are fresher and applying for a job, you are likely to be scrutinised through this lens, though no one tell you so explicitly. Whatever your job, understanding how to cultivate and develop skills is essential for success in your career. Today, management people are looking at your personal traits – character, personality, attitude, social and human skills as prime qualities that make and keep you employable.

Our level of skill, ability and competency is not fixed genetically nor does it develop only in early childhood. These are to be learned and it continues to develop as we grow through life and learn from our experiences and our skills in it keeps growing as age grows. We learned most, all we know from and with each other. That takes social intelligence (social relationship) not just cognitive ability. Many people have trouble because they don't understand how you become part of a human situation, part of relationship. It is easy to focus on cognitive ability and ignore social intelligence. But, it is when you bring those together, there you can create magic. Many a times it is observed that supers, intellect and technical talents alone do not make people great performer. It is the social skill which lubricates the mechanisms of positive relationship network at workplace. Intellectual understanding is a threshold process, necessary for learning, but not sufficient for lasting improvement. Deep change requires the retooling of ingrained habits of thoughts, feeling and behaviour.

There is a crucial difference between declarative knowledge, knowing a concept and its technical details, and procedural knowledge, being able to put those concepts and details into action. Knowing does not equal doing, whether in playing the Piano, or managing a team. Intellectual understanding of a skill or competence may be necessary but it is not sufficient in itself to result in behaviour change. Skills can be seen as coordinated bundle of habits, what we think, feel, assume and do to get a job done. When such habits, feelings, assumptions are dysfunctional; replacing it with a more effective one requires enough learning, understanding and practice to make it better and acceptable.

The set of skills/competencies, well suited to develop personal abilities are listed here for your study and examination. These skills are helpful in developing your personality at work. You can master these skills for successful career planning, if they rightly learnt and practised. As Daniel Goleman in his book "Working with Emotional Intelligence", has rightly pointed out that there are some elements of emotional intelligence that are so basic as to constitute "meta-abilities", which are essential for most other competencies. These basics include self-awareness, self-regulation, motivation, empathy and social skills. These primary capabilities are essential for supporting the emotional competencies that flow from them. For instance, a manager who tries to shift his leadership style may also need to improve in self-awareness in order to make the other change. Following are such of the skills that are essential to build your abilities at work.

SKILLS KIT

(1) Emotional Awareness:

(Recognising one's emotions and their effects.)

The recognition of how our emotions affect our performance, and the ability to use our values to guide decision-making.

People with this skill:

- ❖ Know which emotions they are feeling and why.
- ❖ Realise the links between their feelings and what they think, do, and say.
- ❖ Recognise how their feelings affect their performance.
- ❖ Have a guiding awareness of their values and goals.

Such awareness is our guide in fine-tuning on the job performance of every kind. Managing our untruly feeling, keeping ourselves motivated, tuning in with accuracy to the feelings of those around us, and developing good work related social skills including those essential for leadership and teamwork. It is a focusing ability, knowing the internal meters and subtle signals that tell you what you are feeling and using them as an ongoing guide to how you are doing. A person excelling in this skill is aware of his emotions at any given moment often recognising how those emotions feel physically. He can articulate those feelings, as well as demonstrate social appropriateness in expressing them.

(2) Accurate Self-assessment:

(Knowing one's inner resources, abilities and limits.)

A candid sense of our personal strength and limits, a clear vision of where we need to improve, and the ability to learn from experience.

People with this skill are:

- ❖ Aware of their strengths and weaknesses.
- ❖ Reflects learning from experience.
- ❖ Open to candid feedback, new perspective, continuous learning and self-development.
- ❖ Able to show a sense of humour and perspective about themselves.

Before you can lead others, before you can help others, you have to discover yourself. If you want creativity to take place, if you want the kind of performance that leads to truly exceptional results, you have to be willing to embark on a journey that leads to an alignment between an individual's personal value and aspirations and the values and aspirations of the company. Accuracy in self-assessment is a hallmark of superior performance. It is not that star performers have no limits on their abilities, but they are aware of their limits and so they know where they need to improve or they know to work with someone else who has a strength they lack. Superior performer intentionally seek out feedback; they want to hear how others perceive them, realising that this is valuable information. They may be part of the reason people who are self-aware are also better performers. Presumably their self-awareness and self-assessment help them in a process of continuous improvement. Knowing their strengths and weaknesses and approaching their work accordingly is the skill they possess.

(3) Self-confidence:

(A strong sense of one's self-worth and capabilities.)

The courage that comes from certainty about our capabilities, values and goals.

People with this skill are:

- Present themselves with self-assurance have 'presence'.
- Can voice views that are unpopular and go out on a limb for what is right.
- Are decisive, able to make sound decisions, despite, uncertainties and pressures.

Self-confidence gives us the requisite self-assurance for plunging ahead or stepping in as a leader. Self-confidence can reveal itself in a strong self-presentation, a projection of presence: people with self-confidence typically see themselves as efficacious, able to take on challenges and to master new jobs or skills. They believe themselves to be catalysts, movers and initiators and feel that their abilities start up favourably in comparison to others. Self-confidence gives the strength to make a tough decision or follow a course of action one believes in despite opposition, disagreement or even explicit disapproval from those in authority.

(4) Self-control:

(Keeping disruptive emotions and Iimpulses in check.)

Managing disruptive emotions and impulsive effectively is a skill.

People with this skill are:

- Manage their impulsive feelings and distressing emotions well.
- Stay composed, positive and unflappable even in trying moments.
- Think clearly and stay focused under pressure.

People with this skill are optimistic, action-oriented people. If something goes wrong in their lives; they immediately start to think about how to make it better. This skill is in a sense largely invisible. Self-control manifests largely in the absence of more obvious emotional fireworks. Signs include being unfazed under stress or handling a hostile person without lashing out in return. Hence, the ultimate act of personal responsibility at work may be in taking control of our own state of mind. Moods exert a powerful pull on thought, memory and perception. When we are angry, we more readily remember incidents that support our ire, anger, irritability. Resisting this despotic quality of moods in essential to our ability to work productively.

(5) Trustworthiness and Conscientiousness:

(Maintaining integrity and taking responsibility for personal performance.)

Credibility stems from integrity, stars know that trustworthiness at work translate into letting people know one's values and principles, intentions and feelings and acting in ways that are reliably consistent with them. They are forthright about their own mistakes, confronts others about their lapses.

People with this skill are:

For Trustworthiness

- Act ethically and are above reproach.
- Build trust through their reliability and authenticity.
- Admit their own mistakes and confront unethical actions in others.
- Take tough principled stands even if they are unpopular.

For Conscientiousness

- Meet commitments and keep promises.
- Hold themselves accountable for meeting their objectives.
- Are organised and careful in their work.

Integrity acting openly, honestly and consistently set outstanding performers in jobs of every kind. People with integrity are frank. They are clear-cut in their thinking and doing. So, being trustworthy is all the more important. You will be more successful if you stay in alignment with your personal values.

Conscientiousness is a taproot of success in any field. The everyday signs of conscientiousness are being punctual, careful in doing work, self-disciplined and scrupulous in attending to responsibilities are hallmarks of the model citizen, the people who keep things running as they should. They follow the rules, help out, and are concerned about the people they work with.

(6) Innovation and Adaptability:

Being open to novel ideas and approaches and being flexible in responding to change.

People with this skill are:

For Innovation:

- Seek out fresh ideas from a wide variety of sources.
- Entertain original solutions to problems.
- Generate new ideas.
- Take fresh perspectives and risks in their thinking.

For Adaptability

- Smoothly handle multiple demands shifting priorities and rapid changes.
- Adapt their responses and tactics to fit fluid circumstances.
- Are flexible in how they see events.

Creativity on the job revolves around applying new ideas to achieve results. People who have this skill can quickly identify key issues and simplify problems that seem overwhelmingly complex. The emotional foundation of the innovator at work is taking pleasure in originality. Risk taking and the drive to pursue innovative ideas are the fuel that stokes the entrepreneurial spirit of such people.

(7) Achievement Drive:

(Striving to improve or meet a standard of excellence.)

People with this skill are:

- Are result-oriented with a high drive to meet their objectives and standards.
- Set challenging goals and take calculated risks.
- Pursue information to reduce uncertainty and find way to do better.
- Learn how to improve their performance.

Such people talk about and take more calculated risks; they urge and support enterprising innovations and set challenging goals to achieve, and they throw their support behind others entrepreneurial ideas. The need to achieve is the single strongest competence that sets apart these people from average people. They are driven by the need to achieve, seek ways to track their success.

(8) Commitment:

(Aligning with the goals of a group/organisation.)

People with this skill are:

- Readily make sacrifices to meet larger organisational goals.
- Find a sense of purpose in the larger mission.

- ❖ Use the group's core values in making decisions and clarifying choices.
- ❖ Actively seek out opportunities to fulfil the group's mission.

The essence of commitment is making our goal and those of the organisation one and the same. For them commitment is an emotional issue. They feel a strong attachment to their group's goals when they resonate strongly with their own. They value and embrace an organisation mission are willing not just to make an all-out effort on its behalf; but to make personal sacrifices when needed.

Self-awareness is a building block of commitment. People who know their own guiding values or purpose will have clear, even vivid sense about whether there is a 'fit' with an organisation. When they feel match, their commitment is spontaneous and strong. Their organisational commitment grows from such emotional bonding.

(9) Initiative and Optimism:

(Displaying productivity and persistence.)

People with this skill are:

For Initiative:

- ❖ Are ready to size opportunities.
- ❖ Pursue goals beyond what is required or expected of them.
- ❖ Cut through red tape and bend the rules when necessary to get the job done.
- ❖ Mobilise others through unusual enterprising efforts.

For Optimism:

- ❖ Persist in seeking goals despite goals despite obstacles and set backs.
- ❖ Operate from hope of success rather than fear of failure.
- ❖ See setbacks as due to manageable circumstances rather than a personal flaw.

These people often take anticipatory action to avoid problems before they happen or taking advantage of opportunities before they are visible to anyone else. Possessing this farsightedness may mean taking steps when no one else sees the need to. These people act before being forced to by external events. While initiative is generally laudable, it needs to be balanced with social awareness in order to avoid unintended negative consequences.

Optimism can more readily make a realistic assessment of a setback and admit how they contribute to it. The nearness of optimism is hope knowing the steps needed to get to a goal and having the energy to pursue those steps. It is a primal motivating force for optimism. In some jobs, where stress is high and frustrations common a rosy look may get better results. Hopefulness is crucial when anyone undertakes a tough task. Positive expectations may be especially beneficial in the toughest jobs, where high optimism may be a pragmatic job category.

(10) Understanding Others:

(Sensing others feelings and perspectives and taking an active interest in their concerns.)

People with this skill are:

- ❖ Are attentive to emotional cues and listen well.
- ❖ Show sensitivity and understand others perspectives.
- ❖ Help out based on understanding other people's needs and feelings.

Empathy is essential as an emotional guidance system, piloting us in getting along at work. Beyond mere survival, empathy is critical for superior performance wherever the job focus is on people. Understanding some ones point of view or perspective knowing why they feel as they do – does not inevitably mean embracing it. Particularly in business dealings understanding how someone feels need not lead to giving in but to more skilful negotiation and management. As a result, tough decisions may generate less resentment and lasting it will. People with this competence are trusting people who believe that people are basically good tend to be more highly attuned to feelings.

A finely tuned ear is at the heart of empathy. Listing well is essential for workplace success. Listening well and deeply means going beyond what is said by asking questions, restating in ones words what you hear to be sure you understand. This is 'active' listening. A mark of having truly heard someone is to respond appropriately, even if that means making some change in what you do. Empathetic people cared about other people, their needs and concerns. This is especially true if the empathy go hand-in-hand with the sense that the other people could be trusted.

(11) Developing Others:

(Sensing others development needs and bolstering their abilities.)

People with this skill are:

- ❖ Acknowledge and reward people's strengths and accomplishment.
- ❖ Offer useful feedback and identity people's needs for further growth.
- ❖ Mentor, give timely coaching and offer assignments that challenge and foster a person's skills.

The simple bit of advice exemplifies coaching, which lies at the heart of developing others. The heart of coaching and developing is the act of counselling. And the effectiveness of counselling hinges on empathy and the ability to focus on our own feelings and shared them. Strong coaching and mentoring help employees perform better, enhances loyalty and job satisfaction. An open trusting relationship is the foundation of success in on the job coaching. The best coaches show a genuine personal interest in those they guide and have empathy for and an understanding of their people. Coaches who show respect, trustworthiness and empathy are the best coaches.

(12) Service Orientation:

(Anticipating, recognising and meeting customer's needs.)

People with this skill are:

- Understand customers need and match them to services or products.
- Seek ways to increase customer's satisfaction and loyalty.
- Gladly offer appropriate assistance.
- Grasp a customer's perspective acting as a trusted advisor.

The key to service orientation success lies in the customer services. First of all to make feel good and make everyone comfortable. Superlative service entails being a trusted advisor. This kind of trust based relationship grows overtime. To shine at service we need to monitor the satisfaction of customers, not waiting to hear complaints but freely offering information on that might be helpful without self-interest motivating to gesture. This lays the ground work for trusting relationships. As advocated by P. Drucker, the purpose of business is not to make sale, but to make and keep a customer.

(13) Leveraging Diversity:

(Cultivating opportunities through different kinds of people.)

People with this skill are:

- Respect and relate well to people from varied backgrounds.
- Understand diverse world views and are sensitive to group differences.
- See diversity as opportunity, creating an environment where diverse people can thrive.
- Challenge bias and intolerance.

Success through others who are different from yourself, there is strength of difference, and this makes the ability to leverage diversity an increasingly crucial competence. Variety of people working in organisation of every kind demands a greater awareness of the subtle distortion that stereotypes and bias bring to working relationship. You being able to read people accurately, without distortions of emotionally laden stereotypes, sets superior performers apart from average. Beyond zero tolerance for intolerance, the ability to leverage diversity revolves around three skills; getting along well with people who are different; appreciating the unique ways others may operate; and seizing whatever business opportunity these unique approaches might offer. When leaders of organisations value the insights brought to work by people of diverse background; it can lead to organisational learning that boost competitiveness. Learn, and change and so do better by leveraging diversity.

(14) Political Awareness:

(Reading social and political currents.)

People with this skill are:

- ❖ Accurately read key power relationship.
- ❖ Detect crucial social networks.
- ❖ Understand the forces that shape views and actions of clients, customers or competitors.
- ❖ Accurately read organisational and external realities.

The ability to read political realities is vital to the behind the scene networking and coalition building that allows someone to wield influence no matter what their professional role. Mediocre performer lacks such social acumen and so betrays a distressingly low level of political savvy. Skill at reading the currents that influence the real decision-makrs depends on the ability to empathies on an organisational level, not just inter-personal one. People who maintain rich personal networks in an organisation typically are savvy about what is going on, and this social intelligence extends to understanding the larger realities that affect the organisation.

(15) The Art of Influence:

(Wielding effective tactics for persuasion.)

The art of influence entails handling emotions effectively in other people. Star performers are artful communicators, able to sway an audience. The emotional exchange constitutes an invisible inter-personal economy. Part of every human interaction, but it is usually too subtle to notice. Emotions are attention grabbers; operating as warnings, invitations, alarms, and the like these are powerful messages, conveying critical information without necessarily putting that data into words. Emotions are a hyper efficient mode of communication. Emotion is the sum total of the exchanges of feeling among us. In subtle ways, we all make each other feel a bit better or work as part of any contact we have. Social skill is essential in handling another person's emotion artfully, underlie several competencies. These include: influence-wielding effective tactics of persuasion; communication-sending clear and convincing messages; conflict management-negotiating and resolving disagreements; leadership-inspiring and guiding; change catalyst-initiating, promoting or managing change.

Empathy is crucial for wielding influence. The first step in influence is building rapport. Charm and social polish in themselves do not add up to competence at influence. True influence exhibits in the true competence in harmonising with the collective goal. In the world of work, no matter the business at hand, emotional element plays a crucial role. Emotional competence requires being able to pilot through the emotional under currents always at play rather than being pulled under by the people.

(16) Communication:

(Listening openly and sending convincing messages.)

People with this skill are:

- ❖ Are effective in give and take, registering emotional cues in attuning their message.
- ❖ Deal with difficult issues straightforwardly.
- ❖ Listen well seek mutual understanding and welcome sharing of information fully.
- ❖ Foster open communication and stay receptive to bad news as well as good.

Being an adapt communicator is the keystone of all social skills. Communication competence strongly distinguishes star performers from average or poor ones. Listening well the key to empathy is also crucial to competence in communicating. Listening skills asking astute questions, being open-minded and understanding, seeking suggestions are the skills of effective communicator.

(17) Conflict management:

(Negotiating and resolving disagreements.)

People with this skill are:

- ❖ Handle difficult people and tense situations with diplomacy and tact.
- ❖ Spot potential conflict brings disagreements into the open and helps deescalate.
- ❖ Encourage debate and open discussion.
- ❖ Orchestrate win-win solutions.

One talent of those skilled of conflict resolution is spotting trouble as it is brewing and taking steps to calm those involved. The arts of listening and empathising are crucial for handling conflict management. The ability to read the feelings of the opposition during a negotiation is critical to success. Those who have mastered the art of the deal realise the emotionally charge nature of any negotiation. The best negotiators can sense which points matter most to the other party and gracefully concede there, while pressing for concessions in points that do not carry such emotional weight and that takes empathy. Skill at negotiation obviously matters for excellence in professions like law and diplomacy. Conflict resolution requires that each side be able to understand not just the others point of view, but their needs and fears. This empathy, makes each side better able to influence the other to their benefit, by being responsive to the others needs. In other words, to find ways in which both parties win.

(18) Leadership:

(Inspiring and guiding individuals and groups.)

People with this skill are:

- ❖ Articulate and arouse enthusiasm for a shared vision and mission.
- ❖ Step forward to lead as needed, regardless of position.
- ❖ Guide the performance of others while holding them accountable.
- ❖ Lead by example.

In general emotional charisma depends on three factors: feeling strong emotions, being able to express those emotions forcefully, and being an emotional sender rather than a receiver. Highly expressive people communicate through their facial expression, their voice, their gestures, and their whole body. This ability allows them to move, inspire and captivate others. The ability to convey emotion convincingly, from the heart requires that a leader be sincere about the message being delivered; truly believing the emotional message is what separates the charismatic leader from the self-serving one. To be a charismatic messenger, the leader must act from authentic belief. Leadership entails exciting imagination and inspiring them to move in a desired direction.

It takes more than simple power to motivate and lead. The superior leaders managed to balance a people-oriented personal style with a decisive command role. They did not hesitate to take charge, to be purposeful, assertive and business like. The most effective leaders are more positive and outgoing, more emotionally expressive and dramatic, warmer and more sociable, more democratic, more cooperative, more likable and 'fun to be with', more appreciative and trustful and even gentler than those who were merely average.

(19) Change Catalyst:

(Initiating or managing change.)

People with this skill are:

- ❖ Recognise the need for change and remove barriers.
- ❖ Challenge the *status quo* to acknowledge the need for change.
- ❖ Champion the change and enlist others in its pursuit.
- ❖ Model the change expected of others.

Beyond technical expertise, the change catalyst needs other skills like high level of self-confidence, effective leadership, influence, commitment, initiative and optimism. When you work with a company to help them transform their business, the personal abilities of the leader of their team count immensely. You need someone who takes this change as a mission, not just a job. Transformational leaders go beyond management and as usual such leaders are able to rouse people through the sheer power of their own enthusiasm. Such leaders don't order or direct; they inspire others. And they are committed to nurturing relationships with those they lead. The successful leaders are rated by people who worked for them as highly charismatic and flexible. They seemed to spread their own sense of confidence and competence, and they inspired people to be more imaginative, adaptive and innovative. Leadership of this kind, then is an emotional craft they develop through skills and competence.

(20) Building Bonds:

(Nurturing instrumental relationship.)

People with this skill are:

- ❖ Evaluate and maintain extensive informal networks.
- ❖ Seek out relationships that are mutually beneficial.
- ❖ Build rapport and keep others in the loop.
- ❖ Make and maintain personal friendships among works and associate.

One of the virtues of building relationships is the reservoir of goodwill and trust that arises. Highly effective people are adept at cultivating such relationships. These human links are the routes through which people come to be known for their abilities and skills. Rapport building is central to developing strong, useful relationship. Rapport hinges on empathy and typically emerges naturally in the course of casual conversation about family, sport, children, and the stuff of life. Finally, the building of a close work relationship means establishing an alliance, a relationship that can be counted on. The people we get along with trust, feel simpatico with, are the strongest links in social relationship networks. Web like connectivity is the secret of success in many organisations where people spend their career in a single organisation with high-intensity relationships. Networks of personal contacts are the kind of personal capital.

(21) Collaboration and Cooperation:

(Working with others toward shared goals.)

People with this skill are:

- ❖ Balance a focus on task with attention to relationships.
- ❖ Collaborate, sharing plans, information and resources.
- ❖ Promote a friendly cooperative climate.
- ❖ Spot and nurture opportunities for collaboration.

Building collaborative and fruitful relationships begins with healthy relationship at work. Our relationships with co-workers have a parallel emotional component, something akin to the pleasures, jealousies, etc. This inter-dependence ties together in a way that can become highly charged. If superior and subordinate do well emotionally, if they form a relationship of trust, rapport, understanding and inspired effort, their performance will shine at work. But if things go emotionally awry, the relationship can become a nightmare and their performance shall be a series of minor or major disasters at work.

(22) Team Capabilities:

(Creating group synergy in pursuing collective goals.)

People with this skill are:

- ❖ Model team qualities like respect, helpfulness and cooperation.
- ❖ Draw all members into active and enthusiastic participation.
- ❖ Build team identity, esprit de crops and commitment.
- ❖ Protect the group and its reputation, share credit.

People in teams tend to share common understandings. They are competitive and even handed in matching members to the best role for their talents. They have strong anticipative need, they like people for their own sake, which makes them more harmonious, better able to handle conflicts and offer mutual support. They share a commitment to the group goal. The best team leaders are able to get everyone to buy into a common sense of mission, goals and agenda. The ability to articulate a compelling vision that senses as the guiding force for the group may be the single most important contribution of a good team leader. The competencies of star teams are: empathy or inter-personal understanding, cooperation and unified effort, open communication, setting explicit norms and expectations and confronting underperforming team-members, a drive to improve, so that the team paid attention to performance feedback and sought to learn to do better; self-awareness in the form of evaluating their strengths and weakness as a team, initiative and taking a proactive stance toward solving problems, self-confidence as a team, flexibility in how they went about their collective tasks, building bonds to other teams.

Such competencies/skills let teams work better on problem-solving, decision-making, negotiation and agreement with others. The organisations of all kinds have come to the realisation that the success of people's talent can be orchestrated in a team that cut a cross traditional boundaries for improving business processes, products and troubleshooting.

Learning, practising and presenting there skills at work make you champion of the masses. It is important to realise that there are no great people. There are just ordinary people with great ideas and great courage to learn. We must have the great courage to change our philosophy, our beliefs, assumptions, perceptions, attitude and behaviour. We have to retool our ways of communicating our beliefs in ourselves, people and organisations.

The primary reason, therefore, some people are great champions because they have bon-dip commitment and passion for learning new things and practicing it and thus created their own 'personality brand image' as great persons. Their developments in knowledge, conduct personality are all the creation of coherent mental constructs to represent the surrounding environment has resulted from the interplay between the challenge of complexity and the urge to master it. They reduce complexity first by attempting to simplify realty and then absorb complexity by differentiating restructuring and improving their means to cope with it. They followed innovative learning path. Through such learning they developed the capacity to face new situation of growing complexity of modern world.

Innovative learning involves both anticipation and participation. Participation involves more than the formal sharing of decision, suggestions, guidelines, it is an attitude characterised by cooperation, dialogue and empathy. It means not keeping communications open but also constantly testing your operating rules and values against those of others. Without participation, anticipation becomes futile, and participation without anticipation can be misguided. Cultivating understanding in isolation can lead to reliance on self-defeating, quickly obsolescent and ignoring the context of others, usually run danger of narrow-mindedness and false sense of security. Whereas, anticipation encourages solidarity in time, participation creates solidarity in space.

Therefore your relationships will need to be fashioned and refashioned as a part of the dynamism of social processes like inquiry and dialogue that mediate learning. Such relationships are more intricate because their character derives from specifies of the situation that are always both pragmatic and psychological. Pragmatic takes to get work done best and psychological, what people need to sustain their motivation and commitment. The caring relationship, the interviewing of thought, feeling and action becomes a pre-condition for learning. This type of mental make-up will help change mediocre man into star performer.

10.4 EMOTIONAL INTELLIGENCE

Why Emotional Intelligence? – It is because business culture changes so do the personal traits needed to excel.

The organisations are shrinking through wave of downsizing, VRS or rightsizing or economy recession. People who remained there are more accountable and more visible for getting things done effectively and timely. Earlier they might have easily hide a hot temper or shyness. They might have used fault finding with others than fact finding. Till then it was within tolerance limit of organisations. But now a day's individual competencies such as managing one's emotions, handling encounters well, teamwork and leadership count more than ever to manage desired results.

The globalisation of the workforce demands new kind of productivity norms. For these technical skills, technological advances alone are not enough and they must be supported with other social and soft skills and personal fit to fight back new problems that cry out, for even greater intelligence. Team-building and adopting to change are entirely new capabilities have began to appear as traits of star performers and therefore, these new challenges demand new talents with emotional intelligence. Companies are waking up to the fact that even the most expensive training can go futile and often do. And this ineptness comes at a time when emotional intelligence in individuals and organisation is emerging as missing ingredient in the recipe for competitiveness. Thus, more and more companies are seeking that encouraging emotional intelligence skills is a vital component of any company's philosophy. You don't compete with products/services alone any more, but how well you use your people can establish edge over competition.

With these felt needs the rules for work are fast changing. People are being judged by new standards, not by how smart you are, by your training and expertise but also by how well you handle yourself and others. These standards are increasingly applied in choosing who will be hired and who will not; who will be let go and who retained; and who passed over and who promoted. The new rules of business management predict who is most likely to become a star performer and who is solid citizen, question mark employees? Organisation measures employee's personal traits, soft skills that are crucial to marketability for future business or services. The new standards take for granted having enough intellectual ability and technical knowledge to do the jobs; it focuses instead on personal qualities: initiative, empathy, adaptability and persuasiveness. If you are part of a management team, you need to consider whether your organisation fosters these competencies or discourages them.

WHAT IS EMOTIONAL INTELLIGENCE?

It is nothing but creating personal excellence at work.

In today's world of work job security is eroded, where the very concept of job is rapidly being replaced by "Portable skills" – character, personality traits, potentials, soft skills competence all are now named as emotional intelligence. E.I. refers to the capacity for recognising our own feelings and those of others for motivating ourselves and for managing emotions well in ourselves and in our relationship: Psychologist Peter Shalvey and John Mayer of University of New Hampshire defined E. I. in terms of being able to monitor and regulate one's own and others feelings and to use feelings to guide thoughts and action. They developed five basic emotional and social competencies of self-awareness, motivation, self-regulations, empathy and adeptness of life and learn from the experiences – our competence in it can keep growing.

In olden days employees of meritocracy who were taught education and technical skills, supposed to be the permanent ticket holders of success. But today people began to realise that success takes more than intellectual excellence or technical prowess and that we need another sort of skills just to survive and certainly to thrive in the increasingly turbulent job market of the future. Internal qualities such as resilience, initiative, optimism and adaptability are taking on a new valuation. A common core of personal and social abilities has proven to be the key ingredient in people's success: E.I. It is the E.I. abilities that matter more for superior performance. Sometimes out of controlled emotions can make smart people stupid. The aptitudes you need to succeed start with intellectual horsepower but people need emotional competence too, to get the full potential of their talents.

An emotional competence is a learned capability based on emotional intelligence that results in outstanding performance at work. E.I determines our potential for learning the practical skills of self-awareness, motivation, etc. Thus, our emotional competence shows how much of the potential we have translated into capabilities. For instance, being good at servicing is an emotional competence based on empathy. Likewise trustworthiness is a competence based on self-regulations or handling impulses and emotional well. Both customer service and trustworthiness are competencies that can make people outstanding in their work.

Each company has its own emotional ecology and the most adaptive traits for employee will differ accordingly. Company has styles like people. If they have been arrogant or duplications to their vendors, employees or customers, these karmic debts can comeback to haunt them. Beyond professional qualification the person needs personal qualities and competencies that would mesh with the unique environment of performance. Hence, you need to be able to work in a team, make decisions by consensus, cooperate. You can't be a prima-doma. E.I can be an inoculation that preserves health and encourages growth. If a company has the competencies that flow from self-awareness, self-regulation, motivation, empathy, leadership skills and open communication, it would prove more resilient no matter what the future brings. And that in turn, places a premium on people who themselves are emotionally intelligent.

To be sure E.I. is no magic bullet, no guarantee of more market share or healthier bottom line. The ecology of a company is extra ordinary fluid and complex and no single intervention or change can fix every problem. It is all done with people and if this human ingredient is ignored, then nothing else will work. Companies in which people collaborate best will have a competitive edge and so to that extent E.I. will be more vital.

COMPETENCIES

EMOTIONAL COMPETENCIES:

Our emotional intelligence is a base for learning, developing and practicing our emotional competencies, skills, traits and potentials. The competencies one need for success may change as one rise through the ranks of management hierarchies. Following are some of the competencies we developed from our emotional intelligence:

1. Personal Competence:

Self-awareness knowing one's internal states, preference resources and intuitions:

(a) Emotional awareness – recognising one's emotions and their effect.

(b) Self-assessment – knowing one's strengths and limits.

(c) Self-confidence – A strong sense of one's self-worth and capabilities.

2. Self-regulations:

Managing one's internal states, impulses and resources:

(a) Self-control – keeping disruptive emotions and impulses in check.

(b) Trustworthiness – maintaining std. of honesty and integrity.

(c) Conscientiousness – taking responsibility for personal performance.

(d) Adaptability – flexibility in handling change.

(e) Innovation – being comfortable with novel ideas, approaches and new information.

3. Motivation:

Emotional tendencies that guide or facilitate reaching goals:

(a) Achievement drive – striving to improve or meet a std. of excellence.

(b) Commitment – aligning with the goals of the group or organisation.

(c) Initiative – readiness to act on opportunities.

(d) Optimism – persistence in pursuing goals despite obstacle and setbacks.

4. Social Competence:

These competences determine how we handle relationship.

5. Empathy:

Awareness of others feelings, needs and concerns understanding others, developing others, service orientation, political awareness are the competencies under this.

6. Social Skills:

Adeptness at inducing responses in others influence communication, conflict management, leadership, change catalyst, building bonds of relationship collaborations and cooperation – working with others towards shared goals, team capabilities, creating group synergy in pursuing collective goals, etc.

These competences are employee's abilities to listen, to influence, to collaborate and to get people motivated and to work together well. In today's workplace, with its emphasis on flexibility, teams and a strong customer orientation: this crucial set of emotional competencies is becoming increasingly essential for excellence in every job.

EQ AND IQ COMPARISONS

Definition – EQ:

Understanding your own emotions and those of others, and being able to use this information to bring about the best outcome for all concerned. Knowing where emotions come from and being able to manage your own and those of others. Knowing what emotions mean and what information they are providing. Being able to work with others as well as alone. Being able to combine cognitive knowledge with emotional knowledge and use them in tandem.

Definition – IQ: Cognitive Intelligence –

Intellectual abilities such as logic, reasoning, reading, writing, analysing and prioritising. These go on in your own head and utilise only the neocortex, not the emotional centre of the brain which also provides crucial information. These abilities do not require any social/soft skills. *Per se,* i.e., you can solve a math equation by yourself, or write an essay, or balance a business books by yourself.

COMPARISONS:

Sr. No.	EQ	IQ
1	Being effective both alone and as a team player.	Only effective when working alone.
2	Being able to manage your own emotions	Having temper tantrums, sulking or withdrawing.
3	Being able to empathise with others and knowing where they are coming from.	Not being able to grasp the feelings of others and understand how the emotions are affecting the situation.
4	Knowing that motivation is a feeling word.	Thinking that motivation is a thinking word.

Example:

Vasant was brilliant in his field and the best IT person in the office as to technical skills, but his people skills were very low. He was abrasive, arrogant, short tempered and a perfectionist. Other people did not like to work with him and he was unable to explain things in terms other people could understand.

Vasanti, who was also in IT department, had good intellectual skills and a good education, though it was less than Vasant. However, her emotional intelligence more than made up for this. She was able to handle herself and other people well and to explain things calmly and clearly. People loved to work with her and requested her by name. She received promotion after promotion because of her technical expertise and high emotional intelligence.

Key Point:

Many people with very high IQs (Cognitive Intelligence) do poorly in work and relationships because they have low EQs (Emotional Intelligence). They sabotage themselves because they can't manage their own emotions or those of other people, and they sabotage projects because they may have all the logical, rational and analytical answers, but they do not have the soft skills to move a project forward.

Benefits:

Emotional intelligence accounts for more success and happiness in life than intellectual intelligence. Learn to develop your emotional intelligence as well as you skills and technical expertise and you will do better in your career. Developing your emotional intelligence is also crucial for personal, professional and family relationships. When you recognise the difference between EQ and IQ, you can work to develop your EQ. It can be learned continuously (Source IQ EQ net by Admin).

10.5 LEARNING ORGANISATON

Surprisingly many organisations do not encourage the growth of their people. This result in vast untapped resources. People enter in business/employment as bright, well educated, high-energy people, full of desire to make difference. By the time they turn 30 years the few are on the fast track and rest put in their time to do what matters to them. They lose their commitment, the sense of mission and the excitement when they started their career. Organisations get down little of their energy and almost none of their spirit. This is the general experience of people in such organisation. It is simply a sign of poor turnover of the organisations economy.

Many organisations learn poorly, the way they are designed, structured and managed, the way peoples job are defined and most importantly the way they have been taught to think and interact with each other, customer-suppliers create fundamental learning disabilities. These disabilities operate despite the best efforts of brighter, committed people often the harden they try to solve problems, the worse the result. Organisational break down despite the individual brilliance and innovative products because they are unable to pull their diverse functions and talents into a productive whole. It is, therefore, essential to rediscover about the collective culture of manager and managed and discover new ideas about how to abandon old ideas and how to tap people's commitment, potential and capacity to learn at every level in the company. Business is the only institution that has chance to fundamentally improve the injustice that exists. But leaders have to move through businesses that are keeping them from being truly vision-led and capable of learning. Perhaps the most salient reason for building learning organisations is that we now starting to understand the capabilities.

WHAT IS LEARNING ORGANISATION?

Managers at all levels in an organisation determined to improve its performance and of individual employed in, appreciate their role into fullest sense. They are prepared to contribute to and enable the learning of their colleagues, staff and are fully aware of the benefits accrued from the investment. In this way, the process of establishing a learning organisation starts. Learning organisation is an organisation, which facilitates the learning of all its members and continually transforms itself for continuous organisational improvement. Learning organisation is a place where people are continually discovering how they create their reality and how they can change it. Learning organisation is a place where people continually expand their capacity to create results they truly desire, where new and expansive patterns of thinking are nurtured, where collective aspiration is set free and people are continually learning how to learn together. Learning dose not means acquiring more information, but expanding the ability to produce the results we truly want in our worklife. It is lifelong, generative learning and learning organisation is not possible unless they have people at every level who practise it.

According to Peddler, learning organisation is one which:

- Has a climate in which individual members are encouraged to develop their potential.
- Extend the learning culture to include customers, suppliers and other stakeholders.
- Make human resource development strategy central to business plan policy.
- Is in a continuous process of organisational transformation.

Learning organisation help people think and act together to create the conditions such as:

Learning strategy, participative policy-making inter-co-learning, self-development, internal exchange, enabling structures, control systems, cost systems to empower people to ask questions and take decision based on available data.

THE SPIRIT OF LEARNING ORGANISATION

Organisation learns only through individuals. Without their learning, no organisational learning occurs in corporate offices or manufacturing facilities.

In many aspect of business the active force is "People" they have their will, their own mind, their own way of thinking. If they are not sufficiently motivated to challenge the goals of growth, Development – there will be simply no growth in productivity, quality and no technological development.

Tapping the potential of people, organisation requires new understanding, willpower and action of the heart and sincerity to serve business world.

Manager duty starts with providing for both the material goods and welfare of his employees. His fundamental task is to provide enabling organisational life.

WHY TO BECOME LEARNING ORGANISATION

Organisations are being constantly told that they need to be flexible and make full use of their available resources if they have to survive and prosper. Recession, business down turn have been experienced by organisations, Different solutions are needed to deal with unprecedented business problems. Thus, organisations are being compelled as well as encouraged to look at new ways of working and to take calculated risks. Secondly, most organisations are finding that the skills needed to make significant changes are not readily available. Hence, the need to upgrade existing human resources, reskilled them and retain them, so that organisations are encourage to ensure employees are systematically trained and developed in line with business objectives, quality systems and soft skills. Therefore, for our survival – individually or as companies, we must create a tradition of learning organisation. Organisational learning is not only investing in training, development and learning activity. It is not enough to enable an organisation to become a learning organisation. The need for the development of individual skills *vis-a-vis* organisation must be embedded in the concept, culture, commitment of the organisation.

Obviously, organisational learning is not simply the sum of each employees learning. It builds widespread understandings of both internal and external circumstances through activities and systems that do not depend on particular member. It is not just about rearranging or redesigning the elements of organisation. Rather it is a form of meta-learning that requires the rethinking of patterns that connect and relate the pieces of an organisation and also relates the patterns to the relevant environment. Organisational learning is process that bundles several processes, e.g., attention, interpretation, search, discovery and invention, choice, influence and assessment. It embraces both cognitive elements, e.g., knowledge and insights which are shared by the organisational employees and repetitive organisational activities for routine actions and improvement. There is a legitimate and ongoing process for surfacing and examining organisational practices and their associated explanations. Thus, an organisation's skill is found in its accepted behaviour patterns and it is collective knowledge logged in its shared assumptions. The organisational attitude exists in the core values. If these are developed within individuals in an organisation, there is no reason why this cannot happen for an organisation as a whole. It might be difficult and may take longer time to achieve, but the existence of learning organisation shall be visible to people. "A learning company is one in which learning and working is synonymous." (Peddler)

It is seen that organisations do not organically develop into learning organisation, there are usually factors prompting their change. It has been found that as organisations grow, they lose their natural capacity to learn as company structures and individual thinking becomes rigid. When problems arise in the company the solutions that are proposed often turn out to be only short-term and reemerge in future. To remain competitive, many organisations have restructured, which has resulted in fewer people in the company. This means those who remain need to work more effectively. To create a competitive advantage, companies need to be able to learn faster than their competitors and also develop a customer responsive culture. Secondly, organisations need to maintain knowledge about new products, processes, practices, understand what is happening in the outside environment and produce creative solutions using knowledge and skills of all employed within the organisation. This requires cooperation between individual and groups, free and reliable communication and a culture of trust and togetherness. These needs can be met through embracing the tenants of the learning organisation.

HOW TO BECOME LEARNING ORGANISATION

"The top thinks and the local acts" (Management and employees) must now give way to integrated thinking and acting at all levels. Learning must be at the heart of the company's ability to adapt to a rapidly changing environment. It is the key to being able both to identify opportunities that others might not see and to exploit those opportunities rapidly and fully. Learning and change typically requires the ongoing questioning of an organisation's *status sqo* or *modus operandi.* Individuals throughout the organisation, not just at the top, must reflect on these processes. Michael Hammer and Steven, the consultants, say "Reflection entails awareness of self, of competitors, of customers". It means thinking without preconception. It means questioning cherished assumptions and replacing them with new approaches. It is only way in which a winning company can maintain its leadership position, by which a company with great assets can ensure that they continue to be well deployed.

Successful learning organisations create a proactive, creative approach to the unknown, solicit the involvement of employees at all levels and enable everyone to use their intelligence and apply their imagination. Higher level skills are required of everyone, not just those at the top. A learning environment involves organisation- wide-commitment to change, an action orientation, and applicable tools and methods. It must be viewed by everyone as a guiding philosophy and not simply as another change programme. A critical requirement of all learning organisations is that everyone supports a compelling purpose. Meaningful participation of employees, sharing of certain values is the core requirement to support the purpose of change. Inspiring and motivating people with a mission or purpose are necessary to learn and adapt to a rapidly changing, complex and interconnecting environment. Therefore, investing in employee's skills development right from the lowest level can help maintain the employees through difficult periods and equipments in readiness for the upturn when an organisation is moving forward making investments in the development of people can bring forth untold benefits for individuals and the whole company.

COMPETENT TECHNIQUES OF LEARNING ORGANISATION

Peter Senge, in his book *"The Fifth Discipline"* identified five new competent technologies.

SYSTEM THINKING (INTERCONNECTEDNESS):

Farmers plough their field, clean it, water it, select the season, sow the seed, weed out unwanted, manure it, wait and see and then harvest it and get his grain. All these events are distant in time and space and yet they are all connected with the same pattern. Each has an influence on the rest, an influence that is usually hidden from view. You can only understand the system of harvesting by completing the whole, not any individual part of the pattern.

Business and human beings therein are also systems. Business systems are conceptual framework, a body of knowledge and tools that are developed years together, to make the full pattern clearer and to help us see how to effect business changes. So to say, product is the focal point for organisation purpose and achievement. Quality in process is impossible without the right organisation. The right organisation is meaningless without proper leadership. Strong bottom-up commitment is the support pillar for the rest.

Each pillar depends upon the other four and if one is weak all are: This is a total system thinking of interconnectedness we experienced in our organisational life.

PERSONAL MASTERY (CONNECTEDNESS)

Mastery might suggest gaining dominance over people or things. But mastery can also mean a special level of proficiency. A master craftsman dose not dominates pottery or weaving. His skills allow the best pots or fabrics to emerge from the workshop. Similarly, personal mastery suggests a special level of proficiecy in every aspect of life, personal and professional. Personal mastery people have a special sense of purpose that lies behind their vision and goals. For them vision is a calling rather than simply a good idea. For them vision is a specific destination, a picture of desired future.

Leaders of learning organisation are deeply inquisitive, committed to continually seeing reality more and more accurately. They feel connected to others, they feel they are part of a larger creative process, which they can influence but not by unilateral control. They want the total development of their people, which is essential to achieve business goals of corporate excellence. They see a complete relationship, connectedness rest on a shared commitment to ideas, issues, and values to goals and management process. Personal mastery would be naive and foolish if leader in organisation lacks the capabilities of building shared vision and shared mental model to guide decision-making.

MENTAL MODELS (ATTITUDES)

Our many best ideas never get put into practice, brilliant strategies fail to translate into action, systematic insight never find their way into operating policies. Their new insights fail to get put into practice because they conflict with deeply held internal image, *status quo* thinking of how the world works. Images that limit us to familiar way of thinking and acting. That is why the discipline of managing mental model-surfacing, testing and improving our internal pictures of how the world works promises to be a major break through for building learning organisation. Mental model are deeply ingrained assumptions, generalisation, images or even picture that influence how we understand the world and how we take action. We are always not aware of our mental models or the effects they have on our business, beahviour and culture. That is why insight into new market, attention to customer care and service, development of human resources get missed. Company policies fail to get put into practice because they conflict with powerful, tacit mental models.

Mental models can be simple generalisations such as people are untrustworthy. Since this our mental model is active in our mind grasp most of the things based on our generalisation when we believe people are untrustworthy we act differently from the way we would if we believed they were trustworthy. Mental models are so powerful in effecting what we do? In past, because they affect what we see? Thus, our theories of mental models shape our perception is no less important. Carrot and stick approach to induce motivation and productivity of employees may sound to be good. The problem of this mental model lies not in whether it is right or wrong. But the problem with this model arise when the model is tacit, when it exist below the level of awareness, because management unawareness of their mental models, the model remain unexamined, the model remain unchanged. Unless we influence the mental model, image, the picture of reality held by critical decision-makers our scenarios would be like water on a stone.

In learning organisation the discipline of working with mental models starts with turning the mirror inward, learning to unearth our internal picture of as and the world to them to the surface and hold them rigorously to scrutiny. Mental models and focus on the openness needed to unearth shortcoming in our present ways of seeing the world.

Developing an organisation capacity to work with mental models involve both learning news skills and implementing institutional innovations that helps bring these skills into regular practice. The effectiveness of a leader is related to the continual improvement of the mental models. Leaders worth is measured by their contribution to others mental models.

The learning organisation systemises their ways to bring people together to develop the best possible metal models for facing any situation at hand. Decision by consensus, group planning, scenario planning are some of the positive mental models. We can see in learning organisation's behaviour.

SHARED VISION (COMMONALITY OF PURPOSE)

Shared vision is not an important idea such as freedom. It is rather a force of people's hearts, a force of impressive power. Ones it goes further, it is compelling enough to acquire the support of more people. People being to see it exists. When people truly share a vision they are connected, bound together by a common aspiration. The practice of shared vision involves the skills of unearthing "shared picture of the future". That fosters genuine commitment and enrolment rather than compliance. Shared vision thus create spark, the excitement that lift organisation out of mundane. In company a shared vision changes peoples relationship with company and each other. It is no longer their company, it becomes our company. Shared vision is the first step in allowing people who mistrust each other to begin to work together. It creates a common identity and in fact an organisation shared a sense of purpose. Vision and operating values establish the most basic level of commonality. You can't have a learning organisation without shared vision. Leaders with vision are cult heroes.

Shared vision is vital for learning organisation; it provides the focus and energy for learning. Generative learning occurs only when people are striving to accomplish something that matter deeply to them. Consequently, the IQ of the team can potentially be much greater than the IQ of the individuals.

TEAM LEARNING (ALIGNMENT)

The intelligence of the individuals in the team exceeds the intelligence of the individuals in the team and where teams develop extraordinary capacities for coordinated action. Where teams are truly learning not only they producing extraordinary result but the individuals members are growing more rapidly than could have occurred otherwise. This we know that teams can learn in sports, performing art, in science and in business too. The discipline of team learning starts with discussions, interaction and team-members suspend their assumptions, generalisations and enter into a genuine "thinking together". Thus, team learning is vital because teams, not individuals are the fundamental learning unit in organisations. This where "the rubber meets the road". Unless teams learn, organisation can't learn. When a teams became more aligned, as commonality of direction emerges and individuals energies get harmonised. Alignment is the necessary condition before empowering the individual, who in turn empower the whole team. Once the team starts learning, their insight gained is put into action, skills developed can propagate to other individuals.

The most successful organisation of the 21st Century will be called a learning organisation; the organisation that excels will be that, which discover how to tap their people commitment and capacity to learn at every level in the company.

10.6 WORK EXCELLENCE AND WORLD-CLASS COMPANIES

Changing or creating the culture within an organisation is formed by number of components like: behaviour based on people interactions, norms, values resulting from different work group, dominant values adopted by the organisation and overall climate of company. Culture in the organisation is defined as the beliefs which pervade the organisation about how business should behave and should be treated. Attempting to control performance through systems, procedures or techniques external to the individual is not an effective approach since it relies on controlling other. Individuals should be responsible for their own actions. When individuals are stimulated to commit themselves to a goal and where personal pride and self-esteem are at stake, then the level of motivation is at a peak. For most people the toughest critic and the hardest task master they confront is not the immediate boss, but themselves. So to say, excellence at work is thus user-driven. It can't be imposed from outside. That means ideas for improvement must come from those with knowledge and experience of the process activities and tasks, the process owner handles.

Excellence is not cost-cutting or productivity improvement device alone. It is more concerned with changing attitudes and skills so that the culture of organisation becomes one of the preventing failure – doing the right things, right the first time, every time and as per conformance to requirements will establish the culture of preventing failure. Obviously, then it is true that creating excellence in work and excellent organisation is collective responsibility lie with management, manager and managed in general and in particular lie with individuals/process owners. Managers are in control when their subordinates can exercise self-control. The only efficient way to tackle process, activity improvement is through teams, which allows individuals to grow. Of course, employees will not engaged continual improvement without commitment and an effective mechanism for capturing individual contributions. For any individual or team to succeed, team need to be facilitated through the stages of becoming AWARE, needing to ACCEPT, ADOPT and a ADAPT in order to ACT to achieve desired goals. In such circumstances problems are exposed to a greater diversity of knowledge, skill, and experience and are solved more efficiently.

Knowledge is very much like organic manure – if it is spread around it will fertilise and encourage growth, if it is kept closed in, it will eventually fester and rot. Teamwork throughout organisation is an essential component of organisational excellence as it builds trust, improves communication and develops inter-dependence. This enable people to feel, accept and discharge responsibility and accountability foster pride, job satisfaction and better work and people themselves expand their knowledge, skills and ability to give more to the company.

They themselves ask:

- How can I be worth more to the company?
- How can I help it to achieve more in less time?
- Are there some ways that I could help cut out cost and increase productivity, quality and efficiency?
- What new system could I develop?

WHAT IS EXCELLENCE

Thousand things, a thousand and thousand of times done a tiny bit better is excellence. The emphasis is on doing not onething or few things but on doing thousands of things better. Excellence means doing the right things, right the first time and all the time. It is a continuous process and requires continuous adaptation. The core of excellence must be the customer-supplier interfaces. The vehicle for achieving this interface is the involvement of the entire organisation, all the people and in all the functions is necessary.

- Providing motivation through leadership.
- Recognizing internal customers and discovering their needs.
- Controlling processes including systems and improving their capability.
- Empowering people at all levels to make improvements.

Thus, excellence is built upon built-in-quality through management of the inputs of processes. Following are the prerequisites of excellent organisation and individual:

- The organisation/individual must have long-term commitment to constant improvement. There must be a constancy of purpose and commitment to improve organisation and people therein.
- Adopt zero defects attitude to change the culture to right the first time, conforming to all requirements all the time.
- Educate individuals to understand the customer-supplier relationships. Customer orientation internal and external must be achieved for each and every individual employee.
- Recognise the improvement of the system need to be managed. Defining performance standards expected and the system to achieve them. The system has to be in line with the shared needs and expectations and will be part of continuous improvements process.

- Adopt modern methods of supervision and training – eliminate fear. It is easy to critic's mistakes, but it often seems difficult to praise efforts and achievements. Recognise and publicise efforts and achievements and provide the right sort of facilitation, supervision and training.
- Eliminate barriers between department by managing processes, improved communication and teamwork. Remove the system of silo management. It is advantageous to build teams and improve communication around the processes.
- Eliminate barriers to pride of workmanship and fiction; get facts by using the correct tool. Adopt the principle of fact-finding not fault-finding.
- Encourage employees to measure their own performance and benchmark their performance against the best practices.
- Constantly educate, retrain and develop employees on their skills. The energy which lies within them can be released into the organisation through education, training, encouragement and involvement.
- Develop a systematic approach to present organisational and individual excellence by way of presenting success stories, innovations, excellence, story telling, break-through people have achieved.
- Form various teams like Kaizen, quality circle, think-tank, task-force, smart working teams, project teams, giving them small project on work improvement.

Achieving organisational excellence often requires a mind-set to change old practices with new practices replacement. Creating excellence is more an attitude of mind. People's attitudes and behaviour can be changed by communication and the essence of changing attitudes is to gain acceptance through excellent communication processes. Good leadership is mostly about good communication, the skills of which can be learned through training but must be acquired through practice. Once people understand the strategy, the management must establish the infrastructure.

WORLD-CLASS COMPANIES

World-class companies and best in class companies demonstrate such work excellence in their activities. Their attributes show their excellence at work. We are reproducing some of the attributes of such companies for your knowledge of guidance.

(1) ATTRIBUTES OF WORLD-CLASS COMPANIES:

What makes a company an:

- Innovative company
- World-class company
- Excellent company
- TQM company

They have the following attributes:

(a) They are *the best* companies in all respect in their industrial world.

- They are *growing faster and more profitable* than their competitor.
- They *hire and retain* the best people.
- They *respond quickly to changing market* conditions.
- They are *not satisfied with the* status quo.
- They *continually upgrade facilities, processes, skills,* behaviours and attitudes.

(2) THEIR PRACTICES:

(1) ***They empower their employee:*** Authority and information is given to employees to make wise business decision and to solve problems. When more people are empowered, the more they produce leaders who can set goals and define a (Milliken Co – Textile Manufacturer) vision of where the organisation should go.

(2) ***They are market driven:*** They understand and know what products and services their global customers want to buy. They focus their strategies on the customer's goals and needs their priorities and thus become market driven with the goal of defect-free quality in everything they do. They create innovations in reducing cycle time, technology, delivery, support and service. (IBM Computers).

(3) ***They see the world differently:*** They challenge traditional business thinking *status quo* situation and accordingly go for to tailor the product to fit the needs of customer. (Procter and Gamble Company).

(4) ***They test new ideas:*** They think of implementing TQM in manufacturing and non-manufacturing areas, product strategies for product development and improvement, people strategies for HR department and service strategy to witness. Customer delights are their concern areas of quality improvement. Their act of transplanting people ideas are considered more important than seeing if their ideas bore fruits. Zero defects, conformance to specifications, do it right the first time, the customer is always right to seek perfection in every act of their doing. (AT&T).

(5) ***They make customer satisfaction an obsession:*** Putting quality service ahead of growth and an absolute dedication to quality and customer satisfaction are their main attributes. They believe that success is essentially the result of an unrelenting pursuit of customer satisfaction. For them customer satisfaction means quality. They believe that people who work in an environment are reflected in the company's relationship with its customer. (MBNA credit card Company)

(6) ***They go for big dreams:*** They dream something bigger than what they do and getting employees to buy into the dream is considered important for business survival. Their employees training focuses on values, vision, mission and goals of company's business for comprehensive understanding of the dream. Commitment

to excellent product/service that people take with them to work all the time, create quality beyond imagination. (Disney World Company).

(7) ***They make quality part of their corporate values:*** They consider quality is not a programme but a legacy, passed down to sr. executives. Continuous improvement is a part of their culture. Reinforcing this quality culture is a major priority for them. They always remember that product/service is for our end-user-customer. It is not for profit only. The profit automatically follows. Quality philosophy and specific measurement to safeguard the quality of all company products is highly inducted to each and every employees of the company. (Merck and Company Pharma Company).

(8) ***They don't compromise their quality standards:*** They just don't operate their business to make money. They always looked into and get involved in customer values, because these are critical to their success. Their philosophy of customer satisfaction is quality product, service, with good value to customer. That is their customer winning formula. (MC – Donald – Chain Restaurant Company).

(9) ***They innovate on continuous basis:*** To improve upon quality of worklife, quality of product and services, they create quality champions at every level. Kaizen-the never ending quest for perfection, potential development for H. R., Pursuit for superior quality building, mutual trust, develop team performance, providing stable environment, collaborative problem-solving, total quality management are some of the lessions they follow to create innovative environment in the company. (NUMMI – Joint Venture Company. Of General Motors and Toyota.)

(10) ***They have a vision and a strategy to make it happen:***

- Their vision is – a line of business must have number one in the industry.
- They believe strategy is not a lengthy action plan but rather the evolution or the central idea through continually changing circumstance.
- They believe quality is not a simple thing, but an aura, an atmosphere, an overpowering feeling that a company is doing everything with excellence, and that the customer is elevated, enhanced in his self-worth and image bettered by his relationship with the company.
- "Their mission is, we want a company where people find a better way every-day, of doing things, and where by shaping their own work experience, they make their lives better and your company best." (General Electric Motor.)

(11) ***Their process efficiency:***

- Their outputs (product and services) exceed all customer expectation.
- Their work is defect free, zero defects.
- They are industry leader and even more value than competitors.
- They are benchmarked by others.

(12) *Their process efficiency:*

- Their processes are defect free, low cost, no wasted cycle line.
- There is no output variation, no rework.
- They established zero cost of poor quality (COPQ) and have high productivity and asset utilisation.

With there built-in characteristics they achieved world-class status in their ways of doing the business.

From the attributes of these world-class companies we may learn, following lesson and start with implementing following few guidelines for making our quality company of future.

IMPROVE INTERNAL CUSTOMER SERVICE

(1) Define the major manufacturing and service department's functions and define their roles and responsibilities based on customer-supplier relationship.

(2) Identify customers (employees) requirements and develop measures of their satisfaction.

(3) Identify the requirement and measurement criteria for internal customer and supplier to assess their ongoing performance and decide their reward management issues.

(4) Continually improve the effectiveness, quality, cycle time and cost of all work processes.

(5) Involve employees and empower them to solve possible problems themselves, by establishing work performance improvement team such as Quality Circle, Kaizen, taskforce, etc. Their participation in actual problem-solving shall yield positive performance individually *vis-a-vis* total performance collectively.

DEVELOP PEOPLE AND RECOGNISE THEIR ACHIEVEMENT

(1) Treat employees as partners. Share with them the good news and bad so they strive to excel and allow them to share reward of their achievement.

(2) Encourage employees that challenge the obvious. The road to success includes failing which is part of learning process.

(3) Involve associates to all levels in the decision-making. Manager should share ideas with associates and solicit ideas from them.

(4) Execute the pledge "a promise we make is a promise we keep."

(5) Incalculate walk-the-talk culture believe in: actions speak louder than words.

DEVELOP PRODUCTIVITY STRATEGIES

(1) Maintain challenging, achievable and measurable productivity objective for all employees.

(2) Communicate productivity objectives to employees and make them the subject of regular and meaningful review.

(3) Engage in effective cost reduction programmes at all levels of the company.

(4) Improve product design, manufacturing, engineering and QA techniques.

(5) Keep abreast of developing techniques of measuring and increasing productivity and use new technology and management innovation effectively to improve the efficiency of operations.

(6) Achieve high quality in internal operations with special focus on relationships management with employees.

(7) Achieve superior performance as an economic unit, with special emphasis on high-quality products and services.

(8) Make capital expenditure directed towards the most and efficient use of facilities toward improving.

(9) Design job assignments and work environment with an understanding and awareness of fostering productivity.

(10) Promote two-way communications between employees at all level to understand better the problems and concerns that affect productivity.

(11) Train and retrain employees for new skills and as well as option for their multi-skilling.

INSTALL BENCHMARKING

(1) *Identify* what is to be benchmarked, select product, service or a practice.

(2) *Identify* comparative companies, competitors, non-competitors who are leaders in the area to be benchmarked.

(3) *Determine* data collection methods and collect data. Face-to-face exchanges, visit to company's records.

(4) *Determine* current performance level. Compare their and your data, analyse, and identify gaps in performance.

(5) *Determine* future performance levels. Expected improvement and goals to achieve, new goals to establish.

(6) *Communicate* benchmark finding and gain acceptance methodology, findings, to reach new goals.

(7) *Establish* functional goals, recommendation on change, based on benchmarked finding, to reach new goals.

(8) *Develop* action plan – objectivewise road map for action and organisational support to induct new change.

(9) *Implement* specific action and monitor progress. Adjust and or correct process parameters investigations by problem-solving.

(10) *Recalibrate* benchmarks – Overtime, the benchmarks are to reevaluated, in detail to ensure that they are based on the latest performance data.

CONTINUOUS IMPROVEMENT

The company that wanted to survive and prosper will have to implement continuous improvement in the holy trinity of business survival. Quality; Customer focus and Innovation.

❖ Following are the Ten Commandments of Continuous Improvement:

(1) ***Put the customer first:*** Without him there is no business. Hence, a companies must focus first and foremost on fulfilling the expectations of the market in such manner that they earn and keep the trust of their customer.

(2) ***Innovate constantly:*** Breakthrough are important, for improvement in product, process people.

(3) ***Design quality into product and services:*** Plan for prevention stopping defects before they happen. By anticipating problems you can avoid time and costs associated with inspecting good material from bad and rework.

(4) ***Improve everything continuously:*** Every process can be improved no matter how good it is today. An emphasis on continuous improvement fosters creativity and breakthrough.

(5) ***Create and support a safe and open environment:*** Which seeks out, nurture, reward and recognise the contribution of each employee.

(6) ***Do not shoot the messenger:*** Overcome the barriers to quality and productivity, discuss the undiscussables.

(7) ***Stop imitating others.***

(8) ***Use time wisely:*** Speeding up production or delivery costs, accelerates new product development and improves quality. The fast way to get something done is to do the right thing the first time.

(9) Do not sacrifice long-term improvements for short-term profits.

(10) Today quality is not enough; work on it day-in and day-out to create excellence at work.

❖ Focus Incremental Stages of Continuous Improvement:

- ❖ Technical quality
- ❖ Functional quality
- ❖ Competitive quality
- ❖ Forward quality

(1) ***Technical quality improvement:***

- ❖ Improvement focus on ⇨ Internal product or process
- ❖ Measure ⇨ Doing things right
- ❖ Driver ⇨ Costs
- ❖ Relies on technology ⇨ Quality tools and processes
- ❖ Customer perspective ⇨ *Persuade them*

(2) ***Improvement in functional quality:***

- ❖ Focus on ⇨ External customers
- ❖ Measures ⇨ Customer satisfaction
- ❖ Driver ⇨ Process
- ❖ Customer perspective ⇨ *Satisfy them*

(3) ***Improvement in competitive quality:***

- ❖ Focus on ⇨ Total market
- ❖ Measure ⇨ Market share
- ❖ Relies on ⇨ Time and flexibility
- ❖ Customer perspective ⇨ *Attract them*

(4) ***Improvement in forward quality:***

- ❖ Focus on ⇨ New markets
- ❖ Measures ⇨ New product/service offering
- ❖ Driver ⇨ Innovation
- ❖ Relies on ⇨ Planning and Intuition
- ❖ Customer perspective ⇨ *Build trust*

10.7 TRAINING AND DEVELOPMENT OF PEOPLE

In order change to happen and for that change to lead to the desired results, it is necessary to change our motivation. The development of highly capable employees must be a genuine desire; you must truly have a passion for developing a workforce with the highest skills and know that is doing so the financial gain will take care of itself. This may seem difficult for many executives who do not see the performance of their employees as being directly linked to their own success. It is much easier to complain about what is lacking and not working rather than to make investment in change. Change forces us to confront the unknown. It is risky and sometimes is it believed that such attempt in future will end in no results. But also see the positive side of the change if it happens in positive way.

There is no doubt that working with people can be extremely challenging and at times frustrating. But the fact is that, the process of change would be impossible without people. People are harder to deal with than machines. They have their own opinions, feelings. They are able to think to solve problems and to improve. People are seen as the key to extending and strengthening the company. What is needed is a full and unflinching belief that people are the key to success. If it is so then developing a system to support people in their efforts is management obligation.

It is said that if the student has not learned, then the instructor has not taught. Getting the organisation ready to develop exceptional people, it is necessary to train people right from the entry level. It is generally considered people's native born gifts to be only about to 10% of the total talent. In other words, natural talent gifts accounts for only 10% of the full capability of an individual. Fully 90% of what we consider talent in the life of company employee is actually learned through efforts and related practices. Begin with a good foundation – a person who has the capacity and desire to learn and then develop specific talent through repeated effort and practice. The idea that with a basic capability any person can become, if not the greatest, at least great performer. It is hard to find, the ideal people who have exactly the skills that company wants. You may develop such people. Then gather competent and trainable from the job market and with considerable time and efforts, develop high level of skills within the employees. It is not a few star performers who make a strong team. It is a collection of many employees with good capability working in unison that makes an exceptional team. Work on this known entity – the latest talent in each person who has the desire for personal growth may be your future skill bank of the company. With this clear objective in mind establish training process in your organisation.

We know that if people are not adequately developed, the entire operational systems will grind to a screeching halt. If the manager does not foster a teaching environment, the company's performance will surely suffer. Create a culture in which teaching others is highly valued and viewed as the key to long-term success.

Standardising training to meet global needs is the need of the hour for high performing organisations. Employees skill development occurs with practice and standardised fundamentals taught to them. These fundamentals of training are applicable to developing employee's talent.

TRAINING IN INDUSTRY

Before launching any such interventions, you must have following key assumptions about the right way to teach and manage employee training:

(1) People learn gradually overtime, in small chunks, by doing and being coached and learning small pieces of the process step-by-step.

(2) Putting pieces together into a whole takes additional time beyond learning the pieces and requires ongoing coaching as the work is being done.

(3) The pieces need to be defined and put together into some form of standardised process in order to be effectively taught to the employees.

(4) Training and development is ongoing process at the workplace and create a harmonious relationship between the supervisor (coach) and the employee.

(5) The key role of supervisor (coach) is to be a teacher and to develop the people doing the work.

(6) Ultimately, quality and productivity are the result of this long-term development process.

With the basic philosophy of 'training within industry' we will consider how people learn and develop their value to increase the performance of any organisation. The rest of the chapter tells you how to do this.

TRAINING NEEDS ANALYSIS

In training and development process the trainer and the trainee/learner should feel encourage to excel in their abilities to create special learning experience. The organisation should identify real development opportunities; provide experiences which are dynamic, positive and challenging. Trainer should be curious, have a thirst for knowledge and seek to be inspiring, innovative and wanting to lead in the field of training and development. The organisation must be supportive.

If you are seeking to provide training then one of the first steps is to undertake a Training Needs Assessment (TNA) analysis. However, it is important to remember to set Business Needs Analysis (BNA). Therefore, while undertaking TNA, some basic needs of organisation should be met.

(1) TNA must be in alignment with the overall business objectives. Ultimately any investment in T&D should be matched to the needs of the business. To conclude effective training needs analysis has to be related to the organisation's aims and objectives.

(2) Training solution should be seen in the context of what the organisation is trying to achieve. At the same time it must be in response to the requirements of employees and customers.

(3) The gap that needs to bridge between performance now and performance desired in future must have to be established. This gap, which may not solely, be a training gap, may need more than one step before it is filled.

(4) In conducting your TNA, it is worth keeping in mind the fact that not all solution necessarily involves training. The problem may involve other factors such as the organisational structure, the environment in which the product, services are made and delivered.

(5) Delivery of training solution must meet the learning needs of employees as well as customers.

(6) It is significant for training needs identification and development that you need to undertake analysis at all levels within an organisation. within this process you must cover following questions:

- What are the organisation's goals and desired performance?
- What is the specific business objectives linked to these needs/goals?
- How will the training meet these needs?
- What needs to be developed or improved?
- What new knowledge, skills and competencies are required?
- Who need to attend?
- How you will evaluate and measure the training effectiveness?
- What information is available about the participants?
- What do you perceive to be their needs? (as a trainer)

PINPOINTING TNA

If the purpose of training is to help close the gap between actual performance and desired performance, in organisations operational areas, you must be able to define what the real training needs. There can be a variety of reasons for the need for change. Some of these are:

- Business performance is not up to expectation.
- New legislation introduce by government.
- Customer complaints rising.
- Employee issues such as poor morale and motivation, high employee turnover, strain management – union relations, etc.

- The need to move into new market or develop new products.
- Latest technology demands altogether new skills and or reskilling or multiskilling of employees.
- New technology ties up with foreign collaborator.

Whatever the need of training, organisation must delect that real need before starting effective training solutions. In conclusions, effective training needs analysis has to be related to the organisation's own aim and goals. The solution should be seen in the context of what the organisation is trying to achieve. Having established the need for TNA, you may also dig further to get more information on TNA by using research techniques such as observation, interviews, structured questionnaires, nominal group technique, brain storming and sampling. And after analysis of data on TNA, you must be able to convince your top management, line managers, and unionists by providing ground realities of training needs. In the systematic cycle of training TNA plays a major part providing essential information to all concerned.

TRAINING NEEDS PRIORITIES

Another aspect of T&D is prioritising training needs.

- **Urgent and important:** Critical training needs that often arise because of changes within business cycle. For e.g., cost reduction, productivity improvement, quality, safety, etc.
- **Important but not urgent:** These areas which need attention and putting into a plan, but do not require an immediate responses. For e.g., new legislation, multi-skilling, etc.
- **Routine needs:** Which are ongoing need relating to day-to-day jobs.
- **Urgent but not important:** For e.g., employee's skill development in an area completely unrelated to their position.
- **Not urgent – not important:** Anything which have no relevance to the business.

This classification of priority training needs at organisational level will help you to focus and to identify where to channel your energies and resources. You as a trainer need to detect what real need are before you then start to suggest fully effective solutions.

CRITICAL FACTORS IN TRAINING

Intellectual learning differs from behaviour change in fundamental way. For intellectual skills, the classroom is an appropriate setting and simply learning about or hearing a concept once is enough to master it. Strategic thinking, computer programing can be taught effectively in this mode. For behavioural change, on the other hand, life itself in the true arena for learning. Learning an emotional competence requires that we also engage our emotional circuitry where social and emotional habits are stored. Changing such habits, feeling, opinions, perceptions, learning to approach people positively instead of avoiding them, to listen better, or to give feedback skillfuly is a more challenging task. Nowadays in professional organisation gradually the focus has getting shifted from organisation development to people development. And in this context, working one-to-one, developing effective coaching and mentoring and having positive and motivational conversation with people may have more impact than any other training intervention. When people genuinely care for each other and the organisation, people can feel the pulse. They feel they have found the heart of the organisation and trainer know why it is important to do it critically and differently too. The philosophy of developing people Toyota way is most relevant to quote here.

(1) Base management decision on long-term philosophy, even at the expense of short-term financial goal: Perhaps the most important long-term investment Toyota makes is in its people and the passion to keep team associates employed for their careers reflect that value.

(2) Standardised processes are the foundation of continuous improvement: Standardised work and job instruction training go hand-in-hand, and long-term team associates need to learn to see waste and make improvement.

(3) Growing leaders who thoroughly understand the work and who live the philosophy and teach to it to others: Teaching is the most highly valued skill of leaders, and leaders have to deeply understand the work to teach and coach others.

(4) Develop exceptional people and teams who follow your company's philosophy: Teams depend on well-trained people and part of individual development is learning to work in teams.

(5) Respect your suppliers by challenging them and helping them to improve: Suppliers need to have the same talent level as Toyota team associates and are developed in similar way.

(6) Became a learning organisation through relentless reflection and continuous improvement: This was intentionally at the top of the hierarchy of Toyota way pyramid because becoming a learning organisation is viewed as the highest level of organisational effectiveness.

Toyota, this way develops exceptional people. These critical steps (philosophy) establish a foundation for a successful talent development process.

Unfortunately, for most companies their, human assets has for years been secondary to the primary interest of the company manufacturing. Everyone, it seems, understand the need of training and can see the skill, knowledge deficiency, but too few are willing to set up to the situation and do something about it. Why is this? Because, the cycle of struggle and firefighting we see in most organisation. It is a vicious cycle; there is never a new outcome. Issues are not resolved; they are simply patched for the movement. As with most cycle of problems, it is difficult to determine where the cycle begins and how to intercede to make a change. We believe that training cycle begins with an ineffective training process, which leads to variable and ineffective results. Ineffective results followed by time consuming firefighting approach, no time for training thus lead to ineffective training. To break this vicious cycle of ineffectiveness, you must take the time and invest in your future of T&D. There are three major factors that ultimately lead to a deficiency in information sharing and learning, which must be targeted in order to break the cycle.

- **Defining critical knowledge** – It is not clear what is important for successful completion of work versus what is personal preference, which varies from person-to-person. People will perform the actual work differently from that what has been prescribed. Many employees seem to have their own way of doing the job. Therefore, it is necessary to prescribe critical requirements of job, so that employees will not have their own way of doing the job.
- **Transferring the critical knowledge** – Once the job is well defined, the subsequent step of transferring the critical knowledge to others is of primary importance. New learning be placed with skilled and competent trainers with define guidelines on training implementation and evaluation.
- **Follow-up** – To verify the results of training efforts it is a must. Well defined job requirement and subsequent training it would be possible to determine the effectiveness of the transfer of knowledge. Hence, there must be systematic and defined method to ensure training process is sufficient. The results are predictable, consistent and accurately measured.

It is imperative that all these elements are performed in order to support an effective training process.

TRAINING METHODS

In any manufacturing or service organisation, all jobs are a mix of specific skills, knowledge, tasks and ability. So, one must move into details in a logical and organised manner. Who needs what training approach is the best fit for finding out successful training needs solution. A defined standard is the foundation for teaching. But to effectively teach, it is necessary to break training into different methods to facilitate learning. The four training methods have different objectives and are approached in different way. Thus, the training process is not just initiated as a standalone activity. It is closely linked to standardised work and the development of the basic job methods. The training is based on four basic methods, which outline about teaching the critical aspect of job and skill and help learner to develop his capability. Learning and skill development occurs with practice and all fundamentals are taught in all concerned areas to help employee acquire the necessary skills and knowledge.

- **Job instruction methods** – Training is more than simply telling someone what to do. These are effective techniques that are used to accelerate learning and to increase the retention of information: job instruction provides a method whereby the trainer will tell, show and explain the task. The job instruction method can be used to teach anyone any task. The job instruction method in its pure form is better suited for teaching the task element of the work, but the principles can also be applied to the development of job knowledge. The job instruction training method ID known as the four-step method: prepare the student, present the operation, try out performance and follow-up. This is the heart of the process for transferring knowledge effectively. Job instruction is the foundation for talent development. In this method, first, identify the job to be taught what to do step-by-step, and then identify what is important about how to perform the step. If these two elements are achieved successfully the results of training will surely improve. This method can be taught through on-the-job and classroom approach.

- **Job method** – This method provides techniques intended to help supervisors and employees (learners) methodically analyse all aspects of a job and to question every detail to determine necessity, sequence and responsibility for each task. This method advocates the idea of seeking the ideas of the people closest to the process, the workers, and employees and provides some guidance on age-old problems, overcoming resistance to change. Thus, the questioning and evaluation and guidance will lead to increase productivity, motivating by eliminating unnecessary steps and activities.

- **Job relation method** – This method used to aim at providing supervisors with methods for handling issues and for improving work relations. Many new executives have no knowledge of how to effectively handle employee's issues and concerns, so this method is developed. Topics such as handling of employee's grievances, performance, facilities, feedback and communication are included. Job methods are generally incorporated in technical manuals, system manuals covering technical, social and general methods of doing the work.

- **Programme development method:** This is specifically intended for the person or persons within plant, who will identify training needs, develop a training plan, get support of management, implement the plan, train executive and employees, and verify the effectiveness of the programme.

APPROACHES TO TRAINING

With the above training methods, training in industries is carried out. Different industries have many different jobs to learn. This learning, knowledge and skill development is generally grouped into five domain areas, irrespective of nature of industries.

- **Interacting with environment:** Providing goods and services to customer, addressing competition, influencing and negotiating to maintain organisations position, handling conflict, uncertainty, complexity and change, preparing for diversification, developing partnerships, etc.

- **Managing the job:** Using management techniques, identifying and making choices, decision, establishing policies and practices, designing budget and cost control, flow of fund, using information and technology, designing job, job role, KRAs, allocating work and resources, selecting assessing and rewarding employees, making use of available skills, time and resources.

- **Developing the organisation:** Recognising culture, working for company goals, building team and cooperation, implementing changes and diversities. Promoting equality, harmony, recognising political dimensions and power relationship.
- **Working with others:** Guiding, directing, enabling, applying values, using conceptual abilities, using personal power, etc.
- **Managing self:** Asking for and receiving feedback, organising staff, organising self, professional skills, balancing work and personal needs. Being flexible and able to adopt, being resourceful and reachable.
- **Knowing self:** Reevaluating beliefs, maintaining ethics and values, requirement of soft skills, leadership traits, team-building, assertive behaviour, cooperative and collaborative, self-discipline and time management, etc. Knowledge, skill development in above areas are general to all people in any organisation. This demands suitable training approach to gain knowledge and to learn skills. Many training and learning events/approaches are available to the trainer and learner some are listed below and highlight whatever they involve high or low participation on the part of learner. There are situations where they might be appropriate and beneficial for learning.

TRAINING APPROACHES

Are as follows:

(1) Lecture/presentation: Lectures/presentations are useful where it is necessary to give the same information to a large number of people at the same time. It is most appropriate where information needs to be conveyed.

(2) Role play: The learner is asked to take on a role and to act out the scenario presented. For e.g., superior is asked to take on role of departmental head in disciplinary action against other superior situation. Thus, it is most relevant where learner wishes to experience the situation in a safe environment and draw learning inputs from the experience. The learner can try out skills and approaches to the situation and receive feedback from the trainer and colleagues on how to improve their approach.

(3) Case study: It is a description of situation which usually takes place in an imaginary organisation and the learner is asked to answer a series of questions. For e.g., the question are structures around the learner acting as the departmental head, based on the information given in the case study. The learner may be asked to do this alone or as part of group. The learning event is similar to the role play in that the trainer guides the learner receives feedback from the trainer and colleagues. In this approach, the learner can try out approaches and ideas to the situation. It is as near to the real life situation as possible. The trainer can show how theory can be applied to practice.

(4) **Discussion groups:** Discussion groups allow learners to share experiences and ideas. It allows learners to actively contribute. It is most useful with small groups of learners containing not more than eight to ten people. The topic of discussion can be chosen by the trainer, or in some situations, the learners. The groups decide the issue to be discussed and the trainer act as a facilitator to the group.

(5) **Project assignments:** The learner is allocated a specific project to complete within given time. He receives specific instructions on what is required. For e.g., HR manager is asked to review the training needs of executives of the company. The result of project will be a presentation to Senior management with the proposals. Such assignments are real and the training is directly related to the situation.

(6) **Business games:** These can include computer simulation or board games, exercises. They are usually played in team of four to six people. The trainer acts as umpire. Often they centre on an imaginary organisation, but some organisations create their own business games which simulate their own organisation. These game plays can develop decision-making, planning skills, team-building skills and leadership skills.

(7) **In tray exercise:** This consists of series of memo, letters, forms, statements and other documents. Similar to the work situation of the learner alone or in pairs. The object is to put the paper-work in order of priority and state what should happen to each items. There is a time limit to complete the exercise. The results are discussed and analysed by the trainer and learner individually or in a group situation. Such exercise develops decision-making and problem-solving abilities. It develops planning skills and the effective use of time.

(8) **Job rotation:** This is when an individual moves around the organisation from one post to another, usually spend minimum one year in each position. It enables the individual to appreciate the different function within an organisation. It gives wide spectrum of experience for the individual. The organisation can assess the individual in a number of different situations and the individual has the opportunity to explore the organisation in order to decision concerning his long-term plans.

(9) **Programmed learning:** This includes computer based training and interactive videos. Computer base and interactive videos ask the learner to make decision or answer questions after receiving information. The program then tells the learner whether he has answered the questions correctly or made the appropriate decisions or answers questions after receiving information. The program then tells the learner whether he has answered the questions correctly or make the appropriate decisions. Interactive videos by comparison are more expensive and cover a wider spectrum of topics. Under this learning the individual can make mistakes and has immediate 1. Feedback on his progress. 2. The training can be undertaken, by the individual independently of the trainer and therefore is flexible to the work environment.

(10) **Mentoring:** This is a form of career development where the employees has a mentor or guide who is someone other than line manager/department and is usually senior person. The mentor and the employee meet regularly over a period of time and the mentor acts as a guide, teacher, and adviser and confidante to the employee. It gives the employee a role model within the organisation and also it encourages the retention of personnel within the organisation.

Above are the various approaches through which appropriate training is imparted to the learner. Choosing a method appropriate to the level of learning required, careful analysis of needs and its applicable solutions. To get desired results from training process, training objectives need to be specific, measurable, actio-oriented, relevant and time-bound. Objectives should address in improvement of knowledge, skills, should change behaviour and attitude of the learner.

TRAINING PLAN

While designing and developing training it is necessary to consider the training needs identified, classification of identified training needs (technical and behavioural), priority of training and facilities available inhouse and external. Reviewing all these factors training plan can be initiated for implementation. Secondly, we have to consider level of the training the basic level of acquisition of knowledge; understanding of information; knowing how to apply the information, etc. putting together all the above information training design can be prepared condensing following points:

- Taking commitment from trainer HODs and learner employees to attend the requisite training.
- To ensure that you have addressed the level of learning, learning style as per identified training needs.
- To ensure that sufficient time is allotted to each part of the trainees.
- To ensure that the content of training meets the objectives and relevant to those receiving the training.
- To ensure learning can be transferred successfully at the workplace.

Now the next step is to implement training design/plan as per the conformance to requirement. Training can be imparted inhouse or with the help of external trainer. However, for internal and external training the process of identifying needs remains the same. The trainer has to assess whether the expertise in meeting the given training need is available within the organisation. If not decision to use of external resources, whether by using external consultant or external public courses is to be made. Based on the training needs, priorities, training plan, resources availability training programmes are implemented into different classified training types.

CLASSIFICATION OF TRAINING PROGRAMMES

- *Internal / on-the-job training* – Conducted by own faculties.
- *In-house training* – Can be conducted by internal faculties or inviting external faculty at the workplace to conduct training.
- *External training* – Under this programme, employees are deputed to attend training under the supervision of professional training institute or individual trainer.
- *In-plant training* – Generally, it is to facilitate college students for undertaking summer/in-plant training to make them aware of industrial cultures, their products, practices and services.

TRAINING BATCHES

After assessing individual employees training needs by superior, by individual, those are classified as technical or behavioural training needs and then the individuals are classified for joining training batch as per their positions/status in the department. Based on position/designation following batches are classified.

- **MDP** – Management Development Programme – for senior management personnel.
- **EDP (I)** – Executive Development Programme – For middle level executives.
- **EDP (II)** – Engineer Development Programme – For engineers and supervisors.
- **TDP** – Technician Development Programme – For skilled workers.
- **WDP** – Workmen Development Programme – For general category workers.
- **CWT** – Contractual Workmen Training – For contractual man force.

TRAINING CALENDAR

Once training need identification exercise is over, training priority is decided and accordingly, training calendar is prepared as per priority. It can be weekly, monthly or on annual basis. While preparing training calendar batch, training module, training faculty and training duration is taken into consideration. Advance notice of training date, duration, faculty and trainees is given to HODs by training head.

TRAINING EVALUATION

Feedback on training infrastructural facilities such as sitting arrangement, training aids, refreshments, etc., along with training faculty, training literature, presentation, relevance of teaching is also assessed by trainee so that further improvement can be undertaken in future. In the same manner feedback on external training programmes is also collected by training head in a specially devised format for this purpose.

The process of evaluating training or learning in itself can provide for additional development. Most evaluation tends to focus on the cost of activity. But evaluation as a process can support managers and employees development in other ways also. A good quality evaluation process enables the individual to move through the following stages:

- **Positive activity assessment:** Did the intended activity of training achieve its intended result. Was it fit for the purpose?
- **Assessment of the application of learning:** Was the training worth acquiring in terms of time, effort and money. Has it led to any improvement in the employee's knowledge, skills and abilities? It is possible to act upon the training?
- Was the learning/training that required was the need accurately identified in the first place?
- Has any unintended learning resulted been it worth acquiring? Can it be applied?
- Can the learning be shared with other employees? Does it enhance the performance of other individuals and the team's collective work?
- Does the training help the individual and his team achieve the business objectives.
- Does the training help to add value to the organisation?

Investment in people development expects that evaluation is more than simply costing and recognizing benefits. It demands that managers actively participate in the whole development cycle – the identification of training need, its satisfaction and follow-up. Evaluation, as a process, can support this way to people development. However, it is important to establish baseline data related to employees skills, knowledge, behaviour or attitudes if you intend to compare their pre-training and post-training results. Hard and soft data may be useful in evaluation. Which type of data you use depends on what you are measuring and what is available in the organisation.

Generally, objective type of questionnaire is often used to collect. Participant's reactions to the training. Immediately after training courses such questionnaire capture immediate feeling, opinion about the course and its infrastructural activities. This information is helpful in modifying the content of course, training facilities, presentation of faculty, etc., thus the purpose of an evaluation report is to explain the findings of the evaluation study to individuals who may not have involved in it, usually senior management personnel. Producing an evaluation report is also a good way of raising the profile of training in the organisation and depending on the evaluation, can help you sell the concept of additional training.

TRAINING TARGETS

In some organisations, training hours per employee, per year target exercise is also administered. The target is given to training head and concerned HODs in their annual performance exercise.

TRAINING APPLICATION

Once training is over, inputs received from such training are expected to convert in to training output. This exercise is shouldered to HODs in coordination with training head. This way employee knowledge and skill development process is continued and according to the assessment employee career plan is charted out.

XYZ Co. Ltd.

EXTERNAL TRAINING FEEDBACK FORM

Name:_______________________ **E. No.:** _________ **Designation:** ____________

Training Topic : ______________________________ **Training Date:** ____________

Conducted by : ____________________________

1. Infrastructural Facilities	**R A**	**T I**	**N G**
(A) How was the faculty?	Very Effective	Effective	Not Effective
(B) Training coverage	Very Relevant	Relevant	Not Relevant
(C) Reading material	Very Useful	Useful	Not Useful
(D) Participants' profile (category)	Mixed	Specific	Not Known
(E) Presentatiom method (was it a combination of):	Classroom Lecture	Exercise	Case Study/On The Job
2. Training Inputs			
(A) Which topic did you find it most interesting and relevant to your nature of job?			
(B) Which topic did you find least interesting or not relevant?			
(C) Can you implement these training inputs in your Dept./Section/Factory?			
(D) Can you suggest further participants from your Dept./Section/Factory?			
(E) What other benefits this training extended to you and to our company?			
(F) What are the most important modules from this training programme which you can implement?			
(G) Does this programme add knowledge and skill for doing your present job better?			
(H) Can you propose youself as a faculty to this programme in our company?			
3. Have you received any training material?	**YES**		**NO**
(A) If yes, have you deposited one set of material in Training Department ?	**YES**		**NO**
SIGNATURE OF EMPLOYEE			

XYZ Co. Ltd.

ATTENDANCE-CUM-INTERNAL TRAINING EVALUATION FEEDBACK FORM

Training Date:	
Timings:	
Venue:	
Faculty:	
Training Module:	
Module Contents:	
Type of Training:	
Division:	

Note:

For Office Use Only

S.No.	Emp.No.	Name	Designation	Divn.	Dept.	Training Rating			Signature	Max Marks:	
						Very Effective	Effective	Less Effecteve		Pretest Score	Post Test Score

10.8 SDC-65 – SCIENCE OF DISCIPLINE AND CREATIVITY

W. D. Deming, one of the Quality Guru stated that "Employees work within a system that is beyond their control. It is the system not their individual skills, knowledge and initiative determine how they perform". Thus, when you put knowledgeable worker to perform in bad systems, most of the time systems win. Therefore, it is management responsibility to change the *status sqo* situation and improve upon the systems. Through this SDC-65 scale one can judge whether the company is quality or unquality company?

Any company's culture can be judged by the way it responds to various organisational situations. These responses are the results of company's history, actions, attitudes developed by past and present management leaders and managers who have established practices; evaluation methods, control systems and management of men, materials, methods and money. All these issues set the way in which people at various levels think, respond and change or do not change the way they think. When they do not change, the companies as a whole can't recognise impending threats, understand the implications of these threats or come up with alternative solutions, such company and its people then witness trouble for survival and gradually vanish from the business world. Their *status quo* mind-set makes them poor learners of new things. They as a company, survive but never live up to their potential.

The situation that arises in such company can be classified as:

- **Disaster:** It remains unattended or symbolic or superficial actions are initiated. The results are: Loss of product, market, loss of profit, high manufacturing cost and high employee turnover. No proper diagnosis of the issues is undertaken.
- **Major problems:** Poor quality of products, dissatisfied customers, dissatisfied employees, this results in negative effect on revenue generation.
- **Minor problems:** Strain relations between/among depts., manager's, employees and external customers.
- **Symptoms of problems:** Productivity is poor, high cost on account of poor quality, no technological and social upgradation seen. Gradually company succumbs to sickness. In such situations the company responses can be;
    - (a) **Reactive:** React after situation is occurred. Firefighting approach is undertaken.
    - (b) **Predictive:** Use information of events to analyse causes and predict possibilities and take actions to avoid such events.
    - (c) **Preventive:** Prevent even symptoms from occurring and treat even a symptom as seriously as disaster.

To assess such situation of business health, SDC-65 is the best and most educative management intervention. SDC-65 stands for productivity and quality status of the company. It is a science of discipline and creativity. 6 – stands for quality level of the company, while 5 – stands for productivity level. Those are considered as a standard on which the company performance is assessed in different areas of its operations. (As narrated here in this chapter.)

QUALITY

Level of quality delivered at each step of design, process engineering, manufacturing or assembly. THESE LEVELS ARE DETERMINED BY RULES USED BY OPERATORS OR PERSONS CARRYING OUT ACITIVITY TO STOP THE PROCESS FOR UNACCEPTABLE QUALITY.

Quality – Different Levels of Qulity Standards

Level 1 Make somehow-No botheration of specifications. Manufacturing stops only when totally unusable output produced or machine breaks down.

Level 2 Some concepts of limits for manufacturing. These may not be specifications. Manufacturing stops if output is beyond limits decided.

Level 3 In addition to limits, there is also sensitivity to target value. Efforts are made to run the process near the target value. Some reduction in deviation limits compared to level 2.

Level 4 Company is very strict with technical specifications. No deviation at the stage of manufacturing, also sensitive to target value.

Level 5 X-R method – In this company technical specifications are met routinely at the stage of manufacturing. In these organisations, people are concerned with average (X) and range (R) of the process. Actions are taken if X or R has changed beyond predetermined limits even if jobs are still produced within tolerance.

Level 6 Process capability – Predetermined process capability is maintained on every process. Actions are taken if process capability changes (drop or increase) to bring capability to required value and maintain better value if achieved.

PRODUCTIVITY

These are assessed by how the output norm per shift is obtained by the organisation. This is also determined by assessing when the operator stops as he believes that he has completed his task for the day.

Productivity – Different Levels of Productivity Standards

Level 1 This organisation follows shop practice. There are no official norms for daily output. Even if studies are conducted and detailed norms exist, they are not conformed to on the shop floor and the norms remain only in the files. In short, these organisations accept what worker delivers.

Level 2 In these organisations, cycle time measurement is followed as a norm. This may be even wristwatch study, not necessarily stopwatch time study. The total time is measured and daily work is accepted based on this measurement. Detailed stopwatch studies may be conducted but they remain in some files. What shop follows is cycle time studies.

Level 3 Detailed stopwatch studies or Time and Motion studies are carried out, understood by all concerned and conformed by all. Obvious method improvements implemented during the study are also agreed. However, once agreed, it is very difficult to improve method and set improved norm between agreements.

Level 4 In these organisations, it is possible to make improvements and change the norm and the new norms are implemented. These efforts are made mostly by the management and these organisations are able to revise almost every norm at least once or twice a year.

Level 5 In level 5 company, the norm is only a guideline and everyone (including all workers) are constantly on the lookout for raising the level of productivity. Workers, supervisors, engineers, managers all participate in raising productivity continuously. As against level 4, in these organisations, one will find as many as one or two revisions every month.

COMPANY LEVELS

Company levels mapping reveal some of following characteristics:

LEVEL 1: Company

(a) There is no graph near the machine, operating staff does not have gauge and he uses only judgement or sporadic checking for quality.

(b) Graph, gauges, measuring instruments present near the machine. But these do not really affect manufacturing quality. Graph not up to date, gauge and measuring instruments not in working condition and manufacturing does not stop even if bad quality is produced.

(c) Graphs near the machine show picture but in reality quality produced is not as per graph. This is worse than not having the graph.

(d) Different operating staffs follow different procedures. No standard written work instructions or there is no conformance to written instructions. (SOP).

(e) What inspector does and what operating staff does are not related. Generally, production stops if only unusable or absolutely unacceptable parts or products are produced. In general people are not aware that there are limits of variation for manufacturing quality. Even if they are aware of limits, there is no botheration for adherence to these limits.

(f) In case of problems or crisis, limits are the first thing to be sacrificed.

LEVEL 2: Company

(a) In this case you will find that people are aware of limits of manufacturing quality although limits used may be well beyond tolerance. However, production stops if limits are crossed and some corrective action is taken.

(b) Graphs maintained by inspector or operating staff conform to quality produced. These may only be on important stages.

(c) Some relation between inspections, manufacturing and supervisory involvement.

(d) All operating staffs involved in some quality checking.

LEVE.L 3: Company

(a) In this company you will find that operating staffs, supervisors and inspectors will be aware of not only limits but also target value.

(b) There may be some deviations but these will be well known to all. Some efforts for reducing variation.

(c) Inspector, operating staff and supervisor will frequently discuss quality based on graphs. Adjustments are made to bring graph near the centre of tolerance.

(d) Graphs are drawn by inspector or operating staff with predetermined frequency. This is strictly monitored on all important stages.

(e) All the operating staffs involved in checking the quality by gauges or measurement and inspectors/supervisors maintaining graphs which guide quality of manufacturing. Actions and improvements seen on the graph.

Level of inspection increases. Every operating staff involved in inspection and some dedicated inspectors for in-process inspection and final inspection.

LEVEL 4: Company

(a) Specifications for manufacturing are strictly adhered to. Manufacturing stops if values are out of specification.

(b) The specifications are revalidated by reference to technical or international standards.

(c) Parts beyond specifications are not accepted for further processing. In general parts are produced as per required tolerance although with adjustments.

LEVEL 5: Company

Here people are really not worried about tolerance since tolerance is adhered to by process accuracy. Here people are concerned about average of the process which is maintained near the nominal size required. If there is a shift in average, action is taken to bring the average back to nominal size although parts produced have not crossed limits of acceptance. Range of the process is also monitored. If range is reduced then investigation is carried out to identify why it has reduced and efforts are taken to ensure that better conditions are maintained.

LEVEL 6: Company

In this company the manufacturing quality is as per process capability. If manufacturing is not as per process capability, actions are taken to assure process capability. If process capability is improved, investigation is carried out why it has improved and efforts are taken to ensure that these better conditions are maintained.

Effect of Quality Standard on the Organisation
Level 1 to 6

	Level 1	Level 2	Level 3	Level 4	Level 5	Level 6
Type of specification	Disrespect. No botheration	Concept of fit.	Technical standards with some deviations.	As per technical standards.	Variation + technical standard.	Process capability.
Initiation of action	If product "breaks down".	If fitment fails.	Till it works within specified limit (may be deviated).	Till it works within technical specification.	Change in type of variation.	If process capability deteriorates.
Type for corrective actions	On product	On product	On cause, i.e., on process	On cause, i.e., on process	On system	On system
Knowledge of process specification	None	None/Vague	For few obvious parameter	Good	Thorough	Thorough
Mismatch in management expectations and actual performance to be	Very high	Very high	Fairly high	Reasonable	Very low	Negligible
Cost control approach	No concept of process cost, material cost-oriented.		Cost of bad products.	Major elements of conversion cost.		Per unit section-wise total cost.
% inspection (Formal)	2 – 5%	6 – 10%	10 – 15%	15 – 20%	10%	< 5%
% job inspected by worker	30 – 50%	60 – 70%	100%	100%	12 – 20%	< 5%

Type of maintenance % break-down (Stoppage)	Break-down % above 15%	Preventive % 10-15 %	Preventive 5-10 %	Preventive 2-5%	Corrective 1%	Maintenance prevention < 0.5 % TPM
Other staffs role in quality control	Carries burden	Carries burden	Shares burden	Participates in improvement	Fully in controls	Assure comfortably
Management attitude	Indifferent, drastic change expected someone else responsible.	Acceptance of some reasonability and accountability but away from shop floor burden shared.	Sr. Management starts giving attention to shop floor and shop problems. Problem-solving approach used management realises that it can do much more.	In addition to middle management involvement for day-to-day problem-solving and corrective actions.	Start demanding, action-oriented, result-oriented training. Starts understanding concept of variation and problems due to variation.	Full involvement with shop floor, through Understanding.
Effect of improvement actions	Vague actions taken, reversal, recurring problems, fashion approach, no benefit from previous initiatives.	Actions on points of high rejection, high rework. However, control actions are person-oriented.	Results of actions seen. Selective control activity starts.	Prominent corrective actions as a routine, operation-wise rejection/ rework, analysis starts.	All initiative starts giving some results. Positive interaction.	Very quick. Effect of every action can be precisely measured.
Effect of benchmarking	"Our situation is different." Pointout	Some attention but disbelief prevails.	Some actions through benchmarking	Some actions through benchmarking	Better understanding of results of	Can learn effectively from others

	differences rather than similarities.		and some learning.	and some learning.	other companies. Managers start seeing similarities.	even dissimilar organisations
Role of inspection	Weak records generated but no effect on manufacturing process.	Strong 100% on important operations. Feedback used by manufacturing charts maintained on important stages.	Strong use of both 100% and sampling inspection efforts to implement self-inspection. Charts on all operations.	Self-inspection can be established and number of inspectors reduced for audit purpose only. In process inspection and audit charts used for control.	Start reducing sampling inspection becomes more effective and result-oriented. Inspection feedback results in process correction.	Eliminated only 1% time spent in inspection.
Quality standard manufacturing	Make somehow	Somehow but to some deviated tolerance.	Make to deviated tolerance.	Make to technical tolerance.	Average and range method.	Process capability based (Cp / Cpk > = 1.33)
Acceptance standard	Use any how (As it is) use if it fits (for assembly products)	Use as per deviated tolerance.	Strictly as per deviated tolerance.	Use strictly as per tolerance.	As per tolerance.	Cp / Cpk >= 1. 33 or higher goal.
Introducing change, new products, etc.	Very difficult, time-consuming, costly.	Improvement over (1) very difficult, time-consuming.	Improvement over (2) time-consuming.	Company gathers confidence for big change.	Change and new product introductions start becoming smoother, quick and hassle free.	Very quick completely hassle free, gives edge over competitors.

Action on customer complaints	No effective action	Some actions and some effect seen	More clarity. Some specific actions.	Actions with cause and effect analysis good correlation of process variations and customer complaint.	Specific actions start producing specific and desired results.	Very quick and effective.
Staff's role	Carries the burden of quality and productivity. Sporadic checking of jobs.	Carries the burden of quality and productivity. Checking based on predetermined sample action or call supervisor in case of poblem.	Carries the burden of quality and productivity. Sample gauging on all operations. Measurement on important stages.	Move towards self-certification starts, self-inspection can get accepted by workers. Workers see results of management action.	Starts participating in control and improvement actions, charts plotting and action. Needs help for control.	Full participation In improvement and control, master of his process. Rarely needs help for control of his processes.
Effect of New technology and machines.	Confused, no clear-cut effect	Some deviations get reduced or clear-cut.	Specific effects seen, specific benefits obtained.	Clarity about role of new technology and new machines. People start seeing benefits of problem-solving in improving machine performance.	Specific planned results are achieved. Unnecessarily investments technology avoided.	Very effective. Unnecessary new additions avoided

Effect of Productivity Standard on the Organisation
Level 1 To 5

	Level 1	Level 2	Level 3	Level 4	Level 5
Method of derivation of productivity standard.	Shop practice. No official norms.	Supervisor/ engineer's judgement through cycle time observations.	Scientifically derived (use of soft watch studies/ MTM/Most, etc.) norms for all activities.	Norms derived by eliminating wasteful elements.	Continuous improvement of scientific norms.
Conformance to norms	Lack of action	Official Action for conformance. Records are generated and sporadic action taken.	Norms are monitors every day. Serious actions are taken.	Actions are directed at reducing work content where problems are noticed.	Nonperformance is rare. In case of NC reasons are known to all.
Effective utilisation of manpower (Manufacturing Effectiveness)	Management unaware about effectiveness – 20-30%	Management unaware about effectiveness – 20-30 %	Need is felt for some measurement as norm completion does not always give economy effectiveness – 30-50%	Awareness is there and selective use made.	Used as management reporting indicator.
Indirect employees to total employees	High – 30-50%	High – 30-50%	Few standards for indirect activities also – 20-50 %	Indirect workforce is systematically attached to direct operations.	Non-value added activities reduces greatly 10%

				Activities are defined.	
Workers' role	Indifferent. Unaware of productivity.	Carries burden of productivity.	Carries burden of productivity but knows how his work has been organised.	Participate in improvement and report problems without bias.	Solve all productivity related problems in groups.
Supervisors' role	Passive, excuses oriented.	Active. Checks records and asks questions at the end of every shift.	Very active. Daily analysis. Indirect with industrial engineers for possible actions.	Guides workers. Exception reporting is continued.	Guides teams. Declares specific projects and goals to small group activities.
Role of planning	Weak.	Active chasing.	Non-conformance/ exception.	Role reduces in shop. More emphasis on aggregate planning.	May be eliminated.
Role of industrial/ process engineers (manufacturing engineering)	Even if present, carry out role other than real IE/PE.	Efficiency calculation, NC reporting, some process studies.	Calculation of incentives/new schemes, improvement plans, capacity budgets.	Training, support to supervisors. Advisory role for top management.	As a consultant in chronic problems.
Management attitude	Indifferent feels that drastic change is required for improvement.	Productivity is workers job. Burden on lower level.	Productivity bites. Middle management and other support departments take interest in productivity issue.	Productivity benefits business.	Productivity is competitive advantage.
Cost of manufacturing	High	High	Starts reducing	Within control	As per norms

Introducing change	Very difficult and time-consuming and costly	Improvement over	Company gathers confidence for Improvement big change.	Change is smooth and quick.	Change is very quick and hassle free.
Effect of new technology and machines	Confused, no clear-cut results seen.	Some results seen	Clarity about role of new technology partial results.	New technology can be absorbed fully.	Very effective. Technology adopted with innovative changes.
Effect of improvement actions	Vague actions taken. Recurring problems, fashion approach. No benefits from previous initiatives.	Effect of stages of poor conformance seen.	Improvements appreciated and are enthusiastically followed-up. Effects are seen clearly.	Good and stable results.	Improvements actions become part of daily work.
Effect of Benchmarking	"Our situation is different." Point out differences rather than similarities.	Some attention but disbelief prevails.	Some awareness. Few executives ponder over the gap.	Can see/ visualise differences in practice.	Effective learning from others.
Effect of increased variety.	Increase cost, inventory, indirect work.	Increase cost, inventory, indirect work.	Productivity may fall. Efforts made to segregate the problem.	Inventory drops as NVA reduced.	Inventory is kept by improvement in set-up activities.

Training in Organisation
Level 1 to 5

	Level 1	Level 2	Level 3	Level 4	Level 5
Identification of goals of the department	No identification. improvement, strategic intent.	Response to ISO, training needs.	Needs identification based on work Training pushed.	Need for improvement customer, etc.	Needs of system requirements or response to problems.
Evaluation of training effectiveness	Deterioration in key performance indices (KPI).	No deterioration or improvement in key performance indices but large fluctuation in actual values.	Average achievement improved up to 25% of target but ± 25% fluctuations.	Achievement > 50% with 10% fluctuation.	Achievement > = 100% with fluctuation < = 5%.

Performance Measurment in Organisation
Level 1 To Level 5

	Level 1	Level 2	Level 3	Level 4	Level 5
Type of target	Production based	Production and rejection based.	Productivity , quality *, cost delivery based.	Productivity *, quality*, cost, delivery based.	Productivity** , quality**, cost, delivery based.
Coverage levels	Top three levels below chief operating officer	Top three levels Below chief operating officer	Top three levels	Up to middle level (Section in charge)	Every supervisor
Coverage functions	Only sales and manufacturing	Only sales and manufacturing and design	Sales, manufacturing, design, engineering, quality	Level 3 plus all direct support functions such as stores, logistics, purchase, maintenance, human resource.	All organised functions.
Monitoring frequency	Specific only in case of problem	Annual reviews	Quarterly reviews	Monthly	Daily
Result of monitoring	Deterioration in key performance indices	No deterioration or improvement in key performance indices but large fluctuation in actual values.	Average achievement improved up to 25% of target but ± 25% fluctuations.	Achievement > 50% with 10 % fluctuation	Achievement > = 100% with fluctuations < = 5%

Cost Analysis in Organisation
Level 1 To Level 5

	Level 1	Level 2	Level 3	Level 4	Level 5
Cost report	Sporadic analysis at gross level	Periodic report at gross level	Periodic report dept/division-wise	Section-wise reports on cost drivers	Work station-wise reports on cost drivers/ conversation cost daily/weekly/ monthly
Control item for cost	Total expenses + largest cost element	Level 1 + total material cost, conversion cost	Level 2 + consumable cost, cost of bad products, cost of poor quality	Level 3 + activity level cost, i.e., cost per trip of fork lift, cost of reheating, etc.	Level 4 + per unit cost with detailed elemental analysis
Level involved in analysis	Top two levels below chief operating officer	Top three levels below chief operating officer	Top three levels.	Up to middle level (section in-charge)	Every supervisor
Monitoring frequency	Sporadic, only in case of problem	Annual reviews	Quarterly reviews	Monthly	Daily
Use of cost analysis	Profit/ profitability	Customer requirement – focus on special order	For improvements in major items	For internal target setting	For external target setting – competitiveness requirement or company objectives

Communication in Organisation
Level 1 To Level 5

	Level 1	Level 2	Level 3	Level 4	Level 5
Type of communication	Directives for welfare, legal or discipline related.	Production and company related mainly top down. Declarations of achievements or failures. Appeals for better performance.	Deliberate communication of facts and figures regarding company competitiveness, customer complaints, and market, competitive environment. Section-wise level 3 displays.	Company plans and objectives. New project, purpose. Comparative competitive performance. Competitive strengths and weaknesses, threats and opportunities.	Vision and strategic intent progress to world-class. Comparison with world-class bench-marks.
Channels and mechanism of communication	Patchy, irregular. Notice-boards and circulars.	Regular, periodic. Notice-boards and circulars.	House magazines. Plant level meetings, monthly managerial meeting.	Weekly plant management meetings, front-line weekly meetings, functions, event, celebrations.	Daily front-line meetings. Workstation-wise communication boards updated regularly leading to performance improvement.

Employee Relations
Level 1 To Level 5

Level 1	Level 2	Level 3	Level 4	Level 5
Passive relationship. Management feels paying well is good relationship.	New initiatives discussed and some action.	New initiatives accepted and efforts take to implement.	New initiatives show desired results in projected time.	Empowerment at all workplaces.
Employees are expected to follow work instructions.	Management expects employees to contribute more and differently.	Employees suggest new initiatives.	Schemes succeed in some area.	Employees are Considered partners in progress.
Employee feel that are contributing more than what they	Employees take up new tasks reluctantly. get.	Job rotation, career planning and succession planning started.	Employee show enthusiasm and eagerness to take up new tasks, responsibilities and work load.	All measurable the targets achieved or exceeded regularly.
No or very few measurable parameters. If present they show very little or no improvement.	Some measurable parameters show improvement.	All measurable parameters have targets and monitored regularly.	Measurable parameters show a positive trend.	Measurements as per conformance to requirement
Participative schemes evoke poor response. Teams generally fail.	Partial success in participative schemes.	Team work and participation at all levels. (Less than 20% for management and less than 10% and for employees.)	Improved teamwork and participation. (> 75% for managers and > 50% for employees.)	All employees participate in teams.

Vendor Relations in Organisation
Level 1 To Level 5

Level 1	Level 2	Level 3	Level 4	Level 5
Indifferent attitude.	Comparative quotation	Engineering based negotiation	Cost reduction. Quality improvement deployed to vendors.	Cost reduction and quality improvement by vendors.
No selection criteria	Some selection criteria	Performance rating every quarter and used for vendor deletion/ development prioritisation.	Reduction in quality problems leading to PPM less than 1,000.	Reduction quality problems (PPM) and delivery delays.

Customer Focus in Organisation
Level 1 To Level 5

Level 1	Level 2	Level 3	Level 4	Level 5
Employees think sales and marketing look after customer.	Every one realises importance of external customer.	Real survey data on customer satisfaction.	Customer data regularly discussed in top management meetings – quarterly.	Regular surveys and focus groups keep company in touch.
Managers think they know what customers want.	People consider next process as a customer but complaints are treated as nuisance.	Written quality and delivery standards across the department. Customer service is key performance indices (KPI) for every department.	Service standards met and exceeded across the company.	Cycle time, order to delivery at world-class bench-marks (> 99% on time delivery performance.)
Managers think they do not have customer or their actions are rarely customer focused.	80% on time delivery performance.	90% on time delivery performance.	95% on time delivery performance.	Customer complaints. Futuristic product analysis and threat perception.

Visual Control
Level 1 To Level 5

Level 1	Level 2	Level 3	Level 4	Level 5
No display or only figures.	Production (with best achieved.) . Rejection % Rework % Break down hours	+ SOP OEE Suggestions*/Kaizen. safety Customer complaints Efficiency Motivation **	+ Cost drivers PPM CM PI Cycle time Improvement activities.	+ CS CP/CPK Unit cost Work content reduction

General Rating Criteria for Key Processes of Companies

SDC Level	Score	Status	Process effectiveness	Process efficiency
65	5	World-class	Outputs exceed all customer exceptions, defect free, industry leader, more value than competitors, benchmarked by others.	Defect free, low costs, no wasted cycle time, no output variation, no rework, zero COPQ, high productivity and asset utilisation.
54	4	Best in class	Outputs meet all customer expectations, exceed some, customer is delighted and intended to reorder.	Low defects rates, unit costs, wasted time, COPQ, rework, scrap, small variation, good productivity and asset utilisation.
43	3	Satisfactory	Outputs meet customer expectation but never exceed, occasional complaints, needs to be improved to stay competitive, not recognised as industry leader.	Moderate defect rates, costs need to be trimmed, some scrap and rework, resources are sometimes wasted, cycle time needs reduction, moderate COPQ.
32	2	Less satisfactory (High scope for improvement)	Few non-conformances to meet customer requirements, quality variation, defects exist, complaints persist.	High NC rate, COPQ, long cycle time, poor resources utilisation, low productivity.
10	1	Unsatisfactory	Customer dissatisfied with output, defects common, frequent complaints and returns.	Excessive defects, scrap and rework, cost out of control, resources squandered, excessive COPQ (above 40)

General Measurment Parameters of Companies

Input	Process	Output	Customer satisfaction	Drivers
Data	Tasks completed	Defect rate	Customer satisfaction	Market share
Inventory	Errors	Rework	On time deliveries	Share valuation
Designs	Cycle time	Scrap	Returns	Profits
Capital	Parts used	Unit cost	Service costs	Growth

Cost Drivers	Functions			
Power/fuel Acid/LPG, etc. Raw Materials Rejection Wasteful practices	QA - Specification, inspection, visual feedback, control and audit, measurement customer satisfaction.	Production processes, productivity, yield, customer – supplier interface, cost of quality, cost of poor quality, methods, system.	Maintenance – Planned Maint, Predictive Maint, Preventive Maint and Total productive maintenance, inventory of spare down time, OEE, etc.	HR Employees Relations Training Employee performance systems

Use of Modern Manufacturing Concepts a Company Level 10, 21, 32, 43, 54 and Level 65

TOOLS/ CONCEPTS	SDC10	SDC 21	SDC 32	SDC 43	SDC 54	SDC 65
Productivity improvement	Planning system, documentation, bottleneck improvement common sense approaches	Estimated norms and efficiency system, simple method improvements, elimination of work, work sampling, flow analysis.	Down time analysis, multiple activity chart for simple rearrangements, etc., simple layout changes, flow diagram	Improvement in die, fixtures, major layout changes, flow, works simplification.	Minor hassles; ergonomics improvement, fatigue reduction, layouts.	Micro motion analysis, two handed charts, line balancing.
SMED	Preparatory activities on-line. Provision of extra resources. Some obvious rearrangements.		Detailed analysis of multiple activity charts.	Conversion of off-line activities to on-line activities.		Improvement in both, on-line and off-line activities.
TPM	Maintenance, data collection, better break down management, basic spare parts management.	Analysis of break down. Schedule for oiling and cleaning of machines. Preventive maintenance.	Preventive maintenance – obvious, improvement machine parameter + maintenance.	Simple visual control. Predictive maintenance, study for failure patterns.	Visual control system. Corrective maintenance + productive maintenance. Simple maintenance.	Maintenance prevention + operator involvement in maintenance.

5-'S'	Seiri and Seiton – Tidiness, neatness, orderliness, cleanliness		Seiso – Machine cleaning.		Seiketsu- Visual control system, spreading 5-'S'	Shitshuke – Self-discipline Training, workplace ownership.
Problem-solving tools	Check sheet and Pareto	Pareto * stratification for data and analysis	Stratification for causes. Cause and effect diagram, run chart.	Histograms (Preliminary analysis)	Histograms, scatter diagram, X – R charts (Preliminary), DOE.	X – R charts, FMEA.

In conclusion, Quality is considered as the most powerful factor to capture, retain and enlarge customer base in the modern business scenario. Achieving customer satisfaction is the essential business of business and quality management and productivity are the most effective enterprise strategies to fulfill this desired goal. Quality management and productivity is an embodiment of concepts, methods and applications and are fundamentals to the successful operation of an enterprise. It necessitates understanding and managing various dynamics in an organisation in order to set goals and judiciously deploy resources. The efficiency and effectiveness with which resources are obtained and utilised will depend upon the good management practices.

Our SDC - 65 scale system shows how different management systems measure, monitor and improve different metrics related to the business processes and what results are experienced. It defines inter – relationships among the business processes, their metrics and the organisational achievement are influenced by how well an organisation deals with issues related to quality and productivity. We have seen a number of innovative approaches are required for balancing the objectives of the partners of the enterprise and the requirements of customers, as there are many conflicting goals such as high customer service, low inventory, low units cost, improved ROI etc. SDC – 65 system provides a management framework that gives you the necessary SWOT analysis and necessary controls to address and monitor and measure performance of the business. It also guides management to enhance the image and reputation and enable for improvements through internal and external intended solutions.

SDC – 65, a kind of quality management system is relevant to all organisations whether large, small, private, public, manufacturing or service. It can be applied to a single department right up to a large multi unit company. However, the best returns come from companies prepared to implement it through out their organisation rather than particular unit, department or divisions.

SDC – 65 is a management approach or strategy aimed at embedding awareness of quality in all organisational processes, which organisation must strive to continuously improve these processes by incorporating the knowledge and expertise of employees. This will strengthen relationships and quality and productivity processes from the identification of management requirements, customer satisfaction. It supports of all steps of PDCA (Plan, Do, Correct and Apply) performance and employee relationships etc. Thus the solution will also boost efficiency and cutting cost helping to drive success at organisation of any size.